Doing Business in ASEAN Markets

Peter Verhezen • Ian Williamson • Mark Crosby • Natalia Soebagjo
Editors

Doing Business in ASEAN Markets

Leadership Challenges and Governance Solutions across Asian Borders

palgrave
macmillan

Editors

Peter Verhezen
Melbourne Business School
Melbourne, Australia

University of Antwerp, Belgium

Mark Crosby
Monash Business School
Melbourne, Australia

Ian Williamson
Melbourne Business School
Melbourne, Australia

Natalia Soebagjo
University of Indonesia
Depok, Indonesia

ISBN 978-3-319-41789-9   ISBN 978-3-319-41790-5   (eBook)
DOI 10.1007/978-3-319-41790-5

Library of Congress Control Number: 2016954230

Cover image © AF-studio / Getty Images

Printed on acid-free paper

This Palgrave Macmillan imprint is published by Springer Nature
The registered company is Springer International Publishing AG Switzerland

"We sow a thought and reap an act;
We sow an act and reap a habit;
We sow an habit and reap a character;
We sow a character and reap a destiny."
Anonymous proverb

"Solving a problem simply means representing it so
as to make the solution transparent."
Herbert A. Simon

Dedicated to our respective families and beloved ones who taught us the meaning of awareness, compassion, and dedication

Foreword

Prospects of Good Corporate Governance in ASEAN

Corporate governance plays an important role in protecting investors, in the prudent operation of companies and financial institutions, and in the stability of the financial sector. Principles of good governance have been a major component of international financial standards, and many regulators view effective corporate governance as "the first line of defense" in their supervisory activities. Since the Asian crisis of 1997 significant energy and attention has been placed on improving the ability of boards, managers, and owners to steer their companies through rapidly changing and volatile market conditions. A decade later, the global financial crisis did send a stark reminder that better corporate governance is not only a matter for developing countries, but also for advanced economies, where the shockwaves originated. If anything, the agenda has gained more importance.

At the same time the world has never been as ambitious about developments as it is today. After adopting the Sustainable Development Goals and signing the Paris climate deal at the end of 2015, the world is now looking to implement and finance these milestones. Development assistance will remain critical, but won't be sufficient. The private sector will have to play a key role, by creating the jobs and mobilizing the resources in developing countries to end poverty in sustainable ways.

If the world wants to put words into action, corporate governance is a critical step to success and a major contribution to good governance in general. Good corporate governance practices limit the ability of private sector companies to participate in corruption, establish an environment where companies find it more difficult to engage in questionable behavior, and help board members exercise better judgment; investors receive timely and relevant information, and put decision-making more into the open. When companies are more transparent and decision makers are more accountable for their actions, it is harder for companies to provide company resources to government officials in exchange for services. Improved corporate governance also leads to improvements in internal controls, the establishment of compliance systems, and the creation of an ethical "tone at the top".

Finally, good corporate governance complements financial supervision and is an integral factor in implementing effective risk-based financial oversight. The Basel Framework requires banks to maintain strong internal governance procedures and processes. Pillar II (supervisory review) requires that banks maintain well-functioning systems of internal controls and risk measurement, management and mitigation – and adequate review processes by management and directors. Pillar III (market discipline) mandates additional risk disclosures to provide transparency and allow the market to provide discipline on poorly functioning banks that lack the risk systems to handle the institution's risk profiles.

Strong corporate governance frameworks, and responsible and productive institutions, that contribute to economic growth and financial stability are critical elements in achieving the following development impacts:

1. *To help companies and financial institutions improve their access to affordable external financing and lower their cost of capital* – leading to greater investment, higher growth and more employment.
2. *To address the impact of the financial crisis and advance financial stability* – reducing economic and social costs to client economies due to financial crisis. The global financial crisis and the crisis response highlighted the need for robust corporate governance policy frameworks to ensure financial stability.
3. *To help regulatory agencies improve and enforce corporate governance rules* – while balancing the costs of regulation against the benefits of improved compliance.
4. *To help governments increase their capacity to act as owners of companies* – improving economic and social outcomes linked to state-owned companies, and reducing obstacles to privatization.

In Indonesia, the authorities and the private sector have made progress in strengthening the corporate governance framework since the economic crisis of 1997. The financial sector regulators have upgraded their regulations, and have actively enforced these regulations to better protect investors and depositors. In 2006, Bank Indonesia – Indonesia's Central Bank - introduced rules for corporate governance in banks. The Code of Good Corporate Governance (CGCG), first adopted in 1999, was amended in 2006, and sector-specific codes were issued for the banking and insurance sectors. In 2007 a new company law was adopted that introduced explicit duties for board members. The Ministry of State-Owned Enterprises has also carried out significant corporate governance reform in the state owned enterprise sector.

And yet it is important for the government and the private sector to continue the process of reform. The financial crisis tested corporate governance practices in many countries which were considered to have strong corporate governance frameworks. Several broad areas of weakness have been identified, including poorly-performing boards of directors, bad governance of risk and risk-management, problems with remuneration and the alignment of incentive structures, and the lack of engaged shareholders. Corporate governance matters: different financial institutions fared differently during the crisis, depending in part on the strength of their overall governance framework and culture.

All countries will have to increase their efforts to build strong governance institutions and cultures. The key to improving corporate governance will be to build a cadre of qualified, experienced, and professional board members, managers, and engaged owners, who understand the business case for corporate governance and have the tools to implement it.

The World Bank
May 2016

Sri Mulyani Indrawati
Managing Director
Appointed as Minister of Finance
Jakarta, Indonesia
August 2016

Contents

About the Editors

Mark Crosby was Associate Professor of Economics at Melbourne Business School until very recently. Currently, he is a professor at the Monash Business School, Monash University in Melbourne, Australia. Mark graduated with a PhD from Queen's University in Canada in 1993, and since that time Mark has had academic appointments at the University of Toronto, the University of New South Wales, and Melbourne University.

In 2011 Mark moved to Singapore to take up the role of Dean at the S P Jain School of Global Management, before returning to Melbourne Business School in 2013. Mark's academic interests are in international macroeconomics, with particular interest in policy issues in the Australian and Asian regions. His published research has covered topics such as the role of exchange rates in affecting macroeconomic fluctuations, the impact of macroeconomic factors on election outcomes, and the properties of business cycles. Mark has acted as a consultant to the Hong Kong Monetary Authority and to the Monetary Authority of Singapore on a number of projects since 1998, and he has an ongoing Research Fellowship position at the HKMA. He also consults widely to business and government both in Australia and overseas. His most recent consultancies have examined policies for diversifying Negara Brunei Darussalam's economy, and policy issues related to South Africa's increasing current account deficit. Mark is also a regular contributor to the *Australian Financial Review* and *The Age* newspapers, and he is a sought after public speaker on matters relating to the macroeconomy.

Natalia Soebagjo is Chair of the Executive Board of Transparency International Indonesia (TII) and Board Member of Transparency International, based in Berlin. Until October 2015, she was also the Executive Director of the University of Indonesia's Center for the Study of Governance. Currently, she is a Member of the Oversight Committee of the Kalibaru Port and of the Selection Panel for the Commissioners of the KPK 2015–2019. She also chairs the Perkumpulan BHACA which confers the Bung Hatta Anti-Corruption Award to individuals who have made an impact in fighting corruption. She sits on the boards of a few private companies as an independent commissioner or commissioner.

For many years now, Natalia has been lecturing on international relationships and Chinese society, political and economic international affairs at the University of Indonesia. Natalia studied Sarjana Sastra (Literature) at the Faculty of Humanities at the University of Indonesia, and pursued her Master of Arts at the University of California Berkeley (USA). She also holds a professional stockbroker's and underwriter's license.

Peter Verhezen is Adjunct Professor for "Global Corporate Governance", "Strategy, Ethics and Governance" and "Business in Asia" at the Melbourne Business School, and a Visiting Professor of "Strategy and Risk" and "Business in Emerging Markets" at the University of Antwerp, Belgium. He has been a Fellow at the Ash Institute for Governance and Asian Studies at the Harvard Kennedy School, USA, with whom he still collaborates. In the early nineties, he founded CIMAD Pacific and C-Consulting as spin-offs of IBM. He ran the 2 companies for 15 years till C-Consulting was merged with an international consultancy in 2007. During the Asian crisis in 1997, he was senior financial advisor for Indonesian Bank Restructuring Agency (IBRA) (Ministry of Finance of Indonesia).

As the current Principal of Verhezen & Associates Ltd he advises boards on risk management, strategy and governance in the Asia-Pacific region. Moreover, he is also senior consultant at IFC-World Bank in Asia-Pacific for Corporate Governance. Until recently, he facilitated training sessions on governance on behalf of the Australian Institute of Corporate Directors. Peter regularly writes about these interests in international journals and received the award for best ethics paper by IMCA in 2011; he is also the author of *Gifts, Corruption and Philanthropy. The Ambiguity of Gift Practices in Business*, published in 2009 by Peter Lang in Oxford. He co-authored *The Relevance of Corporate Governance in Indonesia*, with Erry Riyana Hardjapamekas and Pri Notowidigdo, published by the University of Indonesia Press in 2012. His most recent book *The Vulnerability of Corporate Reputation* was published by Palgrave in London in 2015. He studied International Relations and Applied Economics (MA at the University of Antwerp in Belgium) and Philosophy at Leuven University in Belgium (MA & PhD). He took his MBA from Leuven Business School in association with Chicago Booth School of Business.

Ian Williamson is the Helen Macpherson Smith Chair of Leadership for Social Impact at the Melbourne Business School. He currently serves as the Associate Dean of International Relations at MBS and is also the Co-Director of the Asia Pacific Social Impact Centre (APSIC) and the Faculty Director of the MBS Executive MBA program. He is an Associated Scholar of the Lorange Institute of Business Zurich (Switzerland) and Rutgers Business School (USA). He received his PhD in Organizational Behavior from the University of North Carolina at Chapel Hill, USA, and a bachelor's degree in business from Miami University, Ohio, USA.

In his role as Associate Dean and Co-Director of APSIC Prof. Williamson's focus is on developing effective cross-sector partnerships to address key economic and social issues across the Asia Pacific region. Prof. Williamson's research focuses on how the development of effective "talent pipelines" can enhance organizational and community outcomes. His research has been published in several leading academic journals including *Academy of Management Journal, MIT Sloan Management Review* and *Journal of Applied Psychology.* He has presented his research worldwide and he is regularly covered in the media. He has served on the editorial boards of the *Academy of Management Journal, Academy Management Review, Academy of Management Education and Learning, Journal of Management* and *Cross Cultural Management: An International Journal.* Ian is the recipient of numerous awards including the Academy of Management Human Resource Division best paper award for his research on the effect of employee mobility on firm performance in the professional services sector and the Academy of Management Best Practices Mentoring Award for his role as the founding President of the Management Faculty of Color Association (MFCA). He is also a recipient of the Academy of Management Ralph Alexander Best Dissertation Award for his research examining the top management team (TMT) selection decisions of *Fortune 500* firms. He also received the University of Melbourne Award for Excellence and Innovation in Indigenous Higher Education for his work in the area of Indigenous entrepreneurship. Williamson has provided consulting services to numerous leading international organisations in over 20 countries in the areas of strategic human resource management, managing organizational innovation and employee engagement and retention.

Notes on Contributors

Tanri Abeng used to be one of the most successful Indonesian CEOs of Bir Bintang-Heineken Beer. Afterwards, he became Minister of State-Owned Enterprises under President Habibie. After his ministerial role, Tanri served for two terms as Chairman of PT Telkom, the biggest telcom company in Indonesia. He is currently chairman of the state-owned gas-and-oil company PT Pertamina. Moreover, he is founder and CEO of ECGL, an executive institute for leadership development (in collaboration with Erasmus Business School) and founder of Tanri Abeng University. His advice is often sought by Indonesian conglomerates.

Ernie Antoine consults in the areas of culture, psychology and leadership for the Melbourne Business School both in Asia as well as in Australia. Trained at Harvard University, University of Melbourne and RMIT & Swinburne University (Melbourne) and specializing in leadership development and coaching in a globalized environment, his approach aims to produce profound and sustainable changes within leaders. Ernie's specializes in developing senior high performance leaders in government, business and not-for-profit organizations, particularly those working in multinational roles and contexts. Ernie has co-authored a book with Deborah Rhodes called, *Practitioners' Guide to Capacity Development: A Cross Cultural Approach,* a guide for those working globally on international development projects.

Peter Chambers is currently advisor on Indonesian-based investments to Farallon Capital, a US-based hedge fund. Previously he served for many years as Managing Director of Strategy and Governance for Rajawali Corpora. The Indonesian Rajawali Corpora is a conglomerate active in a number of industries and across borders. Peter is currently an Independent Commissioner of Axiata XL (IDX listed), Indonesia's second largest mobile communications operator, Director of PT Agrincourt, an Indonesian based gold miner, Chairman of Indomines (ASX listed) an Indonesian-based miner and a member of the Digital Advisory Board for Malaysian-based

Axiata. He started his career as an accountant and became practice leader for Coopers and Lybrand's telecommunications consulting practice in Hong Kong; after which he moved to Indonesia and was appointed Vice President Director and CFO for PT Excelcomindo, Indonesia's third established mobile telecommunications operator. He studied business and management at RMIT in Melbourne.

Howard Dick is a professorial fellow in the Faculty of Business & Economics and Law at the University of Melbourne and Conjoint Professor in the Faculty of Business & Law at the University of Newcastle (NSW). An economist and economic historian by background, his current research focuses on governance, regulation and corruption in Southeast Asia with particular focus on Indonesia. He first visited Indonesia in 1971 and has written several books and various articles covering economic development, transport and logistics and urbanization as well as governance. Within Australia, he is widely seen as one of the leading experts on Indonesian history and Indonesian economics & policy.

Manggi Habir is currently a board member at Bank Danamon and Adira Insurance, two Jakarta-based financial institutions as well as a regular financial columnist for Indonesia's weekly magazine, *Tempo*. He has held several senior positions, among others, Director at Standard and Poor's Singapore, heading Financial Institution Ratings for the Asia-Pacific region (excluding Korea and Japan), President Director of Pefindo, Indonesia's credit rating agency, Director of Research at state-owned Bahana Securities and Head of Financial Institutions Citibank Jakarta. Early in his career he was business correspondent for the Hong Kong weekly, the *Far Eastern Economic Review*. He has a Masters in Public Administration from Harvard University, Masters in Business Administration from the University of Michigan, Ann Arbor and a Bachelor of Arts in Economics from McGill University. He is also faculty member of the IPMI Business School in Jakarta.

Erry Riyana Hardjapamekas sits on the Board of Commissioners of several major Indonesian and multinational companies such as PT Unilever Indonesia, PT Hero Supermarket and PT Kaltim Prima Coal. Erry was formerly CEO of PT Timah Tbk., effectively turning the once-inefficient SOE into a profitable, publicly listed state-owned company. As its Finance Director (prior to becoming the CEO), Erry strengthened the financial integrity of the company, privatized the company and took it public with a listing on the Indonesian Stock Exchange. Based on his vast experience and his contribution to the development of the Indonesian securities industry, he was elected as the Chairman of the Board of Commissioners of the Jakarta Stock Exchange. Besides being a corporate executive, he is also known for championing the fight against corruption. As Vice-Commissioner of the Corruption Eradication Commission in charge of internal auditing and handling public complaints, Erry was committed to improving the integrity of public institutions. A founder of the Indonesian Society for Transparency, he currently sits on the Executive Board of both the Coalition for Governance Reform and the National Commission for Good Governance. He is also a board member of Transparency International Indonesia and of the Partnership for Governance Reform, besides being Chairman of the Founding Board of the UI Center for the Study of Governance. He earned his Accounting degree from Padjadjaran University in 1978.

Merly Khouw is part of the Vice Presidency of the Integrity Office of the World Bank in Washington where she functions as Lead Investigator & Deputy Manager of External Investigations for Asia. She holds a PhD in Criminology of Wharton School at Penn University. Prior to her World Bank position, she was Vice-President of Forensic Investigation and Accounting at the Indonesian Bank Restructuring Agency between 1997 and 2001.

Warren Weeks is an analyst, consultant, researcher & author. After a successful career as a technologist and marketer, he founded Cubit to help organizations drive better results through communication. He has worked closely with executives in many of the world's best-known companies to design monitoring and analytics services that deliver tangible improvements through: (1) improving corporate reputation - crisis prediction and prevention, (2) competitive intelligence - communication benchmarking; (3) brand positioning. Warren has also designed some of the most advanced analysis regimes ever constructed, to allow Government and private sector clients to map traditional media and social channel messaging against shifts in public perceptions and behavior. Warren's collaborative research has been published in the *MIT Sloan Management Review*, the *Journal of Business Strategy*, *Reputation Management*, and an Australian Federal Government Occasional Paper addressing the international media's framing of discussions about human migration. He regularly lectures in the areas of governance, strategy, reputation and communication. Prior to founding Cubit Media Research in 1995, Warren was the regional director of marketing and communication for a Silicon Valley Technology company, working across the Asia-Pacific region and in the USA. His undergraduate studies were in the areas of motivational psychology, information systems, and marketing. He holds a postgraduate diploma and a master's degree in management. Warren is a fellow of the Australian Institute of Management.

List of Figures

List of Tables

1

Introduction: Doing Business in ASEAN Markets: What Is So Different?

Peter Verhezen, Ian Williamson, Natalia Soebagjo, and Mark Crosby

Many scholars and practitioners have anointed the 21st century as the "Asian Century". It is now obvious that an economic shift from the West to the East is underway, having both major economic and socio-political implications China and India are often featured as drivers of this Asian economic renaissance. China and India are the two remaining BRIC countries that still grow at a considerable speed. China is projected to have a growth rate of about 6.5 % over the next several years (lower than the double digit growth it experienced at the turn of the century) and India may pick up some steam and hit 7 % for the next years. However, less well-known and less analyzed is the equally remarkable story of the rise of the ASEAN market, which may generate interesting prospects for many multinational companies (MNC) and global investors in the coming years.

Founded in 1967, ASEAN today encompasses Negara Brunei Darussalam, Cambodia, Indonesia, Laos, Malaysia, Myanmar, the Philippines, Singapore, Thailand, and Vietnam – economies at vastly different stages of development but all sharing immense growth potential. ASEAN may be seen as a major global hub of manufacturing and trade, as well as one of the fastest-growing

P. Verhezen (✉) • I. Williamson • M. Crosby
Melbourne Business School, 200 Leicester Street, Carlton, 3053, VIC, Australia
e-mail: p.verhezen@mbs.edu

N. Soebagjo
UI Center for Governance & Administrative Reform, Jakarta, Indonesia

© The Editor(s) (if applicable) and the Author(s) 2016
P. Verhezen et al. (eds.), *Doing Business in ASEAN Markets*,
DOI 10.1007/978-3-319-41790-5_1

consumer markets in the world. Indeed, ASEAN's 10 economies are a growing force in global affairs. With a gross domestic product of USD 2.7 trillion, the AEC (ASEAN Economic Community) is the seventh-largest economy in the world. With a population of more than 620 million, it is the third largest in Asia after China and India. It can be easily argued that the AEC economies have collectively grown faster than any other Asian economy save China since the beginning of the century. During that time span, GDP has expanded fourfold, per capita income threefold, and foreign direct investment inflows fivefold. The poverty rate has halved.

However, these positive facts and trends notwithstanding, doing business in the ASEAN region often means overcoming barriers and hurdles not present in most Western markets. In many ways the ASEAN context, due in part to its diversity, can be even more difficult to navigate than the Chinese and Indian markets. A failure to appreciate both the systematic and nuanced differences between the ASEAN market and other global settings has caused many MNCs and international investors to experience major financial and reputational losses in the past.

This book attempts to analyze the pitfalls and risks of entering into ASEAN markets and, more crucially, how to overcome those barriers when doing business in the region. In particular, as a response to these challenges the authors of the chapter examine the role of responsible leadership – encompassing wise decision-making by a leadership of the highest integrity – and sound corporate processes and governance in avoiding the pitfalls and reducing the risks in the ASEAN markets.

1   Business Opportunities in ASEAN Markets

Why focus on ASEAN and why now? We believe several recent economic, political, and demographic trends have made the ASEAN region more important than ever to the world's economy and as a result an important consideration for global business leaders.

First, the ASEAN market is currently one of the strongest economic regions in the world.
Despite the recent global economic headwinds, the ASEAN market continues to be a platform for continuous growth. On average market growth is about 4.5 % for the ASEAN region – creating a market worth USD 2.7 trillion. The ASEAN market is projected to become the 4th largest by 2030, behind only the USA, China and India.

As economic growth in other Asian markets slow down (e.g., China), ASEAN may provide alternatives for foreign investment. Moreover, ASEAN's government debt is under 50 % of GDP – far lower than the 90 % share in the United Kingdom or 105 % in the United States. Most of the region has held steady so far, despite concerns about the impact of quantitative easing by the US Federal Reserve on emerging markets. In fact, ASEAN has experienced much lower volatility in economic growth since 2000 than the European Union. Savings levels have also remained fairly steady since 2005, at about a third of GDP, albeit with large differences between high-saving economies, such as Negara Brunei Darussalam, Malaysia, and Singapore, and low-saving economies, such as Cambodia, Laos, and the Philippines. ASEAN has dramatically outpaced the rest of the world on growth in GDP per capita since the late 1970s. Income growth has remained strong since 2000, with average annual real gains of more than 7-10 %.

According to a survey by Boston Consulting Group Global, ASEAN was home to the headquarters of 49 companies in the Forbes Global 2000 about one decade ago. By 2013, that number had risen to 74. ASEAN includes 227 of the world's companies with more than USD1 billion in revenues, or 3 % of the world's total. ASEAN is the seventh-largest host of such companies, according to the 2014 BGC survey.[1] Singapore in particular stands out, ranking fifth in the world for corporate-headquarters density and first for foreign subsidiaries.

Consistent with this growth, foreign direct investment in ASEAN has boomed, surpassing its pre-crisis levels of 1997. In fact, the ASEAN-5 (Indonesia, Malaysia, the Philippines, Singapore, and Thailand) attracted more foreign direct investment than China (USD 128 billion versus USD117 billion) in 2013. In addition to attracting multinationals, ASEAN has become a launching pad for new companies; the region now accounts for 38 % of Asia's market for initial public offerings.

Second, due to recent trade agreements the ASEAN region is likely to entering into a new dynamic period:
ASEAN is an economic community (AEC, ASEAN Economic Community) where the member countries have made a formal declaration to eliminate interregional tariffs. This will probably result in more economic opportunities within the region, while tapping on the integrated production base from 2015 onwards. This is all consistent with the AEC's five core objectives of integration, competitiveness, enhanced connectivity and sectorial cooperation, equitable outcomes, and global engagement. The AEC is pursuing something akin to what came to be known as the four freedoms – similar as in the European integration: freedom of movement of goods, services, capital and labor. The AEC version of the four freedoms is a single market and production base

with the free flow of goods, services, investment and skilled labor, along with freer capital flows, but still with full sovereignty on all the other issues like tax, citizenship, budget control, currency, monetary and fiscal policies. As the AEC progresses toward this vision it will undoubtedly create many new economic opportunities.

Third, the ASEAN market represents a huge opportunity for consumer products with potential consumers of about 620 million:
With a growing population of more than 620 million people, ASEAN is fast becoming an important hub for increased consumer demand. Some member nations have grown at a torrid pace: Vietnam, for example, took just 11 years (from 1995 to 2006) to double its per capita GDP from USD 1300 to USD 2600. By 2050, ASEAN could be the 4th largest economy. Its GDP in 2014 stood at USD 2.395 trillion with a GDP per capita of USD 3832. Extreme poverty is rapidly receding. In 2000, 14 % of the region's population was below the international poverty line of USD 1.25 a day (calculated in purchasing-power-parity terms), but by 2014, that share had fallen to just 3 %. Already some 70 million households in ASEAN states are part of the "middle class consuming class," with incomes exceeding the level at which they can begin to make significant discretionary purchases. That number could almost double to 125 million households by 2025, making ASEAN a pivotal consumer market of the future. There is no typical ASEAN consumer, but some broad trends have emerged: a greater focus on leisure activities, a growing preference for modern retail formats, and increasing brand awareness; Indonesian consumers, for example, are exceptionally loyal to their favorite brands. Moreover, ASEAN's cities are booming and this urbanization process and consumer growth seem to move in tandem. Nearly 40 % of ASEAN's GDP growth through 2025 is expected to come from 142 cities with populations between 200,000 and five millions.[2]

ASEAN consumers are increasingly moving online, with mobile penetration of 110 % and Internet penetration of 25 % across the region. Its member states make up the world's second-largest community of Facebook users, behind only the United States. But there are vast differences in adoption. Hyperconnected Singapore has the fourth-highest smartphone penetration in the world, and almost 75 % of its population is online. By contrast, only 1 % of Myanmar has access to the Internet. Indonesia, with the world's fourth-largest population, is rapidly becoming a digital nation; it already has 282 million mobile subscriptions and is expected to have 100 million Internet users by 2016.

Fourth, due in part to the success of its economic performance the ASEAN region has become more embedded in the global business environment[3]:
Not surprisingly, ASEAN is becoming extremely well positioned in global trade flows. ASEAN is the fourth-largest exporting region in the world,

trailing only the European Union, North America, and China/Hong Kong. It accounts for 7 % of global exports – and as its member states have developed more sophisticated manufacturing capabilities, their exports have diversified. Vietnam specializes in textiles and apparel, while Singapore and Malaysia are leading exporters of electronics. Thailand has joined the ranks of leading vehicle and automotive-parts exporters. Other ASEAN members have built export industries around natural resources. Indonesia is the world's largest producer and exporter of palm oil, the largest exporter of coal, and the second-largest producer of cocoa and tin. While Myanmar is just beginning to open its economy, it has large reserves of oil, gas, and precious minerals. In addition to exporting manufactured and agricultural products, the Philippines has established a thriving business-process-outsourcing industry. China, a competitor, has become a key customer of ASEAN countries. In fact, it is now the most important export market for Malaysia and Singapore. But demand from the United States, Europe, and Japan continues to propel growth.

The region sits at the crossroads of many global flows. Singapore is currently the fourth-highest-ranked country in the McKinsey Global Institute's Connectedness Index, which tracks inflows and outflows of goods, services, finance, and people, as well as the underlying flows of data and communication that enable all types of cross-border exchanges. Malaysia (18th) and Thailand (36th) also rank among the top 50 most connected countries. ASEAN is well positioned to benefit from growth in all these global flows. By 2025, more than half of the world's consuming class will live within a five-hour flight of Yangoon in Myanmar, and within a seven-hour flight from megacity Jakarta in Indonesia.

The ASEAN Economic Community's global trade flows seem to become more and more interdependent: today about 25 % of the region's exports of goods go to other ASEAN partners, a share that has remained roughly constant since 2003. While this is less than half the share of intraregional trade seen in the North American Free Trade Agreement countries of Canada, Mexico, and the United States and in the European Union, the total value is climbing rapidly as the region develops stronger cross-border supply chains.

Intraregional trade in goods – along with other types of cross-border flows – is likely to increase with implementation of the ASEAN Economic Community integration plan, which aims to allow the freer movement of goods, services, skilled labor, and capital. Progress has been uneven, however. While tariffs on goods are now close to zero in many sectors among the original five member states (Indonesia, Malaysia, the Philippines, Singapore, and Thailand), progress on liberalization of services and investment has been slower, and nontariff barriers remain a stumbling block to freer trade.

2   Common Pitfalls and Leadership Challenges in ASEAN Markets

However, while these four trends illustrate the great potential the ASEAN markets might have for organizations, there are also many challenges in the region that make realizing this potential quite difficult.

1. *Public policy:*

    The "ASEAN way" – provided that such a perspective really exists – still shows quite some significant gaps in terms of launching the AEC. In the field of services, for example, AEC economies are among the most closed in some sectors: heavy-handed bank regulation remains a sovereign matter and the 10 different markets for banking are still very closed to outsiders. Service trade policies in ASEAN are perceived to be more restrictive than in any other region in the world except the Persian Gulf, according to a World Bank report published in April 2015.

    In addition, one could argue that not enough has been done to separate the legitimate public policy objectives of non-tariff measures[4] from a desire to protect local interests. Therefore much more will be needed to ensure that non-tariff measures do not degenerate into red tape "non-tariff trade barriers".

2. *Cultural Diversity & Ethical Leadership Challenges:*

    Despite a shared goal, it needs to be mentioned that ASEAN is a heterogeneous market with many economic differences. Within ASEAN, Indonesia for instance represents almost 45 % of the region's economic output and is a member of the G20 (the world's 20 biggest economies). Singapore while much smaller than Indonesia is seen as a haven of legal reliability and economic efficiency, a first world country with enormous wealth per capita even surpassing mature economies such as Canada and the USA. Conversely, Myanmar is emerging from decades of isolation and is still a frontier market working to build its institutions.

    International business leaders will need to take into account this diversity between, and within, ASEAN countries. What is accepted as "proper business conduct and legal contract" in Singapore, may be 'understood', and possibly complied with, in Kuala Lumpur, Jakarta or Bangkok, but may be questioned at more local levels in Penang, Surabaya or Chang Mai. Any multinational will face leadership challenges in those emerging and frontier markets, whether rooted in cultural differences, or specific legal contexts, or different norm systems.

Moreover, these dynamic ASEAN markets are changing very fast. Leaders will need a core [ethical and strategic] compass to navigate these ambiguous and swiftly changing environments to steer their organization towards value creating opportunities, while acknowledging the local context, norms and values. International leadership often complains about, or silently looks away from, allegations of corruption and misbehavior by their employees. And although Western companies have not been spared from unethical behavior resulting in reputational disasters, the chance that one faces some kind of perceived corruption in those emerging markets is more than likely, unless the organization has implemented a very strong ethical culture and governance structures. Some companies, such as Unilever in Indonesia and other Asian countries, have thrived as organizations attracting the best talent, by emphasizing the strong stance towards social, ethical and environmental issues.

3. *Weak Institutional environment:*

Institutional credibility is crucial in generating and monitoring economic prosperity. Indeed, it is often the most important factor that differentiates stable mature economies from volatile and unpredictable emerging markets. The loss of institutional credibility is part of a more general erosion of trust in politicians and the "system" as such. These institutional voids may have negative effects on firms and organizations (for example, in attracting investment).

Moreover, the combination of *institutional weaknesses or institutional voids*[5] at a country level and potential *conflicts of interest* at an *organizational* level – as visualized in Fig. 1.1 – causes many international business ventures to fail.

Encountering structural institutional pitfalls combined with some major potential organizational threats at firm level lead us to focus on two major challenges that make doing business in Indonesia difficult: (A) typical institutional voids in emerging markets that cause *sub-optimal equilibria* (that is, not optimal for the country as a whole), and (B) potential conflicts of interest at a number of levels, but specifically at a firm level, causing *inferior or conflicted decisions,* often at the expense of minority shareholders.

The lack of proper law enforcement and rampant corruption both at the central federal government level and definitely at the decentralized local authority level complicates business in the ASEAN region. The legal system has been characterized by corruption and red tape, and the implementation of the rules and regulations is patchy. Add concentrated ownership, and it is easy to understand that minority shareholder rights are not always

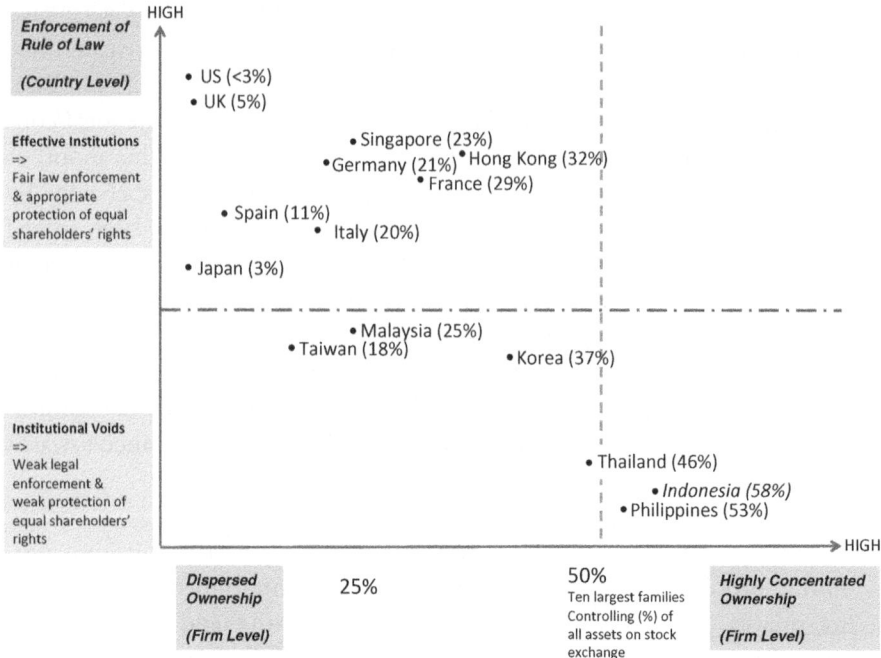

Fig. 1.1 Legal enforcement versus ownership characteristics (*Source*: Verhezen et al. 2016)

protected nor respected as they are in Western common law jurisdictions and to a lesser extent in Western civic law jurisdictions.[6]

4. *Weak corporate governance[7]:*

The fiduciary duties of a board include a duty of care that requires board members to make decisions with due deliberation, a duty of loyalty that addresses conflicts of interest whereby the interest of all shareholders should prevail over the interest of one board member (even if that is the patriarch of the company), and a duty of candor that requires that management and the board inform all shareholders of all information that may be important in their evaluation of the company and its management. However, in most emerging markets, the implementation of corporate governance standards remains rather weak, even though corporate governance significantly improved after the disastrous financial crisis in Asia of 1997. For example, corporate governance in Indonesia lags behind the standards enforced in Singapore, Malaysia, or even Thailand. Analyzing the boards of a number of the top 50 companies on the Indonesian Stock Exchange, only a few could be considered as conforming to best corporate governance practices. When dealing with private non-listed companies, the protection of minority rights remains a serious problem. For example, one of the authors was involved with the IPO of an Indonesian private company. In this IPO the identity of a primary power broker backing the firm was not even disclosed to potential investors. Through a complicated pyramidal structure, the real well connected patriarch was somehow hidden from the public eye to avoid public and government attention.

5. *Social challenges:*

The AEC has the expressed goal of creating a stronger sense of 'community' among its member states. In reality, ASEAN is a region with diverse political systems, from single party rule to democracies and monarchies, with a diverse set of cultures and diverse economic and social settings. Economically, it counts both Singapore as a member with its 2014 GDP of USD 307.9 billion and GNI per capita of USD 55,150 and Myanmar at the other extreme with GDP of USD 64.33 billion and GNI per capita of just USD 1270.

The diversity is also reflected in the Human Development Index (HDI) rankings with Singapore and Negara Brunei Darussalam falling into the category of countries with very high HDI. Malaysia and Thailand have high HDI but the majority of ASEAN countries fall into the medium HDI category. For example, Indonesia, and Cambodia have an HDI rank of 110th and 143rd respectively.

A clear illustration of the diverse social conditions across the ASEAN countries can be seen in the areas of health and education. Life expectancy in Vietnam is high at 75.8 years, comparable to Malaysia (74.7 years) and Thailand (74.4 years), while life expectancy in Indonesia is 68.9 years. In Indonesia only 3.1 % of its GDP is allocated to health, compared to 7.5 % in Cambodia. In terms of education, Indonesians average 13 expected years of schooling which is behind Thailand (13.5 years) but slightly better than Malaysia (12.7 years). Conversely, in an affluent society such as Singapore, the government allocates only 2.9 % of its budget on education but is nevertheless able to achieve 15.4 expected years of schooling. Thailand allocates 7.6 % of its GDP on education, the highest in ASEAN, whilst Indonesia and the Philippines spend less than half of that, at 3.6 % and 3.4 % respectively.

Given the diversity of political systems adopted in the ASEAN Member Countries (AMC), it is noteworthy that the region has been able to maintain stability. Indonesia was able to transition peacefully from an authoritarian system to a democratic system within a relatively short period of time, whereas we have witnessed the reverse in Thailand with politics returning into the hands of the military.

What we see in common in many of the AMCs is the prevalence of corruption, be it blatant or more subtle. The recent case of 1MDB plaguing Najib Razak's government in Malaysia shows how the mishandling of corruption can seriously hurt the credibility of a government. Since the fall of Suharto, Indonesia has openly acknowledged that corruption is a scourge that needs to be seriously addressed and the government has established an Anti-Corruption Agency with the authority independently to investigate corruption cases in all levels of government, as well as in the legislature. In general, the ability of governments to achieve and sustain economic growth to alleviate poverty and their ability to fight corruption are key to unlocking the potential in the region.

3   Structure of Book

Yes, it is true that the ASEAN Economic Community offers an opportunity to create a seamless regional market and production base as in the EuropeanUnion. And yes, the whole is expected to exceed the sum of its 10 individual parts. But it will require enormous investment in infrastructure and human-capital development in order to remain competitive and to grow further in a sustainable manner. However, despite the enormous business opportunities in the ASEAN market, many hidden and less obvious pitfalls remain. This aim of this book is to engage with the reader to share the profound academic research and practical experience of the contributors in how to overcome those risks when doing business in ASEAN.

We would like to thank Dr. Sri Mulyani Indrawati, previously Minister of Finance of Indonesia, and now Managing Director at the World Bank in Washington, who wrote the Foreword of this book, indicating the importance of proper responsible leadership and good corporate governance in Asia and ASEAN countries in achieving their respective development goals. Indeed, reliable public and corporate leadership underpinned by a sound governance framework are the main focus of this book.

Professor Mark Crosby elaborates the economic outlook of the ASEAN countries in the first chapter. The economies of the ASEAN region are large, diverse and very dynamic. Yet the opportunities presented in the ten ASEAN economies have often been hidden behind the bigger regional economies of China and India. In this chapter the outlook for the region is presented, emphasizing the huge advantages in having a young and growing workforce, investment opportunities and abundant natural resources. But some countries have been able to grasp these opportunities more effectively than others, and the challenge is to understand why this has been the case and where future opportunities lie. It is noted that the key thing for businesses to understand is that there are vast differences in political leadership across the region, which give rise to significant differences in prospects.

The second chapter considers the impact of markedly different standards of governance on the emerging pattern of ASEAN integration. Professorial Fellow Howard Dick argues that firms engaged in international business have multiple and often complex legal identities that are necessary both to comply with, and to transcend, the regulations of national governments. The chapter combines the perspectives of Economic History and International Business, examining ASEAN countries in comparison with China and Hong Kong, then reviews historical trends in the role of Singapore within the Southeast Asian archipelago by taking the shipping industry as a case study. Subsequently, Dick looks at the jurisdictional strategies of four case studies – shipping line Samudera Indonesia, food manufacturer Indofood, agribusiness firm Wilmar International and car maker Astra International – providing evidence that their approaches may differ, but better governance is a common thread in trying to remain competitive in this global market.

The third chapter covers the impact of the 1997/98 Asian financial crisis on the evolution of corporate governance in Indonesia's banking sector, in comparison with ASEAN competitors. Manggi Habir assesses the impact of rules-based governance regulations enforced by the regulatory authorities, tax incentives for the top governance ranked banks and market discipline for listed banks, through analysts assessment and credit ratings from global rating agencies. He concludes that progress in improving the banking has been achieved, but there is still quite some room for improvement.

Often-asked questions refer to the relationship between China and ASEAN economies. In this fourth chapter, Professor Marc Crosby assesses to what extent ASEAN economies have become dependent and intertwined with the Chinese economic growth engine. And how to avoid political and military clashes now that an empowered China is making claims on islands in the Pacific? This chapter analyzes China's economy and how it will become more and more engrained – not just with the Western economies but also – with ASEAN growing markets. The inbound and outbound investments from and into China seem to confirm this analysis. In addition, the number of middle-class Chinese tourists visiting neighboring ASEAN destinations will be a boon for their respective economies.

World Bank expert Dr. Merly Khouw provides some insights into why many foreign investors still distrust institutions in ASEAN markets, mainly because of weak governance and unequivocal law enforcement. She argues, however, that these emerging markets will only be able thrive and sustain their current growth rates when proper governance has been implemented. The World Bank and their partners' mission are to assist a number of those ASEAN countries in achieving that goal, and to improve transparency and accountability while reducing corruption. The World Bank even links their aid programs and professional assistance to the implementation of proper governance structures and processes.

In Chap. 6, Peter Chambers and Peter Verhezen try to prove with some practical cases that when companies in Indonesia and Malaysia apply best corporate governance practices, one can solidly assume that their performances will improve. However, the cases here analyzed – more particularly in telecommunications, cement, agriculture and industry – pinpoint to some peculiar critical success factors of how and why specific corporate governance practices make a difference on the ground, especially for joint venture partnerships between block holding investors. These cases indicate how to overcome the many pitfalls caused by institutional voids on a country level and an emphasis of format over substance in governance at a firm level. The cases reveal the importance of some critical success factors to be fulfilled over the more formalistic good corporate governance rules at firm level in a country like Indonesia where the "rule of law" cannot be automatically assumed. The practical recommendations could be interpreted as "rules of thumb" to have the right foundations at the firm level established.

Western companies are already looking to emerging markets as sources of innovation and growth. However, as the three authors Peter Verhezen, Natalia Soebargjo and Erry Riyana Hardjapamekas argue in the seventh chapter, the increasingly interdependent world demands a higher level of corporate and individual accountability. Since Indonesia has been lagging behind in the corporate governance index, compared to quite a number of other ASEAN companies like Singapore, Thailand and Malaysia, the question becomes what measures need to be taken by Indonesian leadership to enhance its competitiveness. The fact that OJK, the Indonesian capital market regulator, has recently issued a clear roadmap is a good start. However, a number of barriers to improving corporate governance remain. Boards should be more diligent and timely in disclosing financial and other information, show more respect for minority shareholders, be accountable to all shareholders and not just the controlling family or state, and be more responsible to relevant stakeholders. In fact, by applying best practices and reducing opaque and often corrupt ways, Indonesian companies might thrive in an open economy, be it within Indonesia, ASEAN or even on a global scale. Unfortunately, sluggish bureaucratic reform and rather weak public governance during the last two decades are not fertile ground for corporate governance to improve.

State-Owned Enterprises remain a specific challenge in ASEAN. Sometimes particular governance structures can hamper or facilitate particular decision-making. Indonesia is characterized by a double-tier board system, whereas most companies with an Anglo-Saxon legal background have single-tier boards. Chapter 8 by Peter Verhezen and Tanri Abeng looks at the experience of two listed State-Owned Enterprises – PT Telkom, the national Indonesian telecommunication company, and PT Pertamina, the infamous Indonesian state owned gas & oil company. This chapter explores the first-hand governance experiences of Dr. Abeng – who was the Minister of State-Owned Enterprises in the late 1990s in Indonesia, Chairman of PT Telkom till 2011, and now serves as Chairman of PT Pertamina. The authors analyze the advantages of a dual-tier board and what should be expected from these boards in big companies like PT Telkom and PT Pertamina.

It takes years for organizations to build a good reputation. Yet bad news or a crisis can destroy it overnight. Being in the headlines for all the wrong reasons can erode the trust of customers or investors in a sudden and dramatic manner undermining the brand equity and reducing revenues and the bottom line. In the ninth Chapter, Warren Weeks and Peter Verhezen discuss the role of corporate leaders as stewards of a firm's reputation. However, the reality in many organizations is that leaders adopt a political or short-term perspective. Whether it is a mining company like Rio Tinto or BHP Billiton, or service companies like KPMG and Deloitte, or a manufacturing company like VW, all need to deal with potential reputational issues when operating in ASEAN countries. This chapter provides guidance on how an international board can be aware of, and address, negative narratives that can undermine an organization's reputation and bottom line.

In the tenth chapter, senior MBS consultant Ernie Antoine focuses on global teams or teams that operate in cross-cultural contexts. Combining leaders' personal insights with practical strategies relevant to their cultural and organizational contexts enables them to optimize their leadership performance. Hence leadership development, negotiations and conflict management, change management, and organizational analysis and development are crucial for such teams to survive and to thrive in an international environment. Findings are derived from such leading companies as Nestle Malaysia Singapore Brunei, Telkom Indonesia, and CIMB in Malaysia.

In our final chapter we are grateful that Aloise Hofbauer, Managing Director of Nestlé Singapore/Malaysia, shares his views on opportunities and dangers in ASEAN in an interview with Ernie Antoine. Hofbauer explains the leadership challenges, emphasizing the importance of good corporate governance practices and Nestlé's efforts to collaborate with Malaysia's government to secure the highest quality of its products possible, in line with the local requirements and norms.

The concluding remarks focus on the integration of proper responsible leadership, rooted in international acceptable practices and the institutionalized foundation of good corporate governance.

Notes

1. Chin, V.; M. Meyer; E. Tan & B. Waltermann, (2014), "Winning in ASEAN. How companies are preparing for economic integration", a *Boston Consulting Group* Publication, October; and Rastogi, V; E. Tamboto; D. Tong & T. Sinburimsit, (2013), "Asia's next Big Opportunity. Indonesia's rising middle class and affluent consumers", a *Boston Consulting Group Publication*, March.
2. Chin et al. (2014), *o.c.*
3. According to some ADB and World Bank surveys, between 2005 and 2012, ASEAN countries have signed mutual recognition arrangements (MRAs) in six sectors – i.e. engineering, nursing, architecture, medicine, dentistry and tourism – as well as framework arrangements on MRAs in surveying and accounting to help facilitate cross-border labor mobility. These agreements allow each member country to recognize education and experience, licenses and certificates granted in another country. However, implementation in these fields have been very slow because in practice, existing national legislation and regulations run counter to regional commitments to labor mobility and discourage cross-border movements by professionals, as recent labor debacles involving Indonesian labor in Malaysia have shown.
4. Chin et al. (2014), "Winning in ASEAN. How companies are preparing for economic integration", a *Boston Consulting Group Publication*, October.
5. The notion of institutional voids was used by Khanna, T., J. Kogan & K. Palepu (2006), "Globalization and Corporate Governance Convergence: a cross-country analysis", *Review of Economics and Statistics*, Vol. 88: 69-90; and Khanna, T., K.P. Palepu & R.J. Bullock (2010), *Winning in Emerging Markets. A Road Map for Strategy and Execution*, Boston, Harvard Business Press.

6. The seminal work by Jensen has greatly influenced the debate of how to govern a firm and how to reduce the agency costs in the USA and other Western countries: Jensen, M.C. & W.H. Meckling (1976), Theory of the Firm: managerial behavior, agency costs and ownership structure, *Journal of Finance Economics*, Vol. 3: 305–360; and Jensen, M.C. (1986), "Agency cost of free cash flow, corporate finance, and takeovers", *American Economic Review*, 76, 323–329.

7. For some research on institutional weaknesses in emerging markets, we refer to the seminal papers by La Porta, R., F. Lopez-De-Silanes & A. Schleifer (1999), "Corporate ownership around the world", *Journal of Finance*, 54(2), 471–517; La Porta, R., F. Lopez-De-Silanes, A. Schleifer & R. Vishny (2000), "Investor protection and corporate governance", *Journal of Financial Economics*, 58, 3–27; and La Porta, Lopez-De-Silanes, Schleifer. & Vishny (2002), "Investor protection and corporate valuation", *Journal of Finance*, Vol. 57; 1147–1170.

Part I

Economic Outlook and Institutional Voids

2

The Economic and Business Outlook for South East Asia

Mark Crosby

Introduction

In August 1967 the Foreign Affairs Ministers of Indonesia, Malaysia, the Philippines, Singapore and Thailand signed the five articles that created the Association of South East Asian Nations (ASEAN). The agreement proclaimed ASEAN as representing "the collective will of the nations of Southeast Asia to bind themselves together in friendship and cooperation and, through joint efforts and sacrifices, secure for their peoples and for posterity the blessings of peace, freedom and prosperity".[1] At the time of its creation ASEAN countries had recently suffered from a number of significant regional confrontations, and as with the European Union, the ambition was to create a region that was more peaceful and stable. In 1967 wars in Indo-China were still continuing, but the newly-created ASEAN was open to participation by any nation in South East Asia that signed up to ASEAN's aims and principles. Today ASEAN includes the original five signatories, plus Vietnam, Cambodia, Laos, Myanmar and Negara Brunei Darussalam.

While the original motivation for the creation of ASEAN was political, the related aim of peaceful regional integration led naturally to the desire for greater economic integration. The push towards greater integration has

M. Crosby (✉)
Monash Business School, Melbourne, Australia
e-mail: mark.crosby@monash.edu

© The Editor(s) (if applicable) and the Author(s) 2016
P. Verhezen et al. (eds.), *Doing Business in ASEAN Markets*,
DOI 10.1007/978-3-319-41790-5_2

increased since the early 2000s, leading up to the agreement to create a new ASEAN economic community (AEC), signed in Kuala Lumpur on 22 November 2015. The vision for ASEAN is to create an integrated, peaceful and stable community with shared prosperity, and so the AEC is a key pillar supporting regional economic integration. Similar to the European Union, the AEC aims to allow the free movement of goods, services and skilled labour. At the time of its creation the ASEAN economy was the 7th largest in the world, with a population of 622 million and a combined GDP in 2014 of $US2.6 trillion. According to the AEC the vision for 2025 is to create a community that is highly integrated and cohesive, competitive, innovative and dynamic, with enhanced connectivity and sectoral cooperation, and a more resilient, inclusive and people-oriented, people-centred community, integrated with the global economy. The aims are ambitious, and the question addressed in this chapter is to what extent these aims might be achieved, as well as some discussion of expected trends for ASEAN as a whole and for the larger economies in the region.

Table 2.1 shows GDP and related data for the ten ASEAN countries plus Australia, China and the United States. The Table shows quite clearly the huge diversity within ASEAN, which will pose enormous challenges to

Table 2.1 Selected indicators

	GDP growth	GDP/capita (USD)	GDP 2005 $US (billions)		Population
	1990–2011	2014	1970	2013	2012
Australia	3.3	61,980	227.3	867.2	22.7
Brunei	1.8	40,980	na	10.1	0.4
Cambodia	7.3	1095	na	10.7	14.8
China	9.9	7590	118.3	4864.0	1350.7
Indonesia	4.7	3492	37.9	452.3	248.0
Laos	6.6	1793	na	5.1	6.5
Malaysia	5.7	11,307	15.1	208.0	29.0
Myanmar	8.9	1204	na	na	52.5
Philippines	3.8	2873	29.6	155.6	96.0
Singapore	6.1	56,284	10.1	199.2	5.3
Thailand	4.2	5977	21.5	230.3	67.1
United States	2.4	54,629	4333.8	14,450.3	314.8
Vietnam	7.1	2052	na	92.3	88.8

Source: World Bank, World Development Indicators, and Asian Productivity Office Database 2013

regional integration. GDP per capita ranges from US$3 per day in Cambodia to US$56,284 per annum in Singapore, a level of per capita income about the same as Australia and the United States. Within ASEAN Singapore and Brunei are high income countries, Malaysia is middle income but all other countries are low income.

In terms of overall size of the economies in ASEAN there is also a very large range. In Laos, Cambodia and Brunei GDP is less than 3 % the size of the Indonesian economy, the largest economy in the region. Malaysia, the Philippines, Singapore and Thailand all have similar sized economies, despite the very large differences in population. However, all of these economies are only about the same size as that of Sydney. And even Indonesia's economy is much smaller than Australia's and dwarfed in size by China. In Chap. 5 we examine the rise of China and the economic impact this has had, and will continue to have, on ASEAN economies.

The other feature of the ASEAN economies is rapid economic growth. The region can still suffer from local political instability, but in general the trend towards greater political and economic stability has supported rapid economic growth across most of the region. The Table shows that Australia's real GDP almost quadrupled between 1970 and 2013, while at the same time China's GDP rose more than 40-fold. While not enjoying quite the spectacular growth of China, the larger ASEAN countries enjoyed growth much greater than that experienced by Australia or the United States. Indonesia, Thailand, Singapore and Malaysia all saw more than ten-fold increases in the size of their economies, with only the Philippines showing relatively slow growth. Some of these differences in economic size can be explained by population, which again varies enormously, from the small state of Brunei to the world's fourth largest population in Indonesia.

Near-Term Economic Outlook

In recent years Asia has been the fast growing region in the global economy, and ASEAN countries as a group have been growing at roughly the same pace as the rest of Asia. According to the IMF (see Table 2.2) Asia is expected to be the most dynamic region in the global economy until 2017, with growth at about 2 % above the world average from 2015 to 2017. While growth in ASEAN is slightly below the Asian average, it is expected to remain comfortably above world growth. Within ASEAN there is considerable variation, with

Table 2.2 Near-term economic outlook

	GDP growth (actual to 2014, projections thereafter)				
	2013	2014	2015	2016	2017
Australia	2.0	2.6	2.5	2.5	3.0
Brunei	−2.1	−2.3	−0.2	−2.0	3.0
Cambodia	7.4	7.1	6.9	7.0	7.0
China	7.7	7.3	6.9	6.5	6.2
Indonesia	5.6	5.0	4.8	4.9	5.3
Laos	8.0	7.4	7.0	7.4	7.4
Malaysia	4.7	6.0	5.0	4.4	4.8
Myanmar	8.4	8.7	7.0	8.6	7.7
Philippines	7.1	6.1	5.8	6.0	6.2
Singapore	4.7	3.3	2.0	1.8	2.2
Thailand	2.7	0.8	2.8	3.0	3.2
Vietnam	5.4	6.0	6.7	6.3	6.2
World	3.3	3.4	3.1	3.2	3.5

Source: IMF, Regional Economic Outlook, Asia and Pacific, May 2016

the oil-dependent economy of Brunei shrinking, while the poorer countries in Indo-China are expected to be among the fastest growing economies globally.

The outlook for future economic growth across the region will be affected by commodity price movements, demographics, the global economic outlook, financial factors and export performance. In addition, local political factors will play a significant role in determining actual outcomes. It is worthwhile considering each of these factors in turn.

Commodity price increases for most base metals, food and fuels over the period from the early 2000s until about 2013 were largely driven by increases in demand from China. As China's economic growth has slowed and as that economy slowly shifts towards services and consumption, commodity prices have fallen significantly, and falls in oil and coal prices in particular have had major effects on some economies. Within ASEAN Brunei is heavily oil-dependent, while Malaysia and Indonesia have seen weakening GDP growth and export and government revenues as a result of commodity price falls. However, as seen from Table 2.2, both Malaysia and Indonesia have still been able to grow reasonably strongly. In both cases these economies are fairly diversified, and other drivers of growth are strong enough partially to offset the dampening effect of falls in commodity prices. In Brunei the economy's heavy reliance on oil has meant that the economy has been severely impacted by falls in oil prices. Many other economies in the region have benefited from falling commodity prices, with commodity import costs and inflation both falling. While the future for commodity prices is quite unpredictable, most analysts are not expecting prices to rise as they did in the 2000s any time soon. While weak commodity prices are likely to continue to drag on growth in Brunei, other factors are likely to play a more important role in other ASEAN economies.

Demographic change across the globe is leading to slower workforce growth, as well as an ageing workforce. Within ASEAN economies there is again a wide range of demographic profiles, ranging from a relatively rapidly ageing Singapore with a profile similar to East Asian countries, to the youthful countries of Indo-China and the Philippines. Thailand and Vietnam both have a higher fraction of the population aged under 15 than Singapore, though in both cases they are have an older population than other countries in the region.

Figure 2.1 shows the fraction of the population aged under 15 and over 65 as a percentage of the total population for all of the ASEAN countries plus Japan, Australia, and the United States, with the countries ordered from highest older population (Japan) to lowest (Laos). Demographic change is starting to have dramatic effects on many economies around the globe, and within Asia an ageing China with fewer workers in the 15–24 year old age group creates significant opportunities for other countries to replace the cheap manufacturing industries that has driven a considerable fraction of China's urban to rural migration and income growth. In particular Indonesia, the Philippines, Vietnam and Myanmar with their large and young population have a considerable opportunity to grow manufacturing in lower skill sectors such as

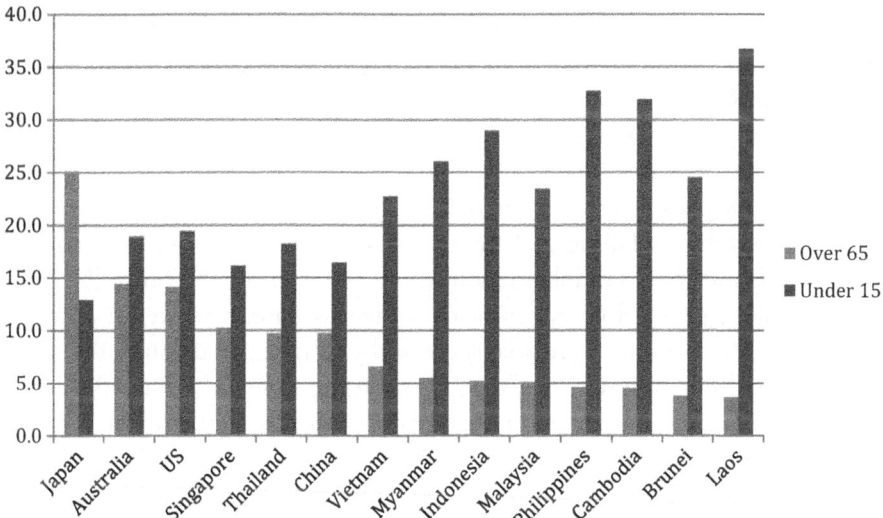

Fig. 2.1 The dependency burden
(*Source*: Population census and Asian Productivity Organization Data Workbook 2015)

textiles, clothing and footwear if such countries can succeed in attracting the foreign capital that is needed to support those industries. Currently growth in those sectors is slow, due to high levels of political risk, weak infrastructure and logistics, and other policies that reduce new business activity (discussed further below).

Weaker demographics is one of the reasons why the global economic outlook since the global financial crisis has been consistently poor. Growth has usually fallen below forecast and there have been many arguments as to why a "new normal" might be lower economic growth.[2] Slower growth in the workforce due to an ageing population and a slowing in that rate of growth of female participation in the labor market will be a drag on future economic growth. A bigger question is around the future of productivity growth. Some, such as Gordon (2016) argue that it is unlikely that we will see productivity growth as fast as the twentieth century, and so future growth in the USA and similar advanced economies will slow considerably. However, others are more optimistic regarding productivity. The IMF forecasts for future growth in Table 2.2 show economic growth considerably lower than in the early 2000s. This is due mainly to slower growth in advanced economies and in China. The main implication of slower growth in the global economy for the ASEAN region is that this will mean slower global trade growth. However in 2015 ASEAN economies were able to withstand the slowdown in global trade and particularly the slowdown in China's trade. One reason for this is the growth in intra-ASEAN trade flows as the consumer market grows and domestic demand growth continues to be strong. Between 2007 and 2014 total trade from ASEAN countries rose from US$1.6 trillion to US$2.5 trillion, with intra-ASEAN trade forming 24 % of the total.[3]

The Asian Financial Crisis in 1997 decimated regional economies. The source of the crisis was financial fragilities relating to pegged exchange rates and large trade and current account deficits. Indonesia, Thailand, and Malaysia were the most hit by falling exchange rates and a corporate and banking sector with high levels of USdollardenominated short term debt. Since the crisis there has been great effort put into strengthening banking systems, and as a result ASEAN countries were able successfully to navigate through the more recent Global Financial Crisis. Currently there are some financial risks in the region such as high asset prices in Singapore but in general the region is much more resilient to financial shocks than in the 1990s. Central banks still try to minimise exchange rate volatility in most cases, but these central banks hold higher reserves, and corporates and banks are not as exposed to foreign currency denominated debt as in the past.

Growth in Major Markets

As noted already in this Chapter, the diversity among the ASEAN economies makes it difficult to make statements about economic outcomes and prospects that apply to all countries in the region. In this section I will use some of the countries in the region to illustrate major economic themes that will continue to affect business and the economy in the future.

Shortly after coming to office the Indonesian President Joko Widodo, better known as Jokowi, announced that his country would aim to achieve 7 % economic growth by the end of his Presidency in 2018. As can be seen in Table 2.1, this is significantly above recent growth performance, though Indonesia was achieving such growth prior to the Asian Financial Crisis in 1997.

In order to achieve higher growth, Jokowi knows that Indonesia will have to shift its economy away from commodities and rely more heavily on manufacturing. Since the days of the spice trade Indonesia has depended upon trade in commodities, with the country being today the world's largest palm oil and tin exporter, as well as a large exporter of rubber, gold, copper and coal. While it is not expected that Indonesia's commodity exports will fall, higher growth requires the greater employment and growth opportunities that can be found in the manufacturing sector. Indonesia did see strong growth in manufacturing in the early 1990s, but this sector stagnated during the Asian Financial Crisis and the 2000s commodity boom. Currently Indonesia has some strong advantages in terms of attracting industry. Wages are 30–40 % below minimum wage levels in Thailand or China, and the median age is about seven years below those countries.

The problem with attracting manufacturing into Indonesia is that infrastructure is very poor so that companies spend up to double on logistics as they would spend in other countries in the region.[4] Jokowi recognises that a lack of infrastructure is a major drag on growth in Indonesia, and he has pledged to start to address this problem. Estimates by PwC suggest that infrastructure spending over the next decade will grow by 7 % per year to $165 billion, making Indonesia one of the bigger infrastructure investors globally.[5] However, the infrastructure deficit is so large that it will be at least a decade before this challenge begins to be addressed.

An equally big problem for Indonesia is bureaucracy, red tape and other business challenges. According to the World Bank's ease of doing business index, Indonesia ranks 109 globally in terms of ease of doing business.[6] In the region Singapore ranks number 1 in the world, Malaysia ranks 18 and Thailand number 49. This ranking for Indonesia reflects a range of factors including difficulties with starting a business and getting services such as electricity, to the complexity of the tax system and challenges with bribery and corruption. The combination of the extreme lack of infrastructure and the difficulties with doing business mean that Jokowi is unlikely to achieve his 7 % goal by 2018. Indonesia does have the potential to grow much more quickly, but that potential won't be reached until the ease of doing business and infrastructure challenges are tackled.

Of the major economies in the region, the Philippines has been the weakest performer for decades. However recent years has seen stronger growth, with the IMF forecasting growth around 6 % in 2016 and 2017. The Philippines is a beneficiary of lower oil prices, and is less dependent on exports to China than other countries in the region, so that as the People's Republic's growth slows down this has less of an impact (see Chap. 3). But the Philippines has had good economic policies under outgoing President Aquino, with budget and fiscal reforms that have raised the country's credit rating. Aquino's government also managed to increase social spending, and increased infrastructure spending from 1.8 % of GDP to 5 %. As in the case of Indonesia, the infrastructure deficit is very large, but is now starting to be addressed. Other policies have improved transparency and governance. The result of this good policy environment has been strong economic growth and large increases of foreign investment into the Philippines. A large, young population with good English-speaking skills has led to a boom in Business Process Outsourcing (BPO), which now makes up around 10 % of GDP.

But the Philippines also illustrates the challenges faced in many parts of the region. Like Indonesia, the Philippines is not an easy place to do business, ranking 103 globally in the World Bank Index. Political stability is also an issue. Despite strong economic performance in recent years, the election in May 2016 brought into office a new populist President in Rodrigo Duterte. It is quite uncertain what President Duterte will implement in terms of economic policies, but his agenda appears to be quite business unfriendly and a reversal from the successful policies of President Aquino. Even if changes in policy are less significant than expected, the uncertainty resulting from the Duterte victory will be enough to deter foreign investment and will likely lead to weaker growth in the short term. Political uncertainty in many parts of the region remains a significant issue, and will continue to lead to volatile growth in Indonesia, Myanmar, the Philippines and Thailand. Even Malaysia is currently suffering from uncertainty surrounding the 1MDB finances that is threatening economic growth.

Unlike other large economies in the region, Vietnam has not had to worry about political instability since the end of the Vietnam War. But the question remains at to whether the government can reform and encourage businesses in the way that has been so successful in China, the other large communist government in Asia. As in the Philippines, the expectation is for very strong growth in the short term, and a big question about Vietnam is whether it will be able to capitalise on the move of manufacturing out of China as that country's labour costs rise. The infrastructure deficit is similar to that found in the Philippines or Indonesia, so that logistics costs remain high. Vietnam's projected infrastructure spend will start to address this problem, and the one advantage that Vietnam has over regional rivals is that the projected spend is more likely to be realised due to the fact that the one-party government can more quickly make and implement infrastructure investment decisions.

Overall Vietnam ranks similarly to China in terms of ease of doing business, and slightly above the Philippines and Indonesia. Unlike China, however, Vietnam's domestic market is small, and so the difficulties in doing business need to be addressed if Vietnam is to attract more foreign investment in sectors such as manufacturing in the future.

The economy of Singapore has been extremely successful in recent decades. When the British started to pull their military out of Singapore beginning in 1968 around 20 % of the population were employed by these bases. Singapore had also been recently ejected from Malaysia, and there were grave fears for its economy. The ruling People's Action Party committed at this time to making Singapore's economy an easy place to do business and attractive for foreign investment. Today, Singapore's high level of workforce skill, excellent infrastructure, lack of corruption, and ease of doing business combine to continue to make Singapore a destination for foreign investment. This investment initially supported low-skill manufacturing industries such as textiles and electronics, but in more recent times has funded financial services and high-tech industries such as biotech. The very successful development path that Singapore followed shows that all countries in the region are capable of reaching middle and high income status. But Singapore also shows that to make such progress requires all of the elements described above – improvements to infrastructure and the business environment, tackling corruption, policy stability and improvements to institutions. Within the region Singapore is now in the position where it is a significant source of foreign investment, as well as a host. The Singapore model has been a source of inspiration for many other countries in the region, and even for China, as described in Chap. 3.

Conclusions

In this Chapter We have outlined the economic and business issues and challenges facing ASEAN countries. It has been noted that while there is considerable diversity between these ten quite different economies, the expectation that the region will be among the most dynamic in the global economy should not disappoint. The region faces huge challenges, but it also has great opportunities. The challenges are to maintain political stability and improve policies that support businesses. Infrastructure weaknesses are a huge issue in most parts of the region except for Singapore. Corruption remains a problem in many countries, and related governance and other institutional shortcomings require addressing. The expressed ASEAN aim of freedom is a challenging one, with freedoms still limited in Vietnam, and Thailand currently ruled by the military. While rights and freedoms seem to be improving in Myanmar, such rights are still far from guaranteed in the future. The aims of the AEC to have full regional integration also is likely to remain many years away as far as the economic sphere is concerned, with difficulties including allowing greater labour mobility in a region with such diversity in incomes and inequality.

Notes

1. http://www.asean.org/asean/about-asean/history/
2. See Robert Gordon, *The Rise and Fall of American Growth: The U.S. Standard of Living since the Civil War*. Princeton University Press, 2016.
3. ASEAN Secretariat, Jakarta, (2015) "A Blueprint for Growth ASEAN Economic Community 2015: Progress and Key Achievements".
4. "Spicing up growth," *The Economist*, May 9 2015.
5. PwC (2014) "A Summary of South East Asian Infrastructure Spending: Outlook to 2025."
6. World Bank Group, Doing Business, available at http://www.doingbusiness.org/data

3

Negotiating Better Governance: Jurisdictional Arbitrage Within ASEAN

Howard Dick

Introduction

The notion that business people should serve the national interests of their country of origin is widely held but also ahistorical, nowhere more so than in Southeast Asia. From the myriad ports of the archipelago, traders have always done business with the wider world and mingled with 'foreigners' from more far-flung places with other languages and religions. The internationalism of commerce was epitomized in the great entrepot of Malacca, whose role eventually passed to Singapore. The European powers seized territories that they consolidated into colonies: in due course these became nation-states in their own right with inherited colonial systems of law and administration and fairly arbitrary peoples and borders. These new nations were not foundational but overlays, albeit intrusive and disruptive. Quite apart from the natural rejection of colonial rule, the timing of independence in the 1940s and 1950s following upon the 1930s world depression and then Japanese occupation, meant that the new nations of Southeast Asia began with a defensive posture towards the world economy. The domestic market had to be protected against 'foreign' imports, exports were begrudged as a loss of resources, and foreign investment was a mode of neocolonialism. Even business itself was often seen as a morally dubious activity. All these views are now widely rejected as not

H. Dick (✉)
Professorial Fellow, University of Melbourne - Australia
e-mail: H.Dick@unimelb.edu.au

© The Editor(s) (if applicable) and the Author(s) 2016
P. Verhezen et al. (eds.), *Doing Business in ASEAN Markets*,
DOI 10.1007/978-3-319-41790-5_3

29

just silly but actually harmful to economic prosperity. Nevertheless, the view that companies should remain loyal to their original national jurisdiction still holds popular sway. The ASEAN single market is a decisive step away from such navel-gazing but there is still residual prejudice that international business, even regional business, should be regarded with suspicion.

Tentative inauguration of an ASEAN Single Market at the end of 2015 potentially moves the region's Economic Community into a new and more dynamic phase. In preparation each member country has been striving to boost its competitiveness by streamlining its trade and investment policies. Nevertheless ASEAN integration is still a muddled and uneven process among the ten quite different polities and economies with as yet only modest progress towards harmonization. Nowhere is this more apparent than in matters of governance, referring here to standards of public administration, corporate governance and relations between business and government. Using the term 'governance' in this way is consistent with the approach of the World Bank's Doing Business surveys and rankings.[1] It puts the focus on processes and outcomes instead of the ideological aspect of government. Moreover, it makes corruption an element of the governance environment instead of being the issue per se.

Firms engaged in international business now enjoy wide choice as to where they base their headquarters and locate their various subsidiary operations. One aspect, much commented upon in regard to foreign investment, has been the shift of production to low-wage countries, most notably China but also ASEAN member states. That shift does not mean, however, that headquarters or even regional offices follow the factories. A second aspect is the search for offshore tax havens in which to vest mobile assets and revenues. These havens used to be mainly European, countries such as Switzerland, Liechtenstein and Monaco but offshore havens have proliferated to include Central America and micro-states in the Caribbean and the Pacific. In the 21st century the principals of Chinese firms also enjoy the benefits of low-tax offshore jurisdictions where profits can be accumulated until reinvested back into China, a practice known as 'round-tripping'.

This chapter considers the impact of markedly different standards of governance on the emerging pattern of ASEAN integration. In the market economy it is private decisions on investment and location that determine business location, which for international business is typically multiple. Firms engaged in international business have often complex legal identities that are necessary both to comply with, and to transcend, the regulations of national governments. The imperative to manage risk, especially to protect the value of assets, including intellectual property, as also to enforce contracts and minimize taxes, is giving rise to increasing jurisdictional arbitrage. The term used to be applied to firms seeking to have international disputes heard in the most favorable legal jurisdiction. Lately there has been much hostile publicity in regard to firms manouvering to declare tax in the most favorable jurisdiction.[2] Nevertheless, jurisdictional arbitrage may also be applied strategically for the good reason of providing a stronger international business platform. It is especially relevant to ASEAN integration as firms seek to leverage their domestic advantage to compete in regional and international markets, the phenomenon referred to somewhat condescendingly in the International Business literature as 'emerging country multinationals'. Because standards of governance in Singapore are much higher than in other member states, ASEAN firms seeking to build international reputation have good strategic reason apart from tax minimization to establish a visible identity in Singapore.

The chapter combines the perspectives of Economic History and International Business. It begins with a brief overview of governance indicators across ASEAN in comparison with China and Hong Kong, then reviews historical trends in the role of Singapore within the Southeast Asian archipelago by taking the shipping industry as a case study. The following section is contemporary and looks at the jurisdictional strategies of four case studies: shipping line Samudera Indonesia, food manufacturer Indofood, agribusiness firm Wilmar International and car maker Astra International. Their approaches differ but better governance is a common thread.

Patterns of Governance

All key governance indicators reveal marked variation in standards across the ten ASEAN countries (Table 3.1).

The World Bank's summary Doing Business Indicator for 2015 ranks Singapore as best in the world out of 189 countries. Malaysia (18) also scores well in the first quartile; Thailand (49), Negara Brunei Darussalam (84) and, narrowly, Vietnam (90) rate in the second quartile but the Philippines (103), Indonesia (109), Cambodia (127), Laos (134) and Myanmar (167) are all below the median of 94.5. By the key indicator of 'enforceability of contracts', ASEAN governance is even less impressive: Singapore is again best in the world but all countries except Vietnam and Laos now perform much worse. The Philippines drops back from 103 to 140 and Indonesia 109 to 170.

Table 3.1 ASEAN member states by Governance Indicators

Nation	DBI rank/189 2015	DBI contracts rank/189	DBI paying taxes rank/189	CPI rank/167 2015	GCB 2013 Judiciary (%)	GCB 2013 Officials (%)
SINGAPORE	1	1	5	8	na	na
Malaysia	18	44	31	54	76	46
Thailand	49	57	70	76	18	58
Brunei	84	113	16	na	na	na
Vietnam	90	74	168	112	53	55
Philippines	103	140	126	95	56	64
Indonesia	109	170	148	88	86	79
Cambodia	127	174	95	150	60	30
Laos	134	92	127	139	na	na
Myanmar	167	187	84	147	na	na
HONG KONG	5	4	4	18	na	na
China	84	7	132	83	na	na

Source: TI (2015a, b), World Bank (2015)

The Doing Business indicators are broadly consistent with the results of Transparency International's Corruption Perceptions Index.[3] According to the 2015 CPI, Singapore ranks a credible 8th out of 167 nations but no other ASEAN country falls in the first quartile and Malaysia and Thailand are the only others to rank below the median of 83.5. The more detailed Global Corruption Barometer (2013) is available for only six of the ASEAN countries (not including Singapore) but it does help to fill out the picture. According to the percentage of informants regarding an institution as corrupt or seriously corrupt, the judiciary in Thailand is the only one of the six that is not regarded by the majority of informants as seriously corrupt. Similar results apply to the corruption of public officials, albeit with Cambodia and Malaysia rating better and Thailand much worse. Police are seen as corrupt by the large majority in all countries except Cambodia.

The general conclusion is that within ASEAN only Singapore has outstanding governance, Malaysia and Thailand are patchy, and all others are more or less deplorable. This creates much more opportunity for jurisdictional arbitrage than is the case in Western Europe. While Singapore is a jurisdiction of global best practice, as well as a hub for global logistics, doing business in other ASEAN countries entails much higher risks. It is therefore sensible as far as possible to vest assets and funds in the safe jurisdiction while carrying out operations in adjacent countries. This calculus applies to both foreign and domestic firms. Foreign firms naturally wish to minimize country risk but, as inward investment restrictions are liberalized, enjoy certain advantages of foreignness. Domestic firms that establish offshore entities in Singapore may also enjoy some of those advantages, a phenomenon known in China as 'round-tripping'. Domestic firms thereby insulate themselves from their own country's pervasive corruption and establish better international respectability.

Some perspective on these findings can be gained from comparing ASEAN states with Hong Kong and China (Table 3.1). Hong Kong ranks only slightly below Singapore in respect to Doing Business and level of corruption and may be regarded as approximating global best practice by most key indicators. China, by contrast, is a mixed bag. According to the summary Doing Business Index, China ranks not much below the median. In terms of enforceability of contracts it ranks just behind Hong Kong but in terms of paying taxes it falls back to near the bottom of the third quartile. Transparency International ranks China's level of corruption as only slightly better than Indonesia's but the Global Corruption Barometer is not available to give finer detail. Unevenness in China's governance has long given Hong Kong a role as a business hub for China, allowing firms to be at once both in and outside China, that is in China for operations and outside China as a vested legal and financial entity, a classic case of jurisdictional arbitrage.

An important analytical distinction can be made between non-transparent and transparent jurisdiction. Profit shifting for tax purposes – what the OECD (2015) refers to as Base Erosion and Profit Shifting – is very much about concealing revenues in the jurisdiction where they are earned and declaring them under brass plate or trading companies in low-tax and non-transparent jurisdictions. In April 2016 the leak of a massive cache of documents by Panamanian corporate lawyers Mossack & Fonseca exposed to the world at large the modus operandi of well-organised international tax avoidance and evasion and the indignation was palpable. Nevertheless, shipowners have long used devices of flag-of-convenience nominee companies to disguise their identity, nationality and country of residence with the aim of evading national maritime regulation and, of course, to minimize tax. Bankers, financial intermediaries and corporate lawyers created what Dick referred to by analogy with physics as 'wormholes'.[4]

Within ASEAN, however, there are virtuous motives for creating transparent entities in a well-governed rule-of-law jurisdiction, notably Singapore but also in adjacent Hong Kong. A company domiciled in Indonesia or the Philippines, for example, suffers a jurisdictional discount to its reputation as well as many practical obstacles to establishing a competitive international business. A visible corporate identity in a globally-recognized jurisdiction such as Singapore is a sensible way to overcome this disadvantage without forgoing regional identity. While domestic operations necessarily remain subject to local law and politics, a growing international business can be vested in a Singaporean or Hong Kong entity without exposing it to the anomalies, vagaries and uncertainties of a chaotic and corrupt legal system, or to extortion by party bosses. Inter-jurisdictional contracts can be negotiated and capital pooled subject to the greater rigor and certainty of enforceable international business law. Even so, law is just the necessary foundation for strategic jurisdictional arbitrage, likewise a low-tax regime that is not onerous in its requirements for disclosure. Just as important is the reality that Singapore and Hong Kong are global markets for banking and business services and a hub of regional information flows in specific markets. Firms that are not tied into these networks of information exchange are outsiders and suffer a competitive disadvantage. A listing on the Singapore or Hong Kong exchange makes that presence highly visible.

Yet notwithstanding the substantial advantages of law, networking and information exchange that flow from a visible business presence in Singapore and/or Hong Kong, this chapter argues that the prime strategic issue is one of governance and, in consequence, reputation. ASEAN firms doing business in their own country have little choice but to adjust to the local political situation and conform with local informal practices. These certainly shade into corruption, and firms make their own decisions as to how aggressively they behave. Even more important is patronage. Whether aggressively or defensively, prominent firms can hardly avoid playing the game of patronage because it has such a big influence on competitive advantage in the domestic market when there is no reliable protection at law. The governance skills for success in the domestic market are therefore very different from those required for sustainable international business. Consequently, ASEAN firms seeking to 'go international' and even to do business elsewhere in the ASEAN single market need to build a new capability in international governance. This involves principals and executives learning to do business by international rules, and it may be accelerated by hiring new managers who already have such skills. Ultimately it will succeed only if a new corporate culture is created and translated into reputation through recognized performance.[5] Hence the prime benefit of setting up a visible entity in Singapore or Hong Kong is that it puts an ASEAN firm in the international spotlight in an international jurisdiction among other international firms who are party to the same markets. If ASEAN's emerging multinationals can thereby build international status and reputation, their domestic economies also stand to benefit, not only from the generation of new business but also through the flow-back of better governance practices.

The Historical Background

The business nexus between Indonesia and Singapore dates back to the island colony's foundation in 1819. Still the definitive work on early trade patterns, Wong Lin Ken (1960) shows that Singapore's regional trade network extended throughout the archipelago, including the Malay Peninsula, Thailand and what is now Vietnam.[6] Despite being a British colony, ethnically and economically Singapore was always primarily a Chinese city.[7] Regional trade was very much in Chinese hands. The typical arrangement was that family members or close associates would control each end of the trade, some in Singapore and some in one or more ports of the archipelago. Traders of substance liked to own at least one vessel to ship their own goods to and from Singapore and top up with the cargo of friendly associates. From the late-nineteenth century, as business incorporation was seen to confer the greater certainty of European corporate law, business entities were established, giving the family dual legal identity, at Singapore under British law and in the Netherlands Indies, for example, under Dutch law. As in Hong Kong and Shanghai, the formation, variation and dissolution of Chinese business firms and partnerships was advertised even in the colonial press and contemporary newspapers show that principals would resort to western law to resolve commercial disputes.

After the opening of the Suez Canal in 1869, steamships soon quickened the pulse of regional shipping and trade.[8] Not being dependent upon the seasonal monsoons, steamers could make more roundtrips in a year but were also more expensive to buy and operate. Among the investors were tycoons who controlled opium and/or mining syndicates in Indonesia, Malaya and Thailand. One of the more notable was Java-based former opium farmer Oei Tiong Ham, who diversified into sugar, banking, property and shipping. In 1912 he transferred his shipping interests to the newly established Heap Eng Moh Steamship Company Ltd in the British jurisdiction of Singapore. In 1921 he became resident of Singapore, moving there in order to minimize inheritance taxes and be able to nominate his heirs under British law from among his twenty-six sons. Four years after his death in 1924, his sons sold the controlling interest in Heap Eng Moh to its main competitor, the Dutch-flag Koninklijke Paketvaart Maatschappij (KPM). The sale and beneficial ownership remained a closely guarded commercial secret until the 1970s, thereby illustrating a further advantage of Singaporean jurisdiction.

Since taking over the monopoly mail contract for the Netherlands East Indies on 1 January 1891, the KPM had sought by rate-discrimination and through-shipment contracts to divert the export trade of the Outer Islands from the British entrepot of Singapore to Dutch ports.[9] The ocean ports of

Belawan (North Sumatra), Tanjung Priok (Jakarta), Tanjung Perak (Surabaya) and Makassar were all developed by the colonial government to assist this trade diversion. Nevertheless, the KPM soon found that Chinese trade and shipping from Sumatra, Riau and West Kalimantan to Singapore was impossible to suppress. In the 1910s the KPM switched tactics to build economic small ships that could compete and share the trade with local interests. Singapore's status was thereby effectively reinforced as one of the five main ports of the Indonesian archipelago.[10] Contemporary postcards of Singapore harbour show how prominent was KPM shipping.

From 1945, Singapore played a vital role in the Indonesian Revolution as a base for smuggling goods in and out of Indonesia through the Dutch naval blockade.[11] After the transfer of sovereignty in December 1949 and the restoration of normal commercial relations between Indonesia and Singapore, a good number of ethnic Chinese born in Indonesia soon found that the business environment was more liberal and stable in British-controlled Singapore, much less regulated and much less corrupt. These up-and-coming entrepreneurs, mostly young men still in their twenties, emigrated to Singapore but left family in Indonesia who as agents could carry on that side of the business.

In no industry was the role of Indonesian expatriates more prominent than cross-border shipping. Leading examples of "Singaporean" shipowners with a family background in Indonesia were the Thay brothers (Kie Hock), Thio brothers (Guan Guan), Tong Djoe (Tunas Group) and Robin Loh (Robin Group).[12] The first two firms played a leading role in the shipping of the archipelago and took good advantage of the suspension of KPM sailings in December 1957, even buying up its ships. The two latter became well known in the 1970s as contractors to the state oil company Pertamina. All the above firms continued to engage in shipping with Indonesia but with registered headquarters in Singapore and ships often flying flags of convenience such as Panama. After late 1963 when Confrontation between Indonesia and the newly-created state of Malaysia (initially including Singapore) led to official suspension of trade between Indonesia and Malaysia, shipping and trade reverted to smuggling with ships renamed and transferred to flags of convenience such as Panama. Some firms also set up businesses in British-controlled Hong Kong and transshipped through that port. By the time normal trade resumed in mid-1966, Singapore had become an independent city-state. In 1968 it sought to consolidate its advantage as a hub of regional shipping and trade by granting the shipping industry exemption from company tax.

After its container port was opened in 1971, Singapore's role was strengthened as the dominant transshipment port in Southeast Asia with a full range of associated maritime and logistics services. As ships became more specialized and their cost increased, financing became more crucial. Singapore offered legal security for mortgages and other forms of ship financing, whereas ships under the Indonesian flag especially were no security at all because of the legal obstacles in the way of repossession in the event of default. Besides the ongoing advantage of tax-exempt status, there was also the consideration of profile and reputation. Finally, besides being the centre of the regional shipping market, Singapore was just a much easier place in which to do business. By the end of the twentieth century Singapore had transcended its traditional role of being a regional entrepot to become not only the busiest container port in the world but also a global centre of the shipping industry alongside London and New York. A parallel evolution could be observed in the financial sector.

Contemporary Case Studies

Samudera Indonesia

One of the first Indonesian companies to seize the new opportunities offered by Singapore as a logistics hub in the containership era was deepsea operator Samudera Indonesia, founded by the late Soedarpo Sastosatomo in 1964.[13] Since the resumption of normal trade with Singapore in 1966, Samudera had a registered Singaporean company Samudera Indonesia Pte Ltd as its local agent to handle calls by its deepsea ships as well as interisland vessels calling at Singapore inbound from Belawan to load backhaul cargo for Jakarta. In 1993, when Samudera sought to extend its interisland container feeder operations into regional networks, it incorporated the subsidiary Samudera Shipping Line Ltd (SSL) in Singapore to manage its regional interests extending from Southeast Asia through to India and the Middle East. SSL listed in Singapore in October 1997.

Despite being Indonesia's leading international shipping operator, Soedarpo had an uneasy relationship with President Suharto. Because of his former association with the Indonesia Socialist Party (PSI), in 1974 he had been arrested on trumped-up political charges and for two years was prevented from leaving the country.[14] After Suharto's downfall in 1998, the group felt more confident to vest in Indonesia. Thus in mid-1999 Samudera Indonesia Tbk was listed on the Jakarta stock exchange as the group's holding company.[15] This gave rise to a dual strategy in which control was exercised from Jakarta but international container operations were managed by SSL from Singapore. The Jakarta parent controls 65 % of SSL with the other 34 % held by the public.[16] After 2000 a similar structure was applied to bulk shipping of dry, liquid and gas cargoes: international shipping was managed from Singapore by Foremost Maritime Pte Ltd, which had been was set up in 1995 as a subsidiary of SSL, while Samudera Shipping Services was set up as an Indonesian subsidiary to take over the group's domestic bulk shipping.[17] As long as Indonesia's shipping and logistics regime continues to be more onerous than that of Singapore, it is commercially sound for Samudera to diversify its operations in this way.

Indofood

Before the Indonesian rupiah collapsed in January 1998 in the midst of the Asian crisis, many families, and not only ethnic Chinese, had already placed most of their liquid funds in Singapore or Hong Kong. Many listed Indonesian companies were thereby left bankrupt, along with their bankers, and were taken under the control of the Indonesia Bank Reconstruction Agency (IBRA). The riots, rapes and the burning of ethnic Chinese property in May 1998 just before the resignation of President Suharto were further cause for many Chinese Indonesians to expatriate their family from Indonesia. Singapore, Hong Kong and Australia were the most popular havens because they were close enough to Indonesia and families held property and funds there. When IBRA later auctioned off its sequestrated companies, the buyers were often nominee companies registered in Singapore, Hong Kong or other tax havens, thereby giving these foreign funds the status of foreign direct investment with the privileges thereof. This was equivalent to Chinese capital 'roundtripping' from Hong Kong or the Virgin Islands and was a sound hedging strategy.

The diversified Salim Group has been described by Borsuk and Chng (2014) as the 'business pillar of Suharto's Indonesia'.[18] Because the patriarch Liem Sioe Liong (Sudono Salim) had been very close to President Suharto and was a prime target of the May 1998 riots, the family evacuated from Indonesia and sought to run what was left of the group, now stripped of Bank Central Asia, from offshore. For the next few years it remained uncertain when it would be safe for the family to return to Indonesia and whether group assets there would be vulnerable to potential legal action against the former president. Since 1967 Liem had owned a small trading company in Singapore and in 1981 set up KPM Pte Ltd as a local umbrella which duly acquired a property portfolio. In May 1998 KPM became the offshore 'crisis centre' but it was not a strategic solution.[19]

For restructuring the group's the profitable Indofood division, Liem turned instead to a Hong Kong investment vehicle, First Pacific Holdings. Since the mid-1970s Liem had dabbled in financial ventures in Hong Kong but First Pacific had been set up in 1982 on the initiative of his eldest son, Anthony, in partnership with merchant banker Manuel Pangilinan.[20] Although funded by the Liem family, it was an arm's length arrangement with management in the hands of Pangilinan, whose main interests were in the Philippines. In 1999 after prolonged negotiations that for some months had included Japanese noodle manufacturer Nissin Food Products, First Pacific bought up 50 % of Indofood. As of 2016, the Jakarta-listed parent entity Indofood Sukses Makmur Tbk is still chaired by Pangilinan with three other First Pacific and three independent commissioners while Antoni Salim in Jakarta serves as President Director and CEO[21]; First Pacific in Hong Kong is more or less a mirror image of this structure with Salim as Chairman and Pangilinan Executive Director and CEO in charge of operations in the Philippines.[22] This unusual and potentially fragile arrangement obviously depends upon a high level of personal trust between Antoni Salim and Pangilinan but it has well served its purpose in transforming Indofood from a crony enterprise to a well-run and transparent business group by Indonesian standards.

Singapore was brought into play by some complex arbitrage. In 2006 Indofood Singapore Holdings Pte Ltd (ISH) was created as an 84 %-owned agribusiness subsidiary of Indofood Sukses Makmur. By way of reverse take-over, a Singapore company Indofood Agri Holdings (IndoAgri) was then created and floated in 2007 with over two-thirds of the shares held by unlisted ISH and just under one third by the public. To its holdings in various Indonesian plantation companies was added a stake in the old Harrison & Crosfield plantation firm London Sumatra, itself listed on the Jakarta exchange. That stake was held though 100 % subsidiary Indofood Oils & Fats Pte Ltd which in turn owned 90 % of Salim Ivomas Pratama (SIMP). The structure was simplified in 2011 by floating SIMP in Jakarta and amalgamating Oils & Fats into IndoAgri. The logic of these moves was financial, not the least benefit being to reduce Indonesian withholding tax on dividends to IndoAgri from 20 % to 10 %.[23] Indofood Singapore Holdings was still owned by the Jakarta-listed parent Indofood Sukses Makmur but now held a string of three listed companies, that is IndoAgri (Singapore), SIMP and London Sumatra (both Jakarta). The arrangement allowed more transparency than is usual in large family conglomerates but the local parent holding company in Singapore remains a closed book. In terms of jurisdiction, the Indofood group is now a web, both Indonesian and offshore at the same time.

Wilmar International
Wilmar originated in Singapore in 1991 as a cross-Straits palm oil trading company jointly owned by William Khoon Hong Kuok, nephew of Malaysian 'sugar king' Robert Kuok, and Medan Chinese "palm oil king" Martua Sitorus, hence the name. After expansion and acquisition the company took

its present form in 2006 and relisted on the Singapore exchange. It has since expanded horizontally from palm oil and sugar into grains and vertically into the whole value chain from plantation through to the consumer and now self-identifies as "Asia's leading agribusiness group".[24] As of April 2015, Forbes rated Wilmar International as #369 in its Global 2000 with a market capitalization of $15.2 billion, sales of $43 billion and a work force of 92,000.[25] Yet despite its massive size, Wilmar retains elements of the original joint venture. While Chairman and CEO William Kuok has prime responsibility for international operations, Martua Sitorus is Executive Deputy Chairman and in charge of operations in Indonesia through a range of subsidiary companies.[26] Thus in sensitive negotiations with the Indonesian government over responsibility for forest fires in Sumatra and Kalimantan and the link with clearance for oil palm plantations, Sitorus has been both an Indonesian national able to liaise at the top level with Indonesian ministers and, through Wilmar, an external party. As it seeks to build global reputation in the face of a barrage of criticism of the oil palm industry, in 2013 Wilmar launched a sustainability policy and is working closely with is main customer, Unilever, to trace all supplies back to source.

Nevertheless, the relative importance of Indonesia in Wilmar's portfolio is steadily declining. In 2015 all Southeast Asia accounted for 44 % of non-current assets but only 20 % of revenues,[27] even though the original footprint has expanded from Indonesia, Malaysia and Singapore to Vietnam (edible oil, refining, oil seed crushing, rice bran extraction, flour milling, special fats and consumer products), the Philippines (edible oils) and Myanmar (sugar mills). The main prize is now China (50 % of revenues and 38 % of non-current assets) along with an increasingly strong presence in India in partnership with Adani Group. The group's global ambitions extend to Africa and Australasia, where in 2015 with First Pacific it acquired food conglomerate Goodman Fielder, plus substantial sales in the Americas and Europe. Wilmar might reasonably claim to be an ASEAN-based company and its jurisdictional structure is well placed to take advantage of the ASEAN single market, even though it has already outgrown ASEAN to become a genuinely global player.

Astra International

A different kind of relationship with Singapore arises in the case of automobile and motor cycle manufacturer P.T. Astra International Tbk. In 1998 Astra was also sequestrated by IBRA. When divested in 2000, it passed under the control of Jardine Cycle & Carriage Ltd, a Singapore-listed subsidiary of the Bermuda-incorporated, London-based Jardine Matheson Group, which holds 50.1 % of the equity.[28] Astra has no significant offshore operations but is enmeshed in joint venture and agency arrangements, mainly with leading Japanese firms, as vehicles for technology transfer for its Indonesian operations. In 2015 Astra sold 50 % of Indonesia's automobiles and 69 % of motor cycles but is also significantly diversified into financial services, heavy equipment and mining, tollroads, IT and even agribusiness with a total work force of 220,000.[29]

Astra is regarded both within and outside the country as one of Indonesia's best public companies in terms of corporate governance and reputation. The group's commitment to good corporate governance is made explicit in its vision:

> *To be one of the best managed corporations in Asia Pacific* with emphasis on sustainable growth by building competence through people development, solid financial structure, customer satisfaction and efficiency (author's italics).[30]

Achieving this vision is the ultimate responsibility of an eleven-member Board of Commissioners of whom four are independent and six are senior people within the Jardine Group. Such structures and accountability processes help to insulate the group from the corrosive pressures of the Indonesian business environment. This may be attributable more to the authority of the controlling British partner than to its immediate offshore domicile in Singapore but it shows what can be done in Indonesia when governance is made a priority from the top down.

Conclusion

Although Samudera, Indofood, Wilmar and Astra have all made sound business decisions to establish a business base in Singapore, nationalist opinion in Indonesia still regards this as problematic. The nationalist impulse causes almost any commercial involvement with Singapore to be seen as a loss for Indonesia in a zero-sum game. There is also an ethnic element: business leaders of Chinese descent are regarded as less Indonesian if they do business offshore. These four cases all suggest that the relationship is too complex to be reduced to such reactive and reductive thinking. Indonesia stands to gain if its leading firms are seen as reliable business partners for foreign investors in Indonesia, as also able to establish their own offshore businesses with a good reputation. However, Indonesia's worldwide reputation for opportunism and corruption makes these things harder to achieve. Given that progress towards good government in Indonesia is painfully slow, and that complicity in a regime of endemic corruption is potentially fatal to international reputation, Indonesian firms act not only in their own self-interest but also in the national interest by seeking to exploit the jurisdictional advantages of Singapore to insulate themselves from the excesses of the Indonesian business environment in order to improve their corporate reputation. Far better that it be done this way, openly and transparently through companies listed on the Singapore stock exchange, than by surreptitiously using Singapore as a safe haven for funds and passive real estate investments. The inflow of capital and entrepreneurship from Indonesia since 1945 has been of enormous benefit to Singapore's economic development, a perverse flow from a poorer to a richer country. It is timely that a more confident Indonesia now seeks to reap some of the synergies for its own benefit.

Within ASEAN, Singapore stands out as the obvious business centre. Indeed, ever since independence in 1965, the Singaporean government has focused its energies on transforming the city-state from its historic role as an entrepot dealing in physical commodities to a service economy that is an integrated logistics, financial and business hub. That in turn has required attention to physical infrastructure and the institutional underpinnings of rule of law, well informed and efficient markets, and minimal corruption. Singapore has thereby achieved credibility as a global business centre as well as a regional one. No other ASEAN member can match these strategic and competitive advantages. Under Prime Minister Mahathir, the Malaysian government made a determined effort to do so but the effort was not sustained by his successors and the considerable gains now look to be eroding. Thailand has been wracked by civil strife that the current military dictatorship has yet to resolve. Indonesia has been transformed into a democracy and resumed a path of rapid growth but institutional weaknesses abound, as in the Philippines. Vietnam, as also Cambodia and Laos, are still in transition from socialist systems while Myanmar is very much a work in progress. While inward foreign direct investment is being facilitated, no ASEAN country apart from Singapore is yet a good base for an outward-looking international business. The outcome of ASEAN integration is therefore likely to be a hub-and-spoke pattern of integration radiating from Singapore rather than a more diffuse process of harmonization on the European model. Hedging political risk and opportunistic financial engineering will as ever play a role but a positive aspect worthy of some attention is the scope for better corporate governance.

Foreign companies looking to benefit from ASEAN economic integration are likely to apply similar logic. Singapore has obvious advantages not only as an international business centre but also because it gives reach across the other nine ASEAN member economies. Partnering with an ASEAN firm that has established a credible presence in Singapore will be much easier than seeking separate partners in each one. As in the case of the Jardine-Astra partnership, it is then feasible to transfer a structure back to those other economies to facilitate good governance and protect international reputation. ASEAN's 'emerging multinationals' such as Wilmar, Indofood and Samudera Indonesia are applying such a strategy by reverse ownership, not least to shield themselves from the corrupt and predatory aspects of local politics. Instead of trying vainly to resist these market forces, ASEAN governments will better share in the benefits and capture more of the higher-end business services flowing from ASEAN integration if they act vigorously to reform their public administration and legal system.

Notes

1. World Bank Group (2015), Doing Business: Rankings. http://www.doing-business.org/rankings [29 March 2016].
2. OECD (2015), http://www.oecd.org/tax/beps-2015-final-reports.htm [6 April 2016].
3. Transparency International (2015a), Corruption Perceptions Index 2010 www.transparency.org/cpi2015 [6 April 2016]; and Transparency International (2015b), Global Corruption Barometer 2013. http://www.transparency.org/gcb2013 [6 April 2016].
4. Dick, H. (2009), 'The Shadow Economy: Markets, Crime and the State', in Government of the Shadows: Parapolitics and Criminal Sovereignty, ed. E. Wilson & T. Lindsey, Pluto Press, London, UK, pp. 97–116.
5. Verhezen, Peter (2015), The Vulnerability of Corporate Reputation. Leadership for Sustainable Long-Term Value. London, Palgrave
6. Wong Lin Ken (1960), The Trade of Singapore, 1819–1869', Journal of the Malayan Branch of the Royal Asiatic Society, 33(4), 5–315.
7. Huff, W.G. (1994), The Economic Growth of Singapore: Trade and development in the twentieth century. Cambridge: Cambridge University Press.
8. Dick, Howard and Peter Rimmer (2003), Cities, Transport and Communications: The Integration of Southeast Asia since 1850, London: Palgrave, Chapter 3.
9. Campo, J.N.F.M. à (1992), Koninklijke Paketvaart Maatschappij: Stoomvaart en staatsvorming in de Indonesische archipel, 1888–1914. Hilversum: erloren.
10. Boer, M.C. de and J.C. Westermann (1941), Een Halve Eeuw Paketvaart, 1891–1941. Amsterdam: De Bussy, pp. 314–44.
11. Twang, Pek Yang (1998), The Chinese Business Elite in Indonesia and the Transition to Independence, 1940–1950, Kuala Lumpur: Oxford U.P.
12. Dick, Howard (1987), The Indonesian Interisland Shipping Industry: An Analysis of Competition and Regulation. Singapore: Institute of Southeast Asian Studies.

13. Anwar, Rosihan (2001). *Bertumbuh Melawan Arus: Soedarpo Sastrosatomo, Suatu Biografi, 1920–2001*. Jakarta: PDP Guntur 49.
14. Anwar, o.c., page 232.
15. Samudera Shipping Line (2010), Corporate Profile. www.samudera.com [3 Dec. 2010]
16. Samudera Shipping Line (2016), Annual Report 2015. http://www1. samudera.com/ssl/investor_samudera.htm [20 April 2016]; and Samudera Shipping Line (2016), Annual Report 2015. http://www1.samudera.com/ ssl/ [20 April 2016].
17. Ibidem.
18. Borsuk, Richard and Nancy Chng (2014), *Liem Sioe Liong's Salim Group: The Business Pillar of Suharto's Indonesia*. Singapore: ISEAS.
19. Ibidem.
20. Ibidem.
21. Indofood Sukses Makmur, Annual Report 2015. www.indofood.com [22 April 2016].
22. First Pacific Company, Annual Report 2015. www.firstpacific.com [22 April 2016].
23. Greenhall, Michael (2011), 'Indofood Agri Resources', BNP Paribas Securities Asia. http://www.bnppresearch.com/?e=bedeakhife [20 April 2016].
24. Wilmar International (2016a), Wilmar in Asia: Annual Report 2015. www. wilmar-international.com [18 April 2016].
25. Forbes (2015), Forbes Global 2000: #369 Wilmar International. www.forbes. com/companies/wilmar-international [18 April 2016].
26. ibidem.
27. Ibidem.
28. Jardine Cycle & Carriage (2016), Corporate Profile. http://www.jcclgroup. com/corporate_profile.html [20 April 2016].
29. Astra International (2016), Annual Report 2015. www.astra.co.id [20 April 2016].
30. Astra (2016), Annual Report 2015. www.astra.co.id [20 April 2016]: page 5; and Astra (2010), Annual Report 2009, P.T. Astra International Tbk, www.astra.co. id/images/upload/articles/files/AR-ASTRA-May11_lowres.pdf [3 Dec. 2010].

4

Indonesia's Bank Governance Trend Post-1998 Crisis

Manggi Habir

Introduction

Indonesian banks have survived relatively unscathed from the 2008 global financial crisis. There has been no failure of big banks and thus no large government-led bank bail-out. Bank failure has been limited to two medium-sized banks, Bank Century and IFI Bank. IFI Bank was closed in the first quarter of 2009 and Bank Century was taken over by the Deposit Guarantee Agency (LPS) inlate 2008, changed management, altered its name to Bank Mutiara and, finally, was sold to a Japanese investment company, JTrust. There has been some controversy as to the government decision to bail out Bank Century, with the bail out funds ballooning beyond LPS' capacity, ultimately involving state budgetary funds. But the overall impact of these two bank failures on the sector was negligible, a far cry from the sector's devastation during the 1997/8 crisis.

Many have attributed the sector's resilience, this time, to the devastation, closures, restructuring and subsequent recovery it went through a decade earlier, during the Asian financial crisis. Bankers were also humbled and acquired a better appreciation and respect for risk. So when the 2008 global crisis hit, Indonesian banks were in better shape. They had higher capital levels, more diversified loan portfolios with manageable non-performing loan levels,

M. Habir (✉)
Independent Commissioner PT Bank, Danamon, Indonesia
e-mail: manggi_habir@yahoo.com

and improved profitability. However, there is scarce mention of improved governance. In this area, there has been tighter regulations, stricter enforcement, and increased market pressure, as banks raised capital from the market. Bank governance was largely regulatory driven, with banks often just complying by "ticking the boxes". However, by going through this exercise, there is growing awareness and appreciation of governance's role in ensuring fairness, accountability, responsibility, transparency and independence. Unfortunately, more often it takes a major crisis for regulators and market players to start addressing these easily forgotten gaps in risk and governance standards.

This chapter will try to shed some light on Indonesia's changing banking landscape since the 1998 crisis and, as a result of this change, how bank governance has evolved. One general lesson from Indonesia's experience, is that issuing regulations alone does not improve governance. It requires a strict and consistent regulatory enforcement, sufficient market pressure to improve standards, and enough awareness and appreciation to nurture necessary change.

A Changing Banking Landscape

So what were the major shifts in the banking landscape since the 1997/8 Asian financial crisis? The first is consolidation. Indonesian banks, which numbered 238 in 1997, at the start of the Asian crisis, have shrunk to 122 by 2008. In 2015, this number is down further to 118. Consolidation has occurred across all four segments of the banking sector, i.e. the state, private national, regional development and foreign banks. The shrinkage, however, was most noticeable among the private national and foreign banks (Table 4.1).

By assets, the largest and fastest grouping comprises private national banks. This category has shown the largest shrinkage in the number of banks, from

Table 4.1 Indonesian bank structure 1997–2008

	State banks		Private banks		Reg'l Dev Bks		Foreign banks	
	1997	2008	1997	2008	1997	2008	1997	2008
No of banks	7	5	*160*	**65**	*27*	26	**44**	**26**
Average branches/ bank	*218*	748	*29*	108	*20*	53	*2*	20
Loans (IDR tn)	*153.3*	523.9	*168.7*	542.1	*7.5*	117.4	*48.6*	182.5
Deposits (IDR tn)	*133.0*	696.4	*177.2*	768.3	*8.8*	173.7	*38.6*	208.7
Loans/deposits	*115 %*	75 %	*95 %*	71 %	*85 %*	68 %	*126 %*	87 %
Capital (IDR tn)	*13.8*	81.7	*25.2*	99.1	*1.3*	19.6	*6.1*	37.5
Assets (IDR tn)	*201.9*	881.8	*248.7*	949.1	*12.3*	210.6	*75.2*	343.1
Capital/assets	*6.8 %*	9.3 %	*10.1 %*	10.4 %	*10.6 %*	9.3 %	*8.1 %*	10.9 %

Source: Bank Indonesia

160 pre-crisis to 65, with the top ten private banks accounting for 32.5 % of total banking assets. If one includes in this list the top three state banks, then the 13 largest banks in the country make up a sizable 65.5 % of the banking sector, reflecting a relatively concentrated banking sector. Among the private banks, Bank Central Asia remains the largest (third nationwide), followed by CIMB Niaga (fifth in the country, after its merger with Lippo Bank), and Bank Danamon (merger of nine banks during the crisis and now in sixth place).

State-owned banks make up the second-largest grouping. This sector which went from seven banks[1] before the crisis to five now, accounts for 37 % of total banking assets. The largest, both in this segment and the country, is Bank Mandiri, a merger of four state banks (Bank Bumi Daya, Bank Dagang Negara, Bank Ekspor Impor Indonesia and Bapindo). The second-largest is Bank Rakyat Indonesia (BRI), followed by Bank Negara Indonesia (BNI is the fourth-largest nationwide). Previously, each state bank was designated to lend to specific sectors, but later this limitation was lifted and now competes across sectors. The exception is Bank Tabungan Negara (BTN), which maintains its focus in mortgage banking, while BRI, although more diversified, has kept its focus in agriculture.

The third grouping is the foreign banks, which numbered just 10[2] back in 1968, but ballooned to 44 after the 1988 bank liberalization, before shrinking back to 26 after the crisis. Foreign banks account for a smaller 14.4 % of total banking assets. However, the actual asset exposure is higher if one includes loans or facilities to Indonesian companies and individuals booked in the foreign bank's offshore branches. After the crisis, several foreign banks and investment companies have entered the Indonesian market through their acquisition of private local banks.

The fourth and last category is made up of the 26 (27 when East Timor was still an Indonesian province) Regional Development Banks (Bank Pembangunan Daerah or BPDs), accounting for 8.8 % of total banking assets. Each province has a BPD owned by the provincial government. It also handles their financial and fiscal transactions, which makes it a net placer of funds in the market and largely a Rupiah bank (Table 4.2).

A second shift is the move to retail and a stronger balance sheet. After the Asian financial crisis, most banks started to become more aware of risk and began to look for ways to reduce and manage their exposure. One strategy adopted was to move away from corporate loans – their main focus pre-crisis – to retail. Retail covers a wide spectrum of consumer loans, mortgages, credit cards, SME (small and medium enterprise) loans and micro-loans to small traders and household producers. The risk of carrying concentrated lumpy corporate exposures, especially those in foreign currency, was painfully felt during the crisis. As a result, most banks wanted to diversify and grew

Table 4.2 Ten largest banks in Indonesia as of December2008 and 2015

(in IDR trillion)	Total assets as of		Bank segment
	Dec 2015	Dec 2008	
Bank Mandiri	910.1	358.4	State bank
Bank Rakyat Indonesia	878.4	246.1	State bank
Bank Central Asia	594.4	245.6	Private national bank
Bank Negara Indonesia	508.6	201.7	State bank
CIMB Niaga	238.9	103.2	Private national bank
Bank Danamon	188.1	107.3	Private national bank
Pan Indonesian Bank	183.1	64.3	Private national bank
Bank Permata	182.7	54.1	Private national bank
Bank Tabungan Negara	171.8	45.0	State bank
Bank International Indonesia	157.6	56.9	Private national bank

Source: Annual reports

their loan portfolio to more granular and smaller-sized, but larger in number, retail loans. The growth of retail loans also had the effect of widening bank spreads, given the higher interest rates these loans carried. However, a retail strategy requires a more extensive branch network and larger investment in automation to gather deposits more efficiently as well as to provide loans. This explains the sharp rise in the number of branches per bank in all four segments, even though the number of banks actually shrunk. Banks adopting this retail strategy have so far been rewarded with improved performance. Non-performing loans were kept below 5 % of total loans, above which Bank Indonesia would get concerned and start monitoring closely. Aside from a portfolio shift to retail loans, there was also better loan portfolio assessment and adequate loan provisioning to cover problem loans. Loans were mostly confined locally in Rupiah and thus the size of foreign currency denominated loans were manageable. None had any significant exposure to US toxic real estate paper, which had devastated many of the major global banks.

The third was improved liquidity, reflected by the bank's lower Loan Deposit Ratio (LDR), which more recently was changed to Loan Funding Ratio (LFR, which adds bond-funding to deposits). Before the 1997/8 crisis there was more reliance on inter-bank borrowing to fund loans and the LDR ratio often exceeded 100 %. After thecrisis this ratio dropped sharply and is slowly trending upward with the August 2015 LDR ratio at 88.8 %. Realizing the higher risk of operating in a weak legal and regulatory environment, most banks have also kept capital levels much above the regulatory required 8 % minimum. The sector improved both its profitability and its financial structure. Its local-currency focus helped it to withstand the 2008 global financial crisis (Table 4.3).

Table 4.3 Indonesian bank sector performance 2001–2008

	2001	2002	2003	2004	2005	2006	2007	2008
CAR	19.9	22.4	19.4	19.4	19.3	21.3	19.3	16.8
NPL	4.6	3.6	3.6	3.1	4.7	3.9	3.0	3.0
RoA	1.5	2.0	2.6	3.5	2.6	2.6	2.8	2.3
LDR	33.0	38.2	43.5	50.0	59.7	61.6	66.3	74.6
Loan	316	371	441	560	696	792	1002	1308
Deposit	797	836	889	963	1128	1287	1511	1753

Source: Bank Indonesia

Bank Governance Pre-Crisis

So how did bank governance evolve in this changing banking landscape? Looking back, there was limited awareness of governance standards before the crisis. After the opening up of the banking sector in the 1980s the sector expanded rapidly. Unfortunately, prudential regulation and tighter bank supervision came later and in phases. Concentrated bank ownership by local corporate groups also led to weak bank governance. Finally, the economic boom and increased international financial integration in the 1980s and 1990s amplified the structural vulnerability of Indonesia's financial system.

In February 1991, the monetary authorities issued prudential regulations, including a comprehensive grading system assessing a bank's capital adequacy, asset quality, management's capability, earning capacity and sufficient liquidity (CAMEL). The system set necessary criteria to fulfill and a time-table for banks to meet Bank for International Settlement (BIS) capital adequacy requirement (CAR) of 8 percent on risk-weighted assets by 1993. There were also stricter information and reporting requirements, as well as tougher limits on lending within a corporate group or to one individual group based on a bank's capital.

Enforcement of these prudential regulations was made difficult, however, because of limited central bank capacity as well as interference from bank-owners close to the government. Despite prudential requirements and regulations, such as legal lending limits, board oversight was weak. There was considerable lending to bank-affiliated group companies exceeding the regulatory limits and, with most of the top private banks owned by major business groups, this practice was widespread. Loan swaps between banks and inter-bank placements to banks, that would then lend these funds to affiliates of the funding bank, were used to overcome the legal lending limits. During boom times, this posed little problem, but during downturns problem loans rose and unwinding these loan swaps and inter-bank loans became problematic (Table 4.4).

Before the 1997/8 crisis there was no effective exit mechanism for failed banks, and well-connected insolvent banks were allowed to remain open. Only one

Table 4.4 The group affiliation of the top ten private banks as of December 1996

Bank	Total assets (in Rp trillion)	Group affiliation	Status after crisis
Bank Central Asia	36.1	Salim Group	Recapitalized
Bank Danamon	22.0	Usman Group	Merged and recapitalized
BII	17.7	Sinar Mas Group	Recapitalized
BDNI	16.7	Gajah Tunggal Group	Closed
Lippo Bank	10.2	Lippo Group	Recapitalized
Bank Bali	8.2	Bali Group	Merged and recapitalized
Bank Niaga	7.9	Hasyim Group	Recapitalized
BUN	7.1	Ongko Group	Closed
Panin	5.4	Panin Group	Survived intact
Bank Duta	5.3	Berdikari Group	Merged

Source: Infobank

private bank, Bank Summa, was closed between 1988 and 1997 with the other problem banks (Bank Duta, affiliated with President Suharto's foundations, and Bank Pacific, owned by the Ibnu Sutowo, former President Director of state-owned oil company, Pertamina) being bailed out directly by the government or by corporations that the government or President Suharto persuaded to step in.

Bank Governance During Crisis

The inability of the government to maintain the Rupiah's stability and, the decision to float the currency in August 1997, led to a steep drop in the Rupiah's value from roughly Rp 2500 per USD to Rp 10,000 per USD by December 1997. The closure of 11 banks in November also had an impact on public confidence in the banking sector, leading to several bank runs.

In January 1998, in an attempt to restore public confidence, the government set up the Indonesian Bank Restructuring Agency (IBRA) and guaranteed all bank liabilities. The Agency's mandate was to close, merge or take over and recapitalize troubled private banks. The state banks, on the other hand, were handled directly by the Ministry of Finance. The private banks, once recapitalized, would eventually be sold or privatized.

A month later, 54 banks were placed under IBRA control. After that, 10 banks were frozen and 3 more taken over. In May, President Suharto stepped down, effectively ending a 30-year military authoritarian regime and handed over the presidency to his Vice President, B.J. Habibie, which sparked considerable capital flight. Bank Indonesia's interest reference rate shot up to 58 % at that time.

In September 1998, with the banking sector's equity turning negative, IBRA launched its bank recapitalization program. The objective was to recapitalize viable banks in the form of government bonds and over time sell the banks to interested investors. Banks were categorized into three groups based on international accounting firm audits.

"Category A" banks, with a CAR above 4 percent, didn't need recapitalization and could resume operations. "Category B" banks, with CAR between 4 and negative 25 percent were candidates for recapitalization, provided that their owners could inject 20 percent of the new capital required to attain a CAR of 4 percent. Banks with a CAR of less than negative 25 percent were put in 'category C' and their owners were given time to inject sufficient equity to push them into a higher category, before becoming eligible for recapitalization. Category B and C banks, whose owners could not provide this additional capital would either be taken over by IBRA or closed.

In October 1998, the four state banks – Bank EXIM, BDN, BBD and Bapindo – merged to become Bank Mandiri. The nonperforming loans of the four banks were transferred to IBRA's Asset Management Unit and Bank Mandiri's top management was largely entrusted to professionals from the private sector, with technical assistance provided by Deutsche Bank. Half of the staff of the four banks was retrenched and branches were closed. Bank Mandiri eventually was recapitalized and publicly listed. The remaining three state banks (BNI, BTN and BRI) were also recapitalized.

For banks under IBRA's supervision, 9 category B banks were eligible for recapitalization, while 38 banks would be closed. Of those remaining, 9 were merged with Danamon. The larger recapitalized banks were BII (affiliated with the Sinar Mas Group), Lippo (Lippo Group) and Universal (Astra Group), while the four smaller ones were Bukopin (Cooperative Bank), Prima Ekspress, Arta Media and Patriot. BCA, Niaga and Bali were recapitalized later.

Bank Governance Post-Crisis

After IBRA's bank-recapitalization, it took a while before loan growth and earnings returned to normal. By the end of 2001, the sector's loan-to-deposit ratio was just 33.0 %, with NPL still relatively high at 4.6 %, but CAR was at a comfortable 19.9 %.

Following Bank Danamon's merger of nine banks, IBRA merged several weaker banks into Bank Bali. These included Bank Universal, Bank Arthamedia, Prima Ekspress and Bank Patriot. The merged bank was renamed Bank Permata.

In 2004, the government's blanket guarantee scheme, helped in maintaining public confidence when three banks, Bank Dagang Bali, Bank Asiatic and Bank Global, experienced financial difficulty and eventually closed. Depositors were able to recover their funds from these three banks, but the blanket guarantee, aside from being costly, didn't provide sufficient market pressure on banks to perform.

In 2005, the government gradually phased out the blanket guarantee on bank liabilities and, in its place, set up the Deposit Insurance Agency (LPS). LPS only guaranteed bank deposits up to IDR 5 billion, which was to have been reduced to IDR 100 million by March 2007. However, with the tightening of domestic liquidity during the global financial crisis in late 2008, and rising concerns about the domestic banks' financial health, the maximum guaranteed deposit was increased to IDR 2 billion to avoid bank runs.

To improve governance and better to coordinate regulatory oversight, which are becoming increasingly intertwined, the government also established a separate Financial Supervisory Authority (OJK). The OJK effectively took over the bank supervisory role from Bank Indonesia and added the supervision of all financial markets and financial institutions (including, among others, insurance, finance, leasing, securities, and fund management companies). In other words, the financial-institution-supervisory role and the monetary-policy role were split between the OJK and the BI, where these two institutions, although expected to work closely together, were independent of each other.

There have been major improvements spurred by the enforcement of tighter governance regulations and market pressure. Aside from tighter rulings, with bank consolidation and bank privatization and divestment, there also has been a marked change in the international ownership of a number of the larger private banks, which has also helped promote transparency, independence and, in so doing, better governance. In addition, foreign banks and investment companies, which have acquired controlling stakes in Indonesian banks, have tightened risk management and governance oversight. Out of the ten top private banks, only three have Indonesian ownership. Djarum, through Farallon Capital owns BCA. Djarum is the second largest clove cigarette producer in the country with diverse businesses in property, retail and electronics. Panin Bank is owned by the Mu'min Ali Gunawan family via Panin Life. The remaining top-10 private bank with local ownership is Bank Mega, owned by CT Corp, which is the holding company of businessman, Chairul Tanjung, who has businesses in retail, media, broadcasting, and property (Table 4.5).

Table 4.5 Ownership of top ten private banks as of 30 March 2009

Bank	Total assets (in Rp trillion)	Controlling shareholder	Year acquired
Bank Central Asia	247.8	Farallon Capital (Djarum Group)	March 2002
Bank Danamon (merged with nine banks, among others Bank Duta)	104.8	Temasek Holdings, Singapore	June 2003
CIMB Niaga (merged with Lippo Bank)	102.9	CIMB Group Sdn Bhd, Malaysia	November 2002
Panin Bank	69.7	Panin Life and Votraint No 1103 PTY Ltd	n.a.
Bank Internasional Indonesia	56.0	Malayan Banking Berhad, Malaysia	September 2008
Bank Permata (merger of Bank Bali, Universal Prima Express, Artamedia and Patriot)	54.1	Standard Chartered plc, UK and Astra Int'l, Indonesia	October 2004
Bank Mega	36.1	Mega Corpora Group	n.a.
Bukopin	34.8	BULOG Cooperative and GOI	n.a.
OCBC NISP	35.5	OCBC, Singapore	March 2004
UOB Buana	22.4	UOB, Singapore	May 2004

Source: Moody's 7 August 2009, Indonesia banking outlook

Tighter Governance Regulation

Board Composition Becoming More Professional

One noticeable trend has been the more professional and independent composition of the two boards, the Board of Commissioners (BOC or Supervisory Board) and the Board of Directors (BOD or Board of Management), among the top Indonesian banks (both in the public and private sectors). In the past, the two Boards have been filled with a mix of professionals, family members of the controlling shareholder, and often retired government officials, including members of the armed forces. Now, the BOD mostly comprises bank professionals and, even when there are one or two family members from the controlling shareholder or founder, they all are bank professionals with considerable banking experience. The BOC composition remains more diversified, but here also the emphasis is on people that have financial knowledge and experience that could add value to the bank.

Appointment of Dedicated Compliance Director

The BI also requires that the every bank should appoint a Compliance Director at the BOD level, whose duty is to assess the bank's compliance with BI regulations. This Director is not involved in direct operations of the bank, but may oversee support functions such as legal and corporate secretary issues. As noted in the below table, the BI has been quite strict in assessing the Compliance Director during the required 'fit and proper' test, with about 27 percent of the candidates failing to pass BI scrutiny (Table 4.6).

This change in board composition has largely been regulatory-driven. In 2007, Bank Indonesia issued its Corporate Governance (CG) regulation noting that BOC membership should be more than three persons and that half of the members should be "independent" Commissioners. "Independence" is defined as not having a family, working and share-owner relationship with

Table 4.6 Top nine banks BOC and BOD composition in 2008

Bank	Controlling shareholder	BOD composition			
		Total Comm	Independent Comm	Total directors	Compliance director
Mandiri	GOI (67 %)	8	5	11	Ogi Prastomiyono
BRI	GOI (57 %)	7	4	10	Bambang Soepeno
BCA	Farralon Capital Management LLC (51 %)	5	3	8	Subur Tan
BNI	GOI (76 %)	7	4	9	Ahdi Jumhari Luddin
CIMB-Niaga	CIMB Group (77 %)	6	3	10	Y.A.Boliona Badilangoe
Danamon	Asia Financial (Indonesia) Pte, Ltd. (67.9 %)	8	4	8	Anika Faisal
Panin	Panin Life and Votraint No 1103 PTY Ltd (75 %)	4	2	10	Iswanto Tjitradi
Permata	Standard Chartered Bank (44.5 %) and Astra International (44.5 %)	8	4	8	Herwidayatmo
BII	Malayan Banking Berhad, Malaysia (97.5 %)	6	3	8	Fransiska Oei

Source: 2008 Bank annual reports

Table 4.7 Bank Indonesia 'fit and proper' test results for 1999–2008

Position	1999–2008		
	No. of candidates	Pass	Fail
BOD	1617	1318	299
Director	*1273*	*1067*	*206*
Compliance Dir.	*344*	*251*	*93*
BOC/supervisor	970	834	136
Shareholder	128	123	5
	2715	2275	440

Source: Bank Indonesia LPP report 2008

any other BOC or BOD members and/or the controlling shareholder, as well as material share ownership in the controlling shareholder that would affect independent judgment.

A former manager should have left the bank for a minimum one-year "cooling off" period before being considered as an "independent"Commissioner. To ensure that the two boards meet the BI's competency and independence standards, candidates have to go through a "fit and proper" test, conducted by the BI. In their annual bank supervision report, Bank Indonesia reports the number of BOC and BOC members they have interviewed and assessed their adequacy as board members and senior management as well as how many have passed or failed these tests. (Table 4.7).

Audit Committees and Internal Audit (SKAI)

At the BOC level, the BI requires that an Audit Committee (AC) should be set up. The bank's internal audit has a dual reporting line, one to the President Director and the other to the AC. Observers would like to see a stronger reporting line to the BOC's AC, but Indonesia's company law makes it difficult to have a sole reporting line to the AC, which explains the dual line compromise.

The AC through SKAI ensures that the operating and support units are following the bank's policy and procedures and the adequacy of the bank's internal controls. SKAI also monitors and investigates frauds, which is reviewed by the AC periodically. SKAI reports to Bank Indonesia on their findings every six months. The AC also monitors the BOD's follow-up corrective action on these findings. Another AC activity is to review the work of the external auditor in its assessment of the bank's financial statements each year. Recently, the capital markets authority limits AC members to two-terms, to ensure that a fresh pair of eyes provides oversight.

Risk and Remuneration Committees

Two other BOC Committees required by the BI are the Risk Monitoring Committee (RMC) and the Nomination and Remuneration Committee (NRC). There are eight key bank risks that the RMC periodically monitors and assesses if any follow up action is necessary. These cover credit, operations, market, liquidity, strategic, legal, regulatory, and reputation risks related to the bank's operations and business. The RMC also reviews any of the bank's related party transactions as well as adherence to BI and Capital Markets Authority regulations. All BOC and BOD members should be nominated and reviewed by the NRC before being recommended by the BOC to, and approved by, the bank's shareholders. The NRC also convenes periodically to choose potential successors for BOC and BOD members, whenever the need arises. This committee also assesses BOD performance annually and recommends to the BOC, and later to shareholders, rates of BOD and BOC compensation.

Although not required, some banks have gone further than the BI and set up Corporate Governance Committees, which review the adequacy of a bank's corporate governance standards and recommend any improvements to the BOC or BOD (Table 4.8).

More Transparent Disclosure

Since the Asian financial crisis, the BI has steadily come out with regulations to incrementally raise disclosure levels. Before the crisis, financial disclosure was rudimentary. After the crisis, the quantity and quality of bank reports to the BI was stepped up. Penalties for late submission have been consistently enforced as well and debited straight away from the bank's account with BI. Now banks have to report their bank financials to the BI on a monthly basis. In addition, to disclosure on loans and deposits from shareholder-related parties, BI requests a more detailed picture on loan quality, covering the likelihood levels of loan repayment and whether bank's have sufficient provisions to cover loans that have repayment difficulties. BOC is also requested to report their assessment of BOD activities to the BI on a six month basis and on its Corporate Governance activities annually. In the annual CG report the BI requests the disclosure of BOD and BOC compensation, their shareholding of bank stock and any other material share holdings (Table 4.9).

Table 4.8 Top nine banks BOC level committee composition and activities in 2008

Banks	BOC meetings in one year	BOC committees							
		Audit committee		Risk committee		Nomination & Remuneration committee		Corporate governance committee	
		Members	Meetings	Members	Meetings	Members	Meetings	Members	Meetings
Mandiri	18	4	24	4	19	8	4	6	3
BRI	33	6	17	4	4	6	9	None	None
BCA	48	4	11	4	6	3	4	None	None
BNI	51	7	30	5	24	6	19	None	None
CIMB-Niaga	23	7	24	5	26	4	12	None	None
Danamon	7	6	11	8	11	5	2	3	3
Panin	12	3	4	3	4	4	2	None	None
Permata	12	4	19	5	10	5	4	None	None
BII	10	3	14	3	6	3	3 and 5[a]	None	None

Source: 2008 bank annual reports

[a]BII had separate Nomination and Remuneration Committees with 3 and 5 meetings in 2008, respectively

Table 4.9 Top nine banks key disclosure in 2008

		Key disclosure items		
Banks	Related party transactions	CSR activities (IDR bn)	BOC/BOD remuneration	BOC/BOD material share ownership
Mandiri	9 (IDR1000bn)	53.9	Aggregate compensation and within different ranges disclosed	No material share ownership. Management Share Ownership Plan (MSOP) breakdown for BOD disclosed
BRI (1.46)	6 (IDR750 bn)	54.5	Aggregate compensation and within different ranges disclosed	Share options to BOD disclosed
BCA (1.35)	90(IDR1924bn)	9.7	Aggregate compensation disclosed	No share option program
BNI	132(IDR1444bn)	38.4	Aggregate compensation and within different ranges disclosed	No material share ownership.
CIMB-Niaga (1.1)	22 (IDR313bn)	6.6	Aggregate compensation and within different ranges disclosed	Employee Stock Option Plan disclosed
Danamon	(IDR 1564bn	10.0	Aggregate compensation and within different ranges disclosed	Employee/Management Share Option Plan disclosed
Panin (1.8)	44(IDR275bn)	0.5	Aggregate compensation and within different ranges disclosed	One Commissioner has 20 % stake in Bank Windu
Permata (1.1)	104(IDR174bn)	0.2	Aggregate compensation and within different ranges disclosed	No share option program
BII (1.28)	47(IDR422bn)	3.2	Aggregate compensation and within different ranges disclosed	No material share ownership. Employee Stock Option Plan disclosed

Source: 2008 bank annual reports

Market Pressure Helps

Rules-driven governance depends very much on the quality of enforcement and the effectiveness of the reward and penalty system in place. This is where market-driven pressure plays an important role as well. Banks need capital to grow and, for those that are listed in the stock market, they would have more flexibility in raising capital, whenever it is needed. In

Table 4.10 Top nine banks listing and rating status 2008

| Banks | Stock exchange listing | | Bank Ratings | | | |
	Year listed	Public share ownership	Pefindo	Moody's	S&P	Fitch
Mandiri	2003	33 %	idAA	Ba3 Fcy subdebt	BB-	LT Fcy BB
BRI	2003	43 %	idAA+	Ba2 Fcy subdebt	n.a.	LT Fcy BB
BCA	2000	46 %	n.a.	n.a	n.a	LT Fcy BB
BNI	1996	24 %	idAA-	Ba2 Fcy subdebt	BB-	LT Fcy BB-
CIMB-Niaga	1989	6 %	n.a.	Ba2 Fcy subdebt	n.a.	LT Fcy BB
Danamon	1989	32.1 %	idAA+	Ba2 Fcy subdebt.	BB-	LT Fcy BB
Panin	1982	25 %	idA+	n.a.	n.a.	LT Fcy BB
Permata	2002	11 %	idA	n.a.	n.a.	n.a.
BII	1989	2.5 %	n.a.	Ba2 Fcy subdebt	BB-	LT Fcy BB

Source: 2008 bank annual reports
Note: FCY Subdebt is foreign currency subordinated debt

addition, market scrutiny by analysts on the bank's share price value and by rating agencies on the bank's bond ratings puts a premium on good corporate governance. This incentivizes banks to meet governance standards, for instance, providing sufficient disclosure so that investors can better assess their financial performance (Table 4.10).

Adherence to stricter governance regulations and the regulators' enforcement of this has no doubt helped the banking sector avoid some of the more reckless pre-crisis behavior. There is more independent oversight at the BOC level and improved compliance to bank regulation at the BOD level. All this helped the banking sector when the 2008 global financial crisis hit Indonesia in 2008.

Latest Sector and Governance Trends

Since 2008, the banking sector has largely kept its total assets composition between state-owned and private banks. Although the weak economic growth in the last two years has slowed down the sector's loan growth and, as a result, increased problem loan levels, thus hurting profitability. China, a major Indonesian export market, has shifted to a lower 6–7 percent growth level from its previous double digit growth, bringing down global commodity prices as well as weakening Indonesian exports. The Rupiah has weakened from the Rupiah 9000 per USD level at December 2012 to Rp 13,000 per USD in April 2016. However, bank sector liquidity and capital levels are still at a comfortable level (Table 4.11).

With OJK – the stock market regulator – taking over governance regulations, there has been a concerted effort to replicate bank governance regulation,

Table 4.11 Indonesian bank sector performance 2009–2015

	2009	2010	2011	2012	2013	2014	2015[a]
CAR (%)	17.4[b]	17.2	16.1	17.4	18.1	19.6	20.7
NPL (%)	2.3	1.9	1.8	1.6	1.5	1.7	2.2
RoA (%)	2.6	2.9	3.0	3.1	3.1	2.9	2.3
LDR (%)	72.9	75.2	78.8	83.6	89.7	89.4	88.8
Loan (Rp trillion)	1438	1766	2217	2726	3320	3707	3917
Deposit (Rp trillion)	1973	2339	2785	3225	3664	4114	4367

Source: Bank Indonesia
[a]August 2015
[b]Does not include operational risk

with relevant changes to suit other financial institutions, starting with finance and insurance companies. Recently, OJK has issued integrated risk and integrated governance regulations for financial conglomerates. These are financial group, that normally has a bank as the main entity, with securities, finance and insurance companies, as subsidiaries. These integrated regulations are meant to better align risk and governance standards among financial group companies.

With the launch of the ASEAN Economic Community (AEC) in 2016, OJK is also looking at synchronizing their governance regulations for listed companies with the ASEAN Scorecard, which has stricter governance criteria in certain areas.

Interestingly, bank governance is now extending its coverage beyond the usual risk areas, such as credit, market, liquidity and operations, to include reputation, legal and regulatory compliance risks. Banks competing for the annual report awards (ARA) are highlighting their Corporate Social Responsibility activities, their non-discriminating employee policies and their customer protection. Some are even starting to issue sustainability reports along with their annual reports. These additional reports cover, among other things, their bank's efforts to protect the environment, such as cutting carbon emissions (by becoming more paperless), reducing the use of plastics, and being more efficient in consuming energy.

Lessons Learnt and Future Trends

Recession has a Cleansing Role to Play

Governance issues, which often are overlooked and hidden during boom times, frequently surface during a downturn. It is only then that these problems get serious attention and are actually addressed. Downturns should never be taken lightly, given the painful human cost and suffering, but it is also an important opportunity to cleanse the economy of deadwood, get a reality check on asset values, and address difficult regulatory and governance problems.

This is why some analysts consider downturns as necessary phases of any business cycle, so that worrying asset bubbles can be deflated before they grow too large and costly to manage. The darker side of recession needs to be addressed as well. By anticipating and taking downturns more seriously, it also forces governments to ensure that proper mechanisms are in place to manage bank or company failures as well as corporate restructuring, so exit strategies can be executed more efficiently. Governments can also better prepare necessary social safety nets and proper security arrangements to address the social costs.

Regulation Needs Effective Enforcement

Regulation is important in setting the standards for good governance. But regulation, without effective enforcement, has little value. The challenge is to have the clear and unambiguous metrics to assess compliance, the political will to enforce it consistently and the right mix of penalties and rewards to encourage appropriate corporate behavior. The annual report awards, where the top three finalists are free from tax audits, has been particularly attractive and sought after by banks and corporates.

Conducive Market Condition Helps

External market conditions that put considerable pressure on banks to promote good governance is critical in effecting proper behavior. There are three broad sources of market pressure. One is scrutiny from depositors. With the lifting of the government's blanket guarantee, depositors are more careful in selecting where to place their money. The challenge here is to provide more transparency as to the levels of bank health and banks' credit ratings. The second market pressure would come from creditors or bondholders. Here, bond ratings provides a grading scale for bond investors to better differentiate higher risk bonds from those with lower risk. This is important to better price and value bonds. The last comes from shareholders. For publicly-listed banks, shareholders closely monitor analyst views and penalize poor governance and badly-performing banks by selling share or demanding bank management changes.

Good Governance from Within, the Ultimate Challenge

The ultimate challenge is to make good governance an integral part of corporate culture. In this regard it is important to include governance as part of the bank staff's key performance indicators (KPIs). The next step is to link performance measures with an optimal compensation scheme that properly balances short-term profitability and long-term institutional-building goals. BOC oversight also needs to be strengthened by reviewing BOC performance more rigorously and somehow link it with their compensation. The challenge here would be to balance oversight with mechanisms to prevent reckless behavior, but not to stifle much-needed innovative thinking.

Given the nature of the 1998 Asian financial crisis, the conditions were sufficiently ripe to bring about significant improvements in bank governance. As the crisis stabilized and as the world pulls out of the global recession, the momentum for improving governance has slowed. Only a few banks have shown commitment to make governance an integral part of their corporate culture. The challenge is to ensure that banks take governance more seriously, particularly in view of the impending retirement of many bankers with painful memories of the Asian financial crisis.[3]

Notes

1. These were Bank Negara Indonesia 1946 (BNI 46), Bank Bumi Daya (BBD), Bank Dagang Negara (BDN), Bank Rakyat Indonesia (BRI), Bank Ekspor Impor Indonesia (BEII), Bank Pembangunan Indonesia (Bapindo) and Bank Tabungan Negara (BTN). BNI traditionally focused on manufacturing, BBD on plantations, BDN on mining, BRI on agriculture, BEII on trade, Bapindo on long-term lending and BTN on mortgage banking.
2. These were Citibank, Chase Manhattan, American Express, Hongkong and Shanghai Bank, Standard Chartered Bank, Deutsche Bank, ABN-AMRO, Bank of Tokyo, Bank Perdania (Daiwa Bank) and Bangkok Bank.
3. The following sources and annual reports were used for this chapter:

   • Bank Indonesia Annual Report 1998 and 2008.
   • Bank Indonesia Circular Letter No 9/12/DPNP dated 30 May 2007 concerning Good Corporate Governance Implementation by Commercial Banks
   • Bank Indonesia Regulation No 8/4/PBI/2006 concerning Good Corporate Governance Implementation by Commercial Banks
   • Bank Central Asia Annual Report 1998, 2008 and 2015
   • Bank Danamon Annual Report 1998, 2008 and 2015

- Bank International Indonesia Annual Report 1998, 2008 and 2015
- Bank Mandiri Annual Report 2008 and 2015
- Bank Negara Indonesia 1946 Annual Report 1998, 2008 and 2015
- Bank Niaga Annual Report 1998, 2008 and 2015
- Bank Permata Indonesia Annual Report 2008 and 2015
- Bank Rakyat Indonesia Annual Report 1998, 2008 and 2015
- Bank Tabungan Negara 2008 and 2015
- Indonesian Financial Statistics 1997 – 2015
- Indonesian Institute of Corporate Governance (IICG), Mewujudkan GCG sebagai sebuah system di Perbankan
- Mari Pangestu and Manggi Habir, *The Boom, Bust and Restructuring of Indonesian Banks*, IMF Working Paper No. 02/66, April 2002
- Mari Pangestu and Manggi Habir, Survey of Recent Developments, *Bulletin of Indonesian Economic Studies*, Volume 26, Issue 1, April 1990
- Moody's Investors' Service, Indonesia Banking System Outlook , August 2009
- Panin Bank Annual Report 1998, 2008 and 2015
- PT UFJ Institute Indonesia, Forum for Corporate Governance in Indonesia, Corporate Governance of Bank in Indonesia, May 2005.

5

China's Rise and Its Impact on South East Asian Businesses

Mark Crosby

Introduction

For centuries voyagers from China and India have brought goods, people, religions and cultures to the countries of South East Asia. In more modern times one of the most important visitors to the region was Deng Xiaoping, the Chinese leader who visited Bangkok, Kuala Lumpur and Singapore in November 1978. Deng was very impressed with Singapore's economic development in particular, and in discussions with Singapore's then Prime Minister Lee Kuan Yew, Lee described the policies that had allowed Singapore to rise quickly from a third world country to first world income status. During these meetings Lee also requested that Deng stop trying to export communism to the region, with political struggles in the region being a major source of instability.

The meeting between Deng and Lee led to many further delegations from China travelling to Singapore to study Singapore's economic system. In the 1980s and onwards many policy reforms in China, especially in the "Special Economic Zones" of that time, were based on ideas borrowed from Singapore. Business friendly policies such as cheap land, low taxes, and other policies aimed to attract foreign multinational companies into China were very similar to those pursued by Singapore in the 1960s and

M. Crosby (⊠)
Melbourne Business School, 200 Leicester Street,
Carlton, VIC, 3053, Australia

© The Editor(s) (if applicable) and the Author(s) 2016
P. Verhezen et al. (eds.), *Doing Business in ASEAN Markets*,
DOI 10.1007/978-3-319-41790-5_5

1970s, and helped China move millions of workers out of rural poverty and into factories in industries such as electronics and textiles, clothing and footwear. Deng's reforms eventually led to China becoming a socialist market economy, and the fact that Deng did commit to stopping the export of communism to South East Asia aided in making the region more politically stable from the 1980s onwards.

China's reforms since 1979 have led to China being a more capitalist economy, but the reforms have also made China a great trading nation. From China's trade being only around 1 % of global trade in 1979, China now accounts for more than 10 % of world trade. South East Asia benefits greatly from its proximity to China, and as Table 5.1 shows, a number of countries in South East Asia have China as their largest trading partner. For ASEAN as a region China is the largest trading partner, in recent years overtaking the USA and the EU. In this Chapter We discuss the trade and other linkages between South East Asian countries and China today. The reason that China is now so important in the region is firstly because it is the world's second largest economy and its trade linkages are globally very important. While India is also a rising power, its economy is much smaller than China's and its trade linkages are far less extensive so that its economic influence on the region is much smaller. That may change, but for the moment China creates huge opportunities and also huge challenges for SE Asian nations.

Table 5.1 ASEAN trade with China ($US billions)

| | Trade in 1998 | | | Trade in 2013 | | | |
	Exports	Imports	Balance	Exports	Imports	Balance	% of exports
Brunei	0	560	−560	87	1704	−1617	0.8
Cambodia	na	na	na	361	3411	−3050	4.1
Indonesia	2462	1172	1290	31,479	36,947	−5469	10.0
Laos	na	na	na	1021	1721	701	34.2
Malaysia	2675	1594	1080	60,068	45,941	14,128	12.1
Myanmar	na	na	na	14,162	10,362	4540	63.0
Philippines	517	1499	−982	18,205	19,836	1631	13.0
Singapore	4226	3901	325	29,969	45,886	−15,918	12.6
Thailand	2423	1170	1253	38,518	32,738	5780	11.0
Vietnam	217	1024	−806	16,886	48,599	−31,714	10.4
ASEAN	12,859	10,919	1670	199,402	244,133	−44,731	12.4

Source: DX database and ASEAN-China Centre, "ASEAN & China in figures 2014"

Trade

Table 5.1 details ASEAN countries trade with China. Between 1998 and 2013 ASEAN's total trade with China rose 19-fold, a compound growth rate of more than 20 % per year. Imports grew more quickly than exports, so that in recent years ASEAN has had a large trade deficit with China. The growth in trade with China over this period accelerated after China's accession to the World Trade Organisation (WTO) in 2001, which has increased China's trade with most of its trade partners, but has also led to integrated supply chains across South East Asia and China.

For most ASEAN member-states other countries within the region are their biggest trade partner, and overall intra-ASEAN trade comprises about one-quarter of total trade. After ASEAN China is the largest trade partner, with trade to the EU and the USA slightly less than China's share. As noted in Chap. 1, there is a huge amount of diversity within ASEAN, and this also applies to the trade relationships with China. Malaysia is China's biggest trading partner in the region, with Malaysia exporting both natural resources, and also electrical and electronic equipment.

The largest trade category for both exports and imports from China is electrical and electronic equipment, reflecting the integration of ASEAN into East Asian supply chains. An auto-maker such as Toyota can utilise the ASEAN free trade arrangement (AFTA) to source parts from numerous countries in the region. Pressed parts are produced in Thailand, engine fuel systems in the Philippines, instrument panels in Malaysia and cyclinder blocks in Indonesia.[1] This integration of South East Asia into regional supply chains is reflected both in the high level of intra-ASEAN trade and the high level of trade between ASEAN and East Asia.

The other major trade category in ASEAN-China trade is mineral fuels, oil and distillation products. While the major producers of oil are Negara Brunei Darussalam (hereafter Brunei) and Malaysia, this category is a major source of export revenue even in Singapore due to the large amount of refining in that country. Together the electrical and fuel categories account for 40 % of export revenues from ASEAN to China.

The global slowdown in trade has been thought to be a major threat to South East Asian countries and to China, and yet as noted in Chap. 1, these countries have been able to weather this slowdown remarkably well. The reason for this is the increase in intra-regional trade, and the increasing reliance on consumption in China and wealthier countries elsewhere in Asia. With incomes growing across the region, as well as the AFTA and other free trade agreements, one should expect to see strong growth in trade in Asia even as the traditional markets in the United States and the EU see much slower economic growth.

Table 5.1 also shows that ASEAN as a whole has a large trade deficit with China. However, while Singapore and Vietnam have large deficits, Malaysia in particular enjoys a trade surplus with China. ASEAN was running trade surpluses with China prior to the global financial crisis, and falling trade balances reflect in part falling commodity prices as well as slower growth in China's economy leading to weaker import demand there.

Foreign Investment

Until recent years China's outbound foreign investment flows were very small. Total global outbound flows were only US$34 billion in 2003, but by 2013 had risen to US$525 billion.[2] ASEAN's share of this flow is however very small. The total stock of Chinese investment into ASEAN as at 2013 was only US$35 billion, with the majority of this being investments into Singapore. This reflects only 2.3 % of the total stock of foreign direct investment into ASEAN.

Inflows into China from ASEAN are also very small. Singapore's cumulative flows into China amount to US$47 billion, with the next largest inflows coming from Malaysia with just over US$4 billion in 2013. While flows in both directions have been small, there is reason to believe that future flows will be much more significant. China is making significant overseas investments in what it sees as strategic industries such as natural resources, finance, and technology, and the ASEAN region should be well located to receive such flows. China is also investing very heavily in its "One belt, one road" (OBOR) program aimed at improving infrastructure across Asia.

The OBOR program is one of a number of strategic initiatives by China that aim to reinvigorate trade and also increase China's influence within the broader Asian region. OBOR includes planned infrastructure projects that link China's western provinces with central and south Asia, as well as projects that link southern and coastal China with South East Asia. To fund these projects China has sponsored the new Asian Infrastructure Investment Bank (AIIB), which has committed to spending US$100 billion on infrastructure projects in Asia. Shortly after this announcement the Asian Development Bank, which is located in Japan and better reflects Japanese and American interests, announced that it would be co-financing with Japanese state agencies US$110 billion in Asian infrastructure in the next five years.

Support within South East Asia for OBOR varies significantly. Thailand and Myanmar are very supportive, and proposed rail links through those countries will benefit both China and the host countries as infrastructure is significantly upgraded. However the Philippines and Vietnam are much less supportive. Those countries have significant maritime disputes with China, and while the OBOR initiatives will enhance trade opportunities they also have great military and strategic significance. Other ASEAN countries are more neutral about OBOR.

Future investments from China into ASEAN countries are likely to reflect some of the factors above. Chinese investment in Thailand is now concentrated in railways and manufacturing. Projects in Myanmar mainly involve electricity and transportation. China's CITIC Group Corporation recently won a bid to build a deep-sea port in Myanmar[3]. However other investments out of China reflect some of the current business realities in China. With Chinese production costs continuing to rise its companies are looking to cheaper production locations in South East Asia and elsewhere. For example, there are now over fifty Chinese textile and light industrial companies situated in Cambodia's Sihanoukville Special Economic Zone. Monthly minimum wages in Phnom Penh and Yangon are less than US$100 per month, compared with more than four times this amount in Guangdong Province in China, so we should expect to see significant investments in low skill manufacturing in those countries.

Tourism and Education Links

Perhaps the area with the greatest opportunity to increase ASEAN-China linkages is tourism. Tourist arrivals from China to ASEAN countries rose from 5.4 million in 2010 to 12.6 million in 2013. China's share of tourist arrivals rose from 14 % to 23 % of total non-ASEAN arrivals during that period. The strong growth reflects the huge overall growth in outbound Chinese tourism. Outbound travel from China in 2000 was only 10.4 million, but this number rose to 45.8 million by 2008 and further doubled to 98.2 million in 2013.[4]

Thailand benefited the most from the growth in Chinese tourist numbers, with 4.6 million visitors, more than one-third of the total visitors to ASEAN from China in 2014. But Indonesia, Malaysia, Singapore and Vietnam all enjoyed more than one million visitors from China in 2014. Chinese tourism numbers are expected to continue to grow strongly, with increasing numbers of Chinese entering the middle class and travelling internationally, and

Chinese government restrictions on the activities and destinations of Chinese tourists being eliminated.

Compared with tourism, education markets in ASEAN have not been greatly affected by the rise in outbound Chinese students. In 2013 there were 712,157 Chinese Tertiary level students studying overseas. The USA, Japan, Australia and the UK together hosted more than two-thirds of all Chinese overseas students. The largest host country in ASEAN was Singapore, which hosted 3.9 % of the total number of Chinese overseas tertiary students between 2007 and 2013. After Singapore the next largest tertiary student market in ASEAN is Thailand, which hosted only 8444 students from China in 2013.[5] There is also a growing number of Chinese secondary school studying overseas, though in this case also the number travelling to ASEAN countries is small, with the largest market in Singapore attracting only 2.68 % of these students. While the language difficulties would be a factor in the small number of student flows from China into ASEAN, the other issue is that there are no highly-ranked Universities in ASEAN, aside from the National University of Singapore and the Nanyang University, also in Singapore. According to the QS rankings for example, the highest ranked University in ASEAN outside Singapore is the University of Malaya, which is ranked 29 in Asia and number 146 in the world.

Foreign student numbers studying in China are still relatively small, with only 133,000 foreign students studying academic programs in 2012. Including non-academic programs in areas such as language studies the total rises to 328,330. Thailand is the largest host market in ASEAN, sending 16,675 students to China in 2012.[6]

Security

A major challenge for China-ASEAN relations is the number of maritime and border disputes in the region. By far the most problematic dispute for ASEAN countries are the maritime disputes in the South China Sea. Brunei, Malaysia, Vietnam and the Philippines each claim exclusive economic zones in territorial waters governed by the United Nations law of the sea. China bases its claim on much of the South China Sea on a "9 dashed line" dating from the 1940s. The South China Sea is rich in hydrocarbons, but also has great military and strategic significance.

ASEAN and China have tried unsuccessfully to resolve some of the issues in the South China Sea. In 2002 ASEAN and China signed a Declaration on the Conduct of Parties in the South China Sea. In 2005 China and the Philippines cooperated in a Joint Marine Seismic Undertaking to assess oil reserves for joint exploitation. However these and other initiatives have broken down due to China's claim to all of the seas and their aggressive reclamation activities. Unfortunately for ASEAN countries China is unlikely to back down on its claims in the South China Sea. With China facing ongoing clashes and separatist activities in Xinjiang and Tibet it is doubtful that China will give up sovereignty and show weakness in any of its claims for fear that this will lead to further demands for autonomy within China.[7]

Conclusions

Despite the many challenges in the China-ASEAN relationships the business opportunities presented by China are enormous. Trade has flourished within the region, and China's global value chain initiative relies heavily on China maintaining global competitiveness through sourcing cheap inputs in regional markets. This should support manufacturing exports in middle income countries in ASEAN, while the cost competitiveness of low skill manufacturing in Cambodia, Laos and Vietnam should see strong growth in industries such as electronics and textiles, clothing and footwear in those countries. For middle income countries further integration into regional supply chains, such as the example of auto above, is likely to increase intermediate goods trade flows in the region. With rising incomes in China, the ultimate consumer of many of these products is more likely to be in China than in Europe or the United States in the future.

Tourism from China is also likely to grow significantly across the region, and Chinese investments in infrastructure are likely to support trade but also be beneficial to local economies. ASEAN's proximity to China creates large economic benefits for the region, but these benefits do come at the cost of significant strategic tensions. Whether a new ASEAN leader can be as effective as the late former Singaporean Prime Minister Lee in reducing these tensions remains to be seen.

Notes

1. World Trade Organisation (2015) "Trade patterns and global value chains in East Asia: From trade in goods to trade in tasks".
2. "China's Economic Ties with ASEAN: A Country-by-Country Analysis", N. Salidjanova and I. Kock-Weser, U.S.-China Economic and Security Review Commission Staff Research Report, March 2015.

3. Qingzhen Chen, "Risks to China's grand strategy in South East Asia", *Global Risk Insights*, March 13 2016.
4. World Bank, World Development Indicators, October 2015.
5. UNESCO, Institute for Statistics, Global Flow of Tertiary students. Singapore statistics are sourced from "Singapore Still the top of the class", *China Daily*, 3 November 2014.
6. China Ministry of Education, Statistical Report on Foreign Students in China, 2012.
7. For further on the South China Sea dispute see "The South China Sea Disputes: Past, Present, and Future", *The Diplomat*, April 9 2016.

6

From Cross Debarment to Integrity Compliance: Promoting Corporate Governance in Development Across ASEAN

Merly Khouw

Introduction

It has been six years since the signing of the Agreement for Mutual Enforcement of Debarment Decisions by five Multilateral Development Banks (MDBs)[1] on April 9, 2010, whereby these five MDBs agreed to recognize each other's debarment decisions based on a finding of one or more of the four uniform "sanctionable practices".[2] For the 10 countries comprising the Association of Southeast Asian Nations (ASEAN),[3] there are 80 debarred companies and individuals listed on the World Bank's Listing of Ineligible Firms & Individuals[4] from ASEAN, and 85 companies and individuals appearing on the Anti-Corruption Sanctions List published by the Asian Development Bank (ADB).[5] More than one third (40 %) of the ADB ASEAN sanctions are cross debarments from the World Bank; while ADB cross debarments constitute one quarter (25 %) of the World Bank ASEAN debarments.

With the "baseline sanction" of the World Bank now debarment with conditional release, companies and individuals who are sanctioned by the World Bank are not automatically released at the end of the debarment period, but

---

The author is the Lead Investigator at the World Bank Integrity Vice Presidency. The findings, interpretation and conclusions expressed here are those of the author and do not necessarily reflect the views of the Integrity Vice Presidency of the World Bank. The World Bank cannot guarantee the accuracy of the data included in this work.

M. Khouw (✉)
World Bank, Washington
e-mail: mkhouw@worldbank.org

© The Editor(s) (if applicable) and the Author(s) 2016
P. Verhezen et al. (eds.), *Doing Business in ASEAN Markets*,
DOI 10.1007/978-3-319-41790-5_6

have to meet certain conditions of "integrity compliance" to the satisfaction of the World Bank in order to be released from debarment. Since its establishment, the World Bank's Integrity Compliance Office (ICO) has released 17 companies[6] from debarment with an Integrity Compliance Program in place, of which four are ASEAN-based.

This paper examines the sanctions imposed by the World Bank and ADB across ASEAN. Referencing ASEAN company cases available from the World Bank's Sanctions Board Decisions and Evaluation Officer Determinations, which include uncontested proceedings, as well as specific Sanctions Board Decisions relating to companies released from debarment, the paper also discusses some of the corporate governance failures that led to the misconduct and violations and resulted in the sanctions for the companies, as well as the Integrity Compliance Guidelines that could be applied to prevent the reoccurrence of such misconduct in the first place.

Sanctions and Cross Debarments Across ASEAN

Since 1996, the World Bank has been sanctioning firms and individuals found to have engaged in fraud or corruption in connection with the procurement or execution of contracts for goods, works and services financed by the World Bank. Since 2006, the violations for which the World Bank can sanction have been part of four standard definitions of fraud and corruption that are applied by the five MDBs participating in cross debarment.[7] The four definitions are for (i) fraud; (ii) corruption; (iii) collusion; and (iv) coercion:

Corrupt practice: the offering, giving, receiving, or soliciting, directly or indirectly, of anything of value to influence improperly the actions of another party.

Fraudulent practice: any act or omission, including a misrepresentation, that knowingly or recklessly misleads, or attempts to mislead, a party to obtain a financial or other benefit or to avoid an obligation.

Collusive practice: an arrangement between two or more parties designed to achieve an improper purpose, including to influence improperly the actions of another party.

Coercive practice: impairing or harming, or threatening to impair or harm, directly or indirectly, any party or the property of the party to influence improperly the actions of a party.

Together with obstructive practices,[8] these five are collectively referred to as the "sanctionable practices" for which the World Bank sanctions apply. These sanctionable practices are also contained in the World Bank Anti-Corruption Guidelines which were developed in 2006 for the Borrowers of World Bank funds on how to prevent and combat corruption in World Bank-financed projects to ensure that loan proceeds are used for the intended purpose of promoting development and reducing poverty.

The ADB also imposes sanctions for fraud, corruption, collusion, coercion and obstruction, in addition to other integrity violations including:

- *Abuse*: theft, waste or improper use of assets related to ADB-related activity, either committed intentionally or through reckless disregard;
- *Conflict of interest*: any situation in which a party has interests that could improperly influence a party's performance of official duties or responsibilities, contractual obligations, or compliance with applicable laws and regulations.
- *Violations of ADB sanctions*
- *Other violations of ADB's Anticorruption Policy*, including failure to adhere to the highest ethical standards.
- *Retaliation against whistleblowers or witnesses*, which is any detrimental act, direct or indirect, recommended, threatened or taken against a whistle-blower or witness or person associated with a whistleblower or witness in a manner material to a complaint because of the report or cooperation with an ADB investigation by the whistleblower or witness

Since September 2010, the "baseline sanction" imposed by the World Bank is now debarment with conditional release where there is a minimum period of debarment, after which time the sanctioned party may apply for release if it can demonstrate compliance with certain conditions. A sanction decision can also be obtained through a Negotiated Resolution Agreement (NRA) where there is an agreement to settle the case as an alternative option to the World Bank's formal sanctions system. However, either an imposed sanction or an agreed sanction now includes a compliance component requiring the establishment, or improvement and implementation, of an integrity compliance program satisfactory to the World Bank.

The World Bank's Integrity Compliance Officer (ICO)[9] has the responsibility not only to monitor integrity compliance by the sanctioned entities, but also to decide whether the compliance condition and any others imposed as part of the debarment, have been satisfied. The conditions may include, but are not limited to, "verifiable actions taken to improve business governance, including … an integrity compliance program, restitution, and/or disciplinary action against or reassignment of employees."[10]

An analysis of sanctioned entities across ASEAN appearing on the World Bank and ADB lists[11] shows a total of 165 entities[12] from eight of the ASEAN countries.[13] The breakdown of sanctioned entities by country is as follows (Table 6.1):

Table 6.1 Sanctioned entities across ASEAN – World Bank[a] and ADB[b]

Country	WBG	Cross debarments from ADB	Subtotal WBG + CD	ADB	Cross debarments from WBG	Subtotal ADB + CD
Myanmar	0	0	0	0	0	0
Lao PDR	2	0	2	2	2	4
Thailand	3	0	3	0	3	3
Vietnam	15	0	15	0	6	6
Cambodia	11	4	15	4	11	15
Philippines	2	0	2	7	0	7
Brunei	0	0	0	0	0	0
Malaysia	3	0	3	0	3	3
Singapore	2	0	2	0	1	1
Indonesia	21	17	38	36	10	46
TOTAL	59	20	79	49	36	85

[a]As of May 15, 2016
[b]As of May 7, 2016

The ADB has six more entities debarred compared to the World Bank in total; however approximately 42 % of the ADB debarments are from WBG cross debarments, while approximately 25 % of World Bank debarments are from ADB cross debarments. Indonesia has by far the most debarments from both institutions, comprising almost half of all the debarments across ASEAN for both institutions. This is followed by Cambodia with 30 of all debarments, then Vietnam with 21 total debarments. For Vietnam and Thailand, all the debarments are from the World Bank, as there are no ADB only debarments for these two countries.

Comparing debarment periods between institutions excluding the cross debarments, the ADB has eight times more indefinitely debarred entities compared to the WBG permanent debarments. The World Bank has double the ASEAN entities debarred for 10 years or more compared to the ADB, but the ADB has no ASEAN entities debarred for five years or fewer. In contrast, approximately one-third of all WBG ASEAN debarments are for fewer than five years. Most of the indefinitely-debarred entities are from Indonesia, as are the entities with debarment periods of 10 years or more.

Approximately 20 % of all the debarments are either ongoing or without an end date, indicating a continuing ineligibility to participate in WBG or ADB-financed or supported activities. Similar to the World Bank, ADB reinstatement after the minimum sanction period is not automatic and companies may remain ineligible beyond the indicated lapse date (Table 6.2).

Of the 59 ASEAN entities debarred by the World Bank, more than one-third (22 entities or 37 %) were debarred as a result of determinations in

Table 6.2 Comparison of debarment periods – World Bank and ADB[a]

Country	WBG	Permanent	Ongoing	10+ years	5+ years	<5 years
Myanmar	0					
Lao PDR	2					2
Thailand	3				3	
Vietnam	15			2	4	9
Cambodia	11		4			7
Philippines	2	2				
Brunei	0					
Malaysia	3				3	
Singapore	2	1	1			
Indonesia	21		5	14	1	1
TOTAL	59	3	10	19	8	19
Country	ADB	Indefinitely	No date	10+ years	5+ years	<5 years
Myanmar	0					
Lao PDR	2	1	1			
Thailand	0					
Vietnam	0					
Cambodia	4	2		2		
Philippines	7	2		1	4	
Brunei	0					
Malaysia	0					
Singapore	0					
Indonesia	36	19	9	5	3	
TOTAL	**49**	**24**	**10**	**8**	**7**	**0**

[a]Excluding cross debarments

uncontested proceedings.[14] This occurs when the sanction recommended by the World Bank's Evaluation Officer (EO)[15] is not contested by the accused subject within a required 90-day period, and the recommended sanction becomes the default sanction. Half of the ASEAN uncontested determinations were from Cambodia (11 entities) and one-third were from Vietnam (six entities). Indonesia and Thailand each had two entities and there was one entity from Singapore that was a result of a default sanction.

In addition, there are six entities from five ASEAN countries that are subject to sanctions other than debarment. Five of the entities are conditionally non-debarred as ASEAN affiliates of a debarred Canadian firm. The affiliates of the debarred Canadian firm are located in the Philippines, Malaysia, Singapore and Thailand. The conditional non-debarment means that as long as the main sanctioned company meets certain conditions including: (i) implementing a corporate compliance program acceptable to the World Bank; (ii) fully cooperating with the World Bank; and (iii) not attempting to evade the sanction imposed on the company and its affiliates that are directly or indirectly controlled, these affiliates can continue to be eligible to participate in World Bank-financed activities[16].

There is one Indonesian company that received a letter of reprimand on June 16, 2014 for the "reckless submission of a forged bid security during the procurement process", but whose status is listed as "ongoing". According to the letter of reprimand, the posting was for a minimum period of six months, "[...] may be removed only if ... [the company] adopted and implemented adequate policies[...] in a manner satisfactory to the World Bank."[17]

Even in the above cases where the sanction is not debarment, the emphasis is still on integrity compliance. Debarment is not imposed on the Canadian firm affiliates as long as the parent company is implementing a corporate compliance program, and the Indonesian company's letter of reprimand can be removed only if there are "adequate policies" to verify the bid securities – both to the satisfaction of the World Bank.

In more than five years since the ICO's inception in September 2010, the World Bank has debarred 238 entities with conditional release, but less than 10 % (18 entities) have been released with an Integrity Compliance Program in place.[18] As of the end of Fiscal Year 2015 (FY15), the ICO reported actively engaging with 47 entities, and making notifications to 55 newly-debarred entities. The number of entities released from sanctions in FY15 was seven, almost half of all entities released by the ICO to date; while 37 entities received notifications of continued sanctions where conditions for release still had not been met, which is more than three-quarters (79 %) of all the entities with active engagements with the ICO.[19]

Of the 18 entities released from sanctions to date, four are ASEAN companies including one from the Philippines released in 2012; two from Indonesia released in 2014 and 2015 respectively; and one from Thailand released in 2015.

Integrity Compliance Guidelines

The World Bank has issued a "Summary of Integrity Compliance Guidelines"[20] that incorporates standards, principles and components commonly recognized as good governance and anti-fraud and anti-corruption practices. They are not intended to be all-inclusive, exclusive or prescriptive, but serve as guidelines that can be adopted based on any party's particular circumstances.

There are ten guidelines that reflect the core values, policies and practices of good corporate governance. Underlying the guidelines is the explicit prohibition of misconduct (namely fraud, corruption, collusion and coercion) within an organizational culture not to tolerate such misconduct; but instead to commit to ethical conduct and compliance with the law in a framework of accountability. The accountability framework should come from the leadership of the organization ("tone from the top"), be mandatory for all individuals within the organization, and have proper oversight and management.

Prior to establishing a corporate compliance program, there should be an initial comprehensive risk assessment relating to the organization's vulnerability to fraud, corruption and other misconduct that takes into account the organization's particular circumstances in size, sector, location and other operational considerations. This risk assessment should be updated periodically, as should management's monitoring of the program to consider new developments in the field of compliance and to correct any shortcomings of the program.

The guidelines further specify internal policies for the organization to cover (i) conducting due diligence of current and future employees, (ii) restricting arrangements with former public officials, (iii) establishing controls and procedures for gifts, hospitality, entertainment, travel and expenses, (iv) adhering to applicable laws when making political contributions, (v) prohibiting the making of facilitation payments, (vi) maintaining appropriate recordkeeping, and (vii) preventing fraudulent, collusive and coercive practices in addition to fraud and corruption. The guidelines encourage the organization to take a similar approach to its business partners as a way of extending the influence of good corporate governance to the organization's affiliates, joint venture partners, associations as well as agents, advisers, representatives, consultants and sub-consultants, distributors and suppliers, contractors and subcontractors, and other third parties. In doing so, the organization is expected to inform the business partner of its own integrity compliance program and seek a reciprocal commitment from the business partner to comply. As a practice, the guidelines suggest the organization conduct due diligence on its business partners, fully document and monitor the relationship with the business partner, and only make justifiable remuneration to the business partner for legitimate business services through bona fide channels.

Lastly, the guidelines suggest strong internal controls over the organization's financial, accounting and recordkeeping practices with regular internal and external audits. To support the control environment, organizations are expected to have procedures in place to report misconduct and other violations, investigate and respond to such reports including taking disciplinary measures against those involved in misconduct or violations of the program. To maintain the integrity compliance program, the guidelines suggest periodic training and communication in the program for organization members, as well as providing incentives to support adherence to the program.

ASEAN Fraud and Corruption Cases

Tone from the Top

One of the earliest ASEAN cases where the sanction record is publicly available[21] involves the US$84 million Thailand Highways Management Project[22] where the development objectives were to enhance the efficiency, productive use, and management of the road network in Thailand. As part of the project, the implementing agency issued a request for proposal for consultancy services to develop and implement a central roads database system, a bridge management system, and a roads maintenance management system. A consortium of three partners submitted a technical and financial proposal based on 80: 20 scoring system in December 2004. The consortium received the highest technical score of all the proposals, and was recommended for the contract in October 2005. However, shortly before the scheduled signing in June 2006, one of the consortium partners informed the implementing agency that it could not proceed with the contract.

An investigation conducted by the World Bank's then-Department of Institutional Integrity (INT)[23] found that some of the consortium partners had acted corruptly by offering and agreeing to pay, and further soliciting funds to pay, public officials 17 % of the contract price to influence the consortium's technical score during the selection process. The bribe was to be shared proportionally as a "management fee" amongst the consortium partners as their "commitment" in the corrupt scheme. The accused consortium partner argued in part that the silence on the part of the Director during an April 2006 meeting when the bribe payment was discussed was not a sign of assent but rather a lack of English comprehension.

The Sanctions Board ruled that the Director's silence during that meeting was not sufficient in itself to show the consortium partner's agreement to participate in the corrupt scheme; However, viewed together with the Managing Director's statements in a June 2006 meeting, and the Director's continued silence were interpreted during email discussions to reallocate the share of the bribe payment as significant to make the director a suspect. Specifically, the Sanctions Board considered comments made by the Managing Director in the June 2006 meeting that "companies must follow through on their commitments and also that, in certain places in Thailand, though not Bangkok, those who do not keep such commitments would be killed"[24] as a way to assert pressure on the consortium partner to keep its commitment to pay the bribe. Furthermore, the Sanctions Board found that the Director's "persistent silence" throughout the email negotiation amongst consortium partners to reallocate the amount of the bribe payment as a sign that the consortium partner had agreed to the corrupt payment scheme.

Although the accused consortium partner argued that the company could not be held liable for the improper commitments made by the Director and Managing Director in the course of their duties because, under the laws of Thailand, the signature of two authorized directors affixed with the company seal are required for a written commitment which was absent here. The Sanctions Board stated, however, that "A firm's liability cannot be limited to only those official acts it has formally adopted in accordance with internal and local law requirements."[25] In imposing a five-year sanction on the consortium partner, the Sanctions Board noted that "The personal involvement of the Respondent's Director and Managing Director in the payment scheme through direct participation in meetings and negotiations justifies an increased sanction."[26]

The Thailand Highways Management Project case exemplifies the role of the leadership's responsibility in creating and maintaining "a commitment to compliance with the law and a culture in which Misconduct is not tolerated."[27] The expectation, as expressed in the Integrity Compliance Guidelines, is that there should be active support and commitment to the implementation of an Integrity Compliance Program from senior management, and the party's Board of Directors or similar bodies, in both letter and spirit.

Undisclosed Conflict of Interest

In another Sanctions Board Decision involving the US$98 million Vietnam Urban Water Supply Development Project,[28] where the development objectives were to improve water and household sanitation services in selected district towns and large urban centers in participating provinces, a four-party consortium of two related firms and two sub-consultants was awarded a consulting services contract for sub-project preparation and support in February 2008. In July 2010, the implementing agency for the project terminated the contract "due to concerns including fraudulent practices in connection with the selection process and execution of the contract."[29]

The consortium was alleged to have engaged in four frauds including (i) failing to disclose and misrepresenting the existence of a marketing consultant and subsequent payments to the marketing consultant; (ii) failing to disclose a conflict of interest involving one of the sub-consultants who was a public official; and (iii) submitting falsified receipts for reimbursement; and (iv) submitting falsified and timesheets for reimbursements.

The fraudulent practice of relevance from a corporate governance stand-point relates to the non-disclosure of a conflict of interest in the engagement of a sub-consultant firm that included the son and business associate of a World Bank official (now-former World Bank staff member). Not only was it generally known that the Director of the sub-consultant firm was the World Bank official's son, a due diligence report for the consortium's firm confirmed the sub-consultant's relationship with the World Bank official, and the World Bank official's active involvement in the sub-consultant's business.

The Sanction Board ruled that the obligation to disclose covers "the broader range of actual or potential conflicts of interest" that impact consultants' capacity to "serve the best interest of their Client, or that may reasonably be perceived as having this effect."[30] Furthermore, the Sanctions Board found that the Director of the main consortium partner deliberately chose not to disclose the relationship with the World Bank official as the consortium Director had confirmed to INT investigators that the consortium's proposal could be damaged if the rumored relationship with the World Bank official became known. Moreover, even before the proposal submission deadline, the consortium Director had noted the significance of the "close relationship with a local [World Bank] officer" as part of a "Draft Business Strategy for Vietnam" that he had prepared.[31]

Among the Integrity Compliance Guidelines for a company's internal policies is the restriction on "the employment of, or other remunerative arrangements with, public officials, and with entities and persons associated or related to them, … where such activities or employment relate directly to the functions held or supervised by those public officials during their tenure of those functions over which they were or continue to be able to exercise material influence."[32] In the Vietnam case, given the World Bank official's responsibility for the project, and his active involvement with the sub-consultant firm, the consortium firm's failure to disclose the conflict of interest constituted a fraudulent practice.

Remediating Misconduct

An important aspect of an integrity compliance program is the ability to remediate misconduct when it is identified. The Integrity Compliance Guidelines state that "the party should take reasonable steps to respond with appropriate corrective action and to prevent further or similar misconduct and other violations …"[33] The case involving the Indonesia Infrastructure Reconstruction Enabling Project highlights the voluntary corrective action taken by the Australian parent company that not only resulted in mitigation of the sanction, but to its release from debarment altogether.

The US$42 million project provided technical assistance to support the post-earthquake and tsunami emergency rehabilitation and reconstruction strategy in Aceh and other parts of North Sumatra. The Australian consulting company's Indonesian affiliate, together with several local sub-consultants, was awarded a US$18 million contract in February 2007 to provide infrastructure project management services under the project. The INT investigation found that the consultant (i) failed to make the required disclosures about a US$43,000 "marketing fee" paid to its main sub-consultant; (ii) submitted approximately US$210,000 in false reimbursement claims for housing expenses over a 15-month period; and (iii) claimed US$150,000 in vehicle and transportation expenses using false supporting documentation including a fake leasing agreement to conceal an arrangement with a rental firm related to its sub-consultant.[34]

An aggravating factor in this case which the Sanction Board took into account in its decision was the consultant's Manager's interference with the INT investigation by "attempts to destroy potentially inculpatory evidence." In an email exchange with sub-consultants, the consultant's Manager instructed the sub-consultants to destroy evidence of improper gifts and expenditures involving government officials ahead of a visit from INT investigators, stating that "[they] should be deleted from the written account, because this is against [B]ank practices."[35] The Integrity Compliance Guidelines for gifts, hospitality, entertainment, travel and expenses state that appropriate records must be maintained, and controls and procedures established to ensure that such expenses are "reasonable, do not improperly affect the outcome of a business transaction, or otherwise result in an improper advantage."[36]

In its decision, the Sanctions Board also took into account for mitigation several voluntary corrective actions taken by the consultant including: (i) timely cessation of the misconduct as company management terminated the car rental agreement with the related firm, and changed the car rental and housing invoicing practices to reflect actual pricing; (ii) an effective compliance program with the adoption of an upgraded compliance program, the "Integrity Management Policy" that contains a Code of Conduct and other measures suggested in the Integrity Compliance Guidelines. The Sanctions Board noted that the measures included, for example, "an express prohibition of misconduct (Integrity Compliance Guideline #1); senior management support for the compliance program (Integrity Compliance Guideline #2.1); application of compliance requirements to all personnel, including contractors and sub-consultants (Integrity Compliance Guideline #2.2, #5); and policies regarding reporting, investigative, and disciplinary procedures in case of misconduct (Integrity Compliance Guidelines #8.2, #9.1, and #10.1)."[37]

However, the Sanctions Board did not give mitigating credit to the consultant's internal action against the responsible individual whereby the consultant's Manager was first removed from his position and later departed from the company, which also severed ties with the sub-consultant in early 2009. Although the Manager was removed from his position, he was retained in a critical role as the Project Director until January 2009, at which time he left the company. The Sanctions Board found that mitigation was not warranted because of the unexplained delay in the Manager's replacement as the Project Director and the absence of any link between the Manager's change in status and the misconduct at issue. Furthermore, although the consultant eventually ended its relationship with the sub-consultant, the Sanctions Board noted that "ongoing contractual obligations" prevented an earlier termination of the business relationship.[38]

Conclusion

The ASEAN cases are fraud and corruption examples from World Bank-financed projects,where inadequate "tone from the top", conflict of interest policies, and business partner oversight violated World Bank guidelines and led to sanctions. But as shown in the Indonesia case, appropriate remediation of the misconduct by changing improper business practices and enhancing the compliance program can reduce the sanction. With 108 ASEAN entities on the WBG and ADB sanctions lists, and approximately 20 % with ongoing debarments or debarments with no end date, the proportion is likely to increase if corporate governance failures are not taken seriously and addressed meaningfully. Although the World Bank gives mitigation consideration in sanctions for an effective compliance program, a principal condition to ending debarment is now also the establishment, or improvement and implementation of a satisfactory corporate compliance program.

Notes

1. The five participating MDBs are the African Development Bank (AfDB), Asian Development Bank (ADB), European Bank for Reconstruction and Development (EBRD), the Inter-American Development Bank (IADB) and the World Bank.
2. The four uniform sanctionable practices are fraud, corruption, collusion, and coercion.

3. The 10 ASEAN countries are Myanmar, Laos, Thailand, Vietnam, Cambodia, Philippines, Negara Brunei Darussalam, Malaysia, Singapore, and Indonesia.
4. The World Bank's Listing of Ineligible Firms and Individuals can be found at http://web.worldbank.org/external/default/main?theSitePK=84266&content MDK=64069844&menuPK=116730&pagePK=64148989&piPK=64148984
5. The ADB's Sanctions List can be found at https://lnadbg4.adb.org/oga0009p. nsf. The list contains the names of entities who violated the sanctions while ineligible; entities who committed second and subsequent violations; debarred entities who are uncontactable; and cross debarred entities.
6. The World Bank Group Integrity Vice Presidency Annual Update Fiscal Year 2015, page 39. Excludes the release of one individual.
7. Uniform Framework for Preventing and Combating Fraud and Corruption agreed by the International Financial Institutions Anti-Corruption Task Force, September 2006.
8. Obstructive practice is defined as (i) deliberately destroying, falsifying, altering or concealing of evidence material to the investigation or making false statements to investigators in order materially to impede a Bank investigation into allegations of a corrupt, fraudulent, coercive or collusive practice; and/or threatening, harming or intimidating any party to prevent it from disclosing its knowledge of matters relevant to the investigation or from pursuing the investigation; or (ii) acts intended materially to impede the exercise of the Bank's contractual rights of audit or access to information.
9. Established in September 2010, the ICO's authority can be found in Section 9.03 of the World Bank Sanctions Procedures of April 15, 2012.
10. Sanctions Procedures, Section 9.01(d), page 23.
11. The figures arebased on the World Bank's list as of May 14, 2016 and the ADB list as of May 7, 2016.
12. The number is actually 162 but there are three entities that appear twice.
13. There were no sanctioned entities from Brunei and Myanmar.
14. As of May 15, 2016, there were 141 determinations from uncontested-proceedings. See http://web.worldbank.org/WBSITE/EXTERNAL/EXT-ABOUTUS/ORGANIZATION/ORGUNITS/EXTOFFEVASUS/0, content MDK:22911816~menuPK:7926949~pagePK:64168445~piPK:64168309~theSitePK:3601046,00.html
15. The Evaluation Officer (EO) is the World Bank's Office of Suspension and Debarment (OSD) which provides the first level of adjudication in the World Bank's sanctions system.
16. World Bank Listing of Ineligible Firms & Individuals, Table 6.2: Other Sanctions.
17. Sanctions Board Decision No. 67 (Sanctions Case No. 193) issued on June 16, 2014.
18. The World Bank Group Integrity Vice Presidency Annual Update Fiscal Year 2015, page 15.

19. Ibid., page 39.
20. http://www.worldbank.org/en/about/unit/integrity-vice-presidency/sanctions-compliance
21. The World Bank publishes the Sanction Board Decisions and Evaluation Officer Determinations in accordance with Section 10.01 of the World Bank Sanctions Procedures adopted on January 1, 2011.
22. Sanctions Board Decision No. 50 (Sanctions Cases No. 117) issued May 30, 2012.
23. INT is now known as the Integrity Vice Presidency.
24. Sanctions Board Decision No. 50 (Sanctions Cases No. 117) issued May 30, 2012, page 20, paragraph 35.
25. Ibid., page 16, paragraph 51.
26. Ibid., page 18, paragraph 61.
27. Summary World Bank Group Integrity Compliance Guidelines, page 2.
28. Sanctions Board Decision No. 83 (Sanctions Case No. 202) issued September 30, 2015.
29. Ibid., page 4, paragraph 10.
30. Ibid., page 14, paragraph 56.
31. Ibid., page 15, paragraph 58.
32. Summary World Bank Group Integrity Compliance Guidelines, page 2.
33. Ibid., page 4, 10.2.
34. Sanctions Board Decision No. 56 (Sanctions Case No. 177) issued on June 10, 2013.
35. Ibid., page 17, paragraphs 57, 58.
36. Summary World Bank Group Integrity Compliance Guidelines, pages 2–3; 4.3 and 4.7.
37. Sanctions Board Decision No. 56 (Sanctions Case No. 177) issued on June 10, 2013, page 20, paragraphs 64, 68, 69.
38. Ibid., pages 19–20, paragraphs 65–67.

Part II

Company Specific Challenges

7

Corporate Governance Practices Affecting Performance: Some Indonesian Cases Applicable Across ASEAN Borders

Peter Chambers and Peter Verhezen

Introductory Remarks on Corporate Governance

Does corporate governance matter when doing business in Indonesia? Yes it does, but not necessarily the way one would expect.

Corporate governance mechanisms are defined and categorized by Schleifer and Vishny in different ways.[1] The influential academic paper determines on mechanisms that safeguard a decent return of the investment made by the capital providers or owners[2]; emphasizing five categories: (1) incentive contracts, (2) reputation considerations by managers and investor's optimism, (3) legal protection, (4) large investors, and (5) specific governance arrangements, such as debt/equity choice, LBOs, co-operatives and state ownership. Two typical governance mechanisms that address the conflicts of interest between shareholders and managers, and between majority and minority shareholders typically characterize the ASEAN governance context. The first is an internal mechanism consisting of the ownership structure, the board of directors, executive compensation, and information disclosure and transparency. The second is an external mechanism

P. Chambers
Peter Chambers, Independent board member
e-mail: pjch1955@gmail.com

P. Verhezen (✉)
Melbourne Business School, Carlton, VIC, Australia
e-mail: p.verhezen@mbs.edu

© The Editor(s) (if applicable) and the Author(s) 2016
P. Verhezen et al. (eds.), *Doing Business in ASEAN Markets*,
DOI 10.1007/978-3-319-41790-5_7

consisting of a market for corporate control, product market competition, and good legal infrastructure and rigorous law enforcement.

Although most scholars and practitioners agree that one-size-does-not-fit-all, there does seem to be a consensus on how to apply good corporate governance principles. Those principles represent certain common governance characteristics across cultures and national borders: (1) ensuring the basis for an effective corporate governance framework, (2) the rights of shareholders and key ownership function, (3) the equitable treatment of shareholders, (4) the role of stakeholders, (5) disclosure and transparency, (6) the responsibilities of the board.[3] Admittedly, these principles of transparency, disclosure, fairness, equal equity rights, responsibility and accountability are so generic that they need to be translated into specific practices on the ground. But even more importantly, it will require extensive "interpretation" to get the ball rolling and to make effective and efficient governance work in Indonesia.

What are the legal duties? On whose behalf are they governing? What are the obstacles in performing the duties of the board? It seems to be true that governance at the firm level is partially determined by clear description of board members' roles and duties, the board's structure, members and the processes.[4] One often hears that the behavior of top executives and board members is determined by the organizational culture, which itself is affected by the board's structure, membership and processes. A board should be clear about their function, their role and duty.

Sure, structure, composition and processes are the explicit design choices every board must make; call it the hard wiring that has an immediate effect on the soft wiring, or the behavior, of the board. The board is like a system in which the behavior of the directors is shaped by the design elements and the culture of the organization. And thus logically, the more these elements of the board's design – structure, membership and processes – are aligned with each other and with the board's role, and the more explicit the expected culture is, the more likely the system can produce the desired behavior to make a board effective in performing its fiduciary duties.[5] How useful or practical are those principles when dealing with concrete situations on the ground? Let us first look into the usual culprits of weak governance in Indonesia and other emerging markets? We them turn the focus to learn from some cases, allowing us to formulate some guidelines to safeguard ventures from falling apart. How then to interpret these corporate governance principles when applied in a family business or in a joint venture partnership where potential principal-principal clashes are prevailing over the traditional principal-agent problems?

What this chapter wants to prove is that within an Indonesian-Malaysian business context, some particular governance characteristics needs to be fulfilled to guarantee some degree of success. The cases – as one of the authors was personally involved in those – will indicate how and why taking those specific features into account are necessary to steer the company towards those expected opportunities.

"Good" Corporate Governance Practices Applied

The fiduciary duty of care and loyalty of a board and its executive team is to create and to enhance the value of the organization. Nonetheless, often this fiduciary duty is often seen as maximizing the shareholder value, whereby the organization is legally interpreted as equal to the owners of the organization.[6]

However, we will stick to the more neutral definition of fiduciary duty to create and preserve organizational value, that obviously includes shareholder value in the form of increased profitability and stock price but also focusing on non-financial objectives such as customer and employee loyalty and engagement, and respect for broader ethical and socio-ecological objectives. Somehow, corporate governance can be described as the institutional foundation to create corporate trust,[7] based on generic principles of good corporate governance mechanisms or best practices.[8]

Good Corporate Governance in an Indonesian (Malaysian) Context

Traditionally, non-executive directors – called "commissioners" in Indonesia – focus on making sure that the company complies with the regulations and rules of the Capital Market and Corporate Law. Hence the importance of control and monitoring of procedures, processes and principles by the supervisory Board. However, as the cases will reveal, boards increasingly need to be aware of the risks a company is facing and the strategies a company is envisaging.[9] This second important task of a board will require "Leadership partnership" between the non-executives and executives.

With the globalization taking precedence, successful and sustainable organizations need to demonstrate that they can engage with and involve key stakeholders to make wise decisions by embracing a culture of transparency, accountability and responsibility,[10] to be fair and consistent in relations with shareholders and stakeholders, and to have an institutional framework established that ensures corporate trust. The board has the ultimate decision power and therefore is the apex of legal power and accountability. With this it carries the responsibility towards stakeholders and to safeguard the sustainability of the organization. The board's responsibility aims to provide guidance and oversight to the management in order to create or preserve organizational value on a sustainable basis while protecting the interests of key stakeholders.

Governance is much more than compliance. It reflects "a culture and a climate of consistency, responsibility, fairness, responsibility, transparency, and effectiveness[11]" that is deployed throughout the company. One of the major governance challenges in Asian and thus Indonesian firms is to safeguard the rights of minority investors and owners.[12]

What Exactly Does Cause Weak Corporate Governance (at the Firm Level)?

The recent global financial crisis has highlighted that, despite all the progress in the field of corporate governance in the last decade, there are still evident deficiencies. Powerful individuals may be able to exercise too much power without appropriate restraints or without being called to account for: Boards may not perform their oversight duty properly, or may not have the skills and competencies to understand the risks the organization was involved.

And although the consensus on the common core principles has been influential in the setting of codes across the globe, boards should be more aware of their responsibility to steer the organization away from threats and towards viable opportunities. Ideally, boards should define and enshrine their core business priorities in order to allow managers and executives to make decisions whereby these priority principles are wide enough boundaries to empower them and narrow enough to guide them.[13]

What are the usual suspects of "bad" corporate governance at firm level? Often one can refer to lack of independence, overreliance on financial data only or uninformed board decisions and poor management information. When boards are composed by family members only and insiders, governed by informal working procedures, without effective subcommittees, without clear division between board and management, such firms' boards often act as "paper" boards and Worse, when minority rights are not properly protected against the potential "expropriation" investment will stall in one form or another by majority (often family) shareholders.

Preliminary Corporate Governance Suggestions

What are the mechanisms to analyze and understand corporate governance, accountability and its relationships with performance? We will use the following variables – that are considered to affect corporate governance – that have an immediate effect on the accountability of the board that in turn should be able positively to affect financial and non-financial performance:

1. High concentration of ownership
2. Board composition
3. Market discipline
4. Board chairmanship
5. Board size
6. Independency of non-executive board members and professionalism of executive directors
7. Strict rules in the Bylaws/Charter or zero-tolerance for related party transactions
8. Management remuneration
9. Inbreeding: a practice whereby senior executives join the board (of commissioners) after retiring from management
10. Governance culture: ethical leadership sets moral standards for the organization and functions as a role model within the organization.
11. Functioning of sub-committees: Audit committee, Remuneration & Nomination committee, Risk & Strategy committee...

    However, based on long practical experience, we argue that the following critical factors play an even more predominant role in constituting long-term success in Indonesian firms:

12. Negotiating a *long-term shareholder agreement* between the investors or partners that establishes the clear duties, obligations, functions and authority of each;
13. Developing long-term relationships with *the right partners* (who share the same objectives) based on *a collaborative rather than a mere legal approach*; and
14. Having each of the partners or investors involved with their "*skin in the game*", i.e. with a significant pro rata effective financial investment at stake in the firm.

Critical Corporate Governance Factors Out-Weighting "Best CG Practices"

It has been clear for most experienced practitioners, board members, consultants and academics that the usual best practices may not all have the same relevance in Indonesia and other ASEAN countries. We argue that the following three criteria are crucial in explaining good outcomes, such as a fair return for the invested capital: (1) a clear agreement among all shareholders in terms of responsibility and accountability, (2) a collaborative rather than legalistic approach by partners who share the same philosophy and adhere to similar values, and (3) having a real financial commitment to the organization on whose board the owners or their representatives – i.e. fiduciary agents or board members on behalf of the principal – are sitting.

A clear shareholders' agreement is nothing but an expression of the specific duties and roles of the different shareholders and their respective board members, consolidated in the company's By Law, Corporate Constitution or Charter. Such an agreement precludes any confusion in terms of operational and other responsibilities. It also allows the company to apply the strengths of each of the partners in the organization's operations, be it some technical operational excellence or expertise in human resources management and networking, be it access to sophisticated financial assets and sources, or sharing brand equity that is especially useful in an international economy. Combining the resources and capabilities of those different partners or owners allows the company to optimize their combined forces to gain and or sustain competitive advantage in this increasingly global and competitive Indonesian economy. This is even more true with the official opening of ASEAN economic borders since January 2016.

Secondly, taking time to make the right choice in terms of partnership is crucialfor aligning potentially different objectives. When one has nurtured relationships over a long period, one understands better the values of the partners. Once trust has been established, it is easier to collaborate and aim for the same goals. Trying to apply a liability approach – as often practised in Anglo-Saxon contexts – will not work in an Asian or Indonesian context. Collaboration carries a longer shadow that a mere legalistic approach. Asian companies – and Indonesia is no exception – are perceived as families. Very often these Asian firms are run by families. Family members treat their members with respect and patience, as long as the members express loyalty to the family values and the specific philosophy of the family company.

Finally, as every entrepreneur knows, peoplewill put in more effort and perform better when their "skin is in the game". In other words, when one has a real financial stake ina company, the motivation to get a fair return on the invested capital is likely to be stronger. No gain without pain! And we do not count mere equity granted because of one's reputation, social capital or network that has been turned into economic capital. We do not ignore the idea that symbolic and social capital carry much weight in any culture, and especially in high-context cultures like Indonesia.[14] However, it is our belief that, for an organization to be successful, all initial partners or investors should have made a real financial commitment with the underlying understanding that a decent and preferably superior return for the invested capital should be the aim within ethical and environmental constraints. Those partners should have a significant stake in the company so that they will act like real owners and entrepreneurs, and not as mere minority equity-holders who remain passive and will sell off any time the stock price booms or divest when a crisis looms. Real partners stay on board even when storms lash their company's shores.

What Did We Learn from the Following Experiences?

We have noted that the governance framework will vary depending upon the defined regulatory and legal requirements of a country or jurisdiction. There are numerous examples where governance has been successful and also where it has 'broken down'. The reasons for the success or failure can be classified into the following categories:

1. Accountability and Responsibility among all shareholders and board members:

- Agreed and Understood Governance Framework (*UGF*) – there must be agreement between the shareholders and management as to the governance structure
- Responsibility for the Governance Structure (*GR*) – a senior management member must have responsibility for the governance structure
- Simplicity (*S*) – the governance framework should be easy to understand and simple in its approach
- Committee Structure (*CS*) – effective Committee Structure complementing the prevailing Board structure
- Use of an Enterprise System (*ES*) – in large organizations it is advisable to implement an Enterprise System to support the governance disciplines

2. Collaboration among Board Members and Executive Team beyond legal compliance:

- Shareholder Alignment (*SA*) – there must be shareholder alignment and agreement on both the local and, where applicable, overseas legal and regulatory requirements
- Management Alignment (*MA*) – alignment with and between management through the business plan, performance management, key performance indicator and financial remuneration is critical to success
- Continuous Education (*CE*) – governance must be understood by all team members – there should be an ongoing education program

3. A real financial and active commitment by all parties to the venture:

- Local Partner (*LP*) – when investing in a foreign country, the engagement of a local partner is critical to success
- Active Governance (*AG*) – the governance framework should be embedded in day-to-day management

The examples in this section highlight where and why governance has either succeeded or failed. They are examples from Indonesia with occasionally an involvement of Malaysian investors. You will see common threads that define either the success or failure of governance. Let us start with an example where governance was successful.

Telecommunications Case

The telecommunications case study involved the creation of a mobile communications operator. This case study highlights the need for an aligned shareholder group with a clear understanding of how governance should be structured and supported. The key features of the case study are:

- The startup Mobile Telecommunications Operator had a shareholder group that comprised a strong local partner and an international strategic operator
- All shareholders had a material ownership stake with real cash injected as part of the equity position
- The shareholders established a meaningful and workable shareholders agreement that functioned as the overall governance framework
- At the start of the venture there was a clear understanding of the regulatory framework governing the International Strategic Operator – this included an understanding of FCPA (Foreign Corrupt Practices Act) guidelines
- The governance framework incorporated effective Board Committees, clear accountabilities at both the Board and management levels and an effective delegation-of-authority structure – it also included requirements addressing the international regulations and FCPA
- The oversight of governance was allocated to a senior manager reporting to the CEO
- Creation of a Program Management Office that oversaw the operators creation – the Program Office was outsourced

- The education program included a unit on governance – there were regular refresher sessions
- A succession plan was established limiting disruption to the decision-making process and ensuring sustainable good governance understanding
- Implementation of an IT enterprise system – used as the core tool to process key management decisions
- A program where governance was continually reviewed and improved

So why was this case study a success and the governance framework a critical component of the success?

- The shareholders were in agreement and respectful of their relevant regulatory domains
- Key issues regarding FCPA etc. were understood and addressed
- Clear accountabilities were established and executed between the various management levels
- The IT Enterprise System was critical to the establishment of a disciplined approval process – this was supported by ongoing education in the development of the system
- The oversight of the governance framework, by an executive, created an environment of 'seriousness' when it came to the governance
- The relationship between the management structure, decision-making and governance was clearly understood and communicated

Today the mobile communications operator is a market leader with a customer base of over 40 million subscribers. The governance structure established a framework of effective disciplines that are still in place today.

Mining Case

This case study highlights the need for foreign parties, when investing, to engage a local partner who understands and can effectively assist in addressing the local regulatory and community issues. The features of this case study are:

- The mining project had a sole foreign shareholder, who approached the project without engaging a local partner and without researching the local governance requirements
- The governance framework was based on Australian guidelines

- Local [Indonesian] regulation and governance required a two-tier corporate framework – comprising a Board of Commissioners and a Board of Directors – with specific responsibilities and legal duties
- The implemented governance framework did not incorporate the two-tier framework and hence did not incorporate a Board of Commissioners – as a result the Board of Commissioners was in name only
- The project had a number of operational challenges – one of those challenges was, in transporting the resource to port, the resource had to pass across two government regencies – in addressing this challenge there was ineffective communications with and participation from the two regencies.

As a result of the approach by the foreign investor, the following occurred:

- The company's legal structure was challenged and was found not to comply with Company law in Indonesia
- The two local regencies in Indonesia banned the movement of any resource being shipped from the mine
- The contract of work was challenged under Indonesian law due to the legal and board structure imposed by the foreign Australian sole owner.

Not surprisingly the project was suspended and a local company was sold a percentage share of the business. Also as a result of the initial issues the local partner has been able to obtain, from the foreign investor, significant concessions representing an economic interest greater than its formal shareholding.

The foreign investor could have addressed its issues from the commencement of the project by implementing the following:

- Establishing a partnership with a local party and gaining an understanding of local legal and governance requirements
- Implementing a governance structure incorporating local legal and social requirements
- Inclusion of local representatives at various levels of the governance framework, such as the Board of Commissioners
- Partnering with a local group to assist with the transport requirement across the local regencies
- Finally, adopting a true partnership approach in addressing the challenges of the investment
- It should be noted that there are many cases where similar investments have been successful – due to incorporating the above approach

Agriculture Case

- Here we have another example where, due to the lack of shareholder agreement and sponsorship, there was a failure in the Joint Venture. The case study highlights the need for shareholders to agree the governance framework and for the said framework to be implemented and maintained. The case study involved a partnership between two major agriculture companies, one being a local party and one being international. The combination of the two should have resulted in success; however, due to the lack of an effective and workable shareholders' agreement and a working governance structure, the venture failed. The approach to the venture and features of the case study are as follows: a Joint Venture was established between a local investor and international investor
- A shareholders' agreement was established and it included details of the governance framework
- The framework included both a Board of Commissioners, Board of Directors and Board Committees at both the Commissioner and Director levels
- The respective Board and Committee meetings were duly held
- The local partner assumed the operating responsibilities – the CFO was appointed by the international partner
- A product off take agreement was signed by both Joint Venture parties that allowed the international partner the sales rights to the final product

In principle the framework should have be effective – what went wrong?

- Upon the formation of the Joint Venture a shareholders agreement was reached, but – it did not addressthe particular requirements of the respective shareholders – for example the international partner was a listed entity – it, therefore, had to adhere to exchange regulatory and listing guidelines – these regulatory requirements were not understood by the local partner and as a result, the local partner did not provide the information necessary to ensure compliance with the regulations
- Sustainability was a key issue for the international partner, but these requirements were not well understood by the local partner and there was no provision included in the shareholders' agreement
- The Board of Commissioners did not meet on a regular basis – there was overlap between the Board of Commissioners and the Board of Directors due to the international partner not understanding the role of the two

Boards – the international partner was inexperienced in Indonesia, hence it lacked understanding re the local legal requirements

- A lack of importance was placed on the Board of Commissioner meetings – agendas and Board Papers were not submitted prior to the respective gatherings. Inadequate planning and preparation led to ineffective meetings and to key problems not being addressed
- Although the two partners commenced the venture with aligned objectives, those objectives changed and there was a clear divide between the two partners – this was evident when the annual plan was submitted for approval – resulting in the plan not being approved; and, as a result of this division, conflicting communications were generated by the two partners
- The local partner was responsible for the operations of the business, such as the implementation of the Annual Plan. There was, however, a lack of transparency and an absence of explanation regarding performance presented to the Board of Commissioners. This also contributed to the International Partner being frustrated regarding available information to meet its listing regulations
- In total eight Board Committees were established – at the Commissioner and Director levels. This created (i) overlap and a culture where many decisions were escalated to the Board of Commissioners for approval; and (ii) inefficiency
- As mentioned, there was an agreed off take agreement, but distrust between the two parties was created due to a lack of transparency at the Board of Director level
- There was overlap in Committee responsibilities to committees with similar responsibilitiesestablished at both the Board of Commissioners and Board of Director levels

The issues could easily have been addressed with the following approach:

- An understanding between the two shareholders of their respective regulatory constraints and compliance requirements – these requirements should have been incorporated into the shareholders' agreement
- A senior executive should have been made responsible for the governance framework – this person would have understood the shareholder requirements and ensured they were addressed in the governance framework
- The establishment of defined terms of reference for the two boards and the committees – note there were too many committees and this structure should have been simplified

- A requirement where the off take transactions were disclosed to the Board of Directors
- An agreement between the two shareholders regarding the five year objectives of the venture Signoff of key communication releases by the Board of Commissioners.

Industry Case

- This case study illustrates the importance of a strong shareholders' agreement and the establishment and agreement of business objectives and structure. The company was a listed entity in Indonesia
- A local investor acquired a significant equity share and with the majority shareholder agreed a plan to implement an improvement program
- A shareholders' agreement was agreed and signed between the two parties – this agreement incorporated key rights for both shareholders – it also allocated key responsibilities for the two shareholders in business operations
- The governance framework incorporated all aspects of the shareholders' agreement and the various company articles – responsibility for governance oversight was allocated to a Senior Executive
- The shareholders agreed an improvement program
- The approval framework was detailed in the governance framework – the framework included approval for the business plan and budget, appointment of management, key performance indicators and the responsibilities of the Board of Commissioners and the Board of Directors
- The shareholders agreed they must be "as one" in improving the company – hence they agreed the company strategy should be reviewed and , where applicable, revised – this was completed and the shareholders approved the revised strategy with management also agreeing the strategy
- The executive remuneration package was revised and tied to the delivery of the new strategy
- A revised key performance structure was implemented

As a result of the business approach by shareholders and management the company improvement program was implemented over a two-year period and resulted in the following:

- Increase in EBITDA margin by over 50 %
- Market share was maintained

- Production capacity was increased by over 50 %
- An industry class sustainability program was implemented
- Importantly, shareholder dividends and management remuneration were increased
- Equity value was increased more than fourfold.

The governance framework was a key ingredient of success because:

- It aligned shareholders as to their objectives and how key decisions were made in implementing the improvements
- Management was made accountable for the improvement program and the governance framework clearly established their decision boundaries – there was also a clear path to resolve any 'out of plan' issues
- A requirement of the governance framework called for improvements to the Enterprise System – improvements that addressed decision-making discipline
- There was alignment between the shareholder interests and management interests
- There was, also, alignment between the key performance measurement and remuneration structures

Holding Company Case

This case study illustrates that when the management structure is not effectively established and accountabilities not understood the risk of major corporate failure increases significantly. The features of the case study are:

- Three levels of decision-making were established:

  - Shareholders
  - Group Board – comprising a mix of corporate executives and business-unit CEOs
  - Executive Board – comprising the business-unit CEOs

- A committee structure was established – reporting to the Group Board
- The CEO and main shareholder established the Executive Board because he wanted the respective CEOs to work together – he regarded it as a way for a common forum for the CEOs
- Decisions regarding strategy, business plan and investments were made at the Group Board level

- Accountabilities and approvals, at the Executive Board level, mainly focused on operating issues and spending – any key investment decisions were referred to the Group Board
- KPIs were established for both Boards and there was overlap in the KPIs between the two Boards

The governance framework failed and after 12 months the Executive Board was eliminated. What caused the failure?

- There was too much overlap in accountabilities between the two boards
- The Executive Board regarded itself as purely an operating Board with no approval authority – hence any business issues and failures were blamed on the Group Board. For example: when it came to the annual bonus evaluation, the Executive Board blamed the Group Board for non-achievement, the reason being tardiness in the decision making
- The representation of two CEOs on the Group Board created uncertainty and an element of jealousy – the two CEOs were regarded as privileged and the respective Business Units regarded as a priority – amongst the CEO Group
- The Committee structure was also ineffective as the Committee Charters were incomplete and without a statement of objectives and accountability – the Committees were allocated no decision making authority
- Communications to staff were, at times, confusing because the two Board would issue separate communications – sometimes with conflicting messages

The issues could have been addressed by:

- Strengthening the Group Board and the elimination of the Executive Board – the respective CEOs should have had a direct line to the Group Board
- Ensuring the Group Board did not have any CEOs as members or, if there was CEO representation, a clear understanding of their position and the position of the respective business units was understood across the organization
- Creation of a KPI structure that created dependence between the various management levels
- A clear understanding of the responsibilities and accountabilities of the Group Board and of the respective businessunit CEOs – for example the Group Board approving the Annual Business Plans and Budgets and the CEOs implementing those plans and budgets
- Regular review of business-unit performance – review by the Group Board
- Allocation of governance oversight to a Senior Executive

Mining Case Study

This case study highlights the challenges of having the Company's main operations overseas, within one legal and regulatory environment, and the Board and corporate office within another jurisdiction. The features of the case study are:

- The mining company was listed in Australia and, complied with Australian Listing requirements
- The company's mining operations were in Indonesia
- The governance framework incorporated requirements for both the Australian and Indonesian jurisdictions
- At a minimum the Board met every quarter and received monthly operations reports – it was not uncommon for the Board to meet on a more regular basis
- Clear accountabilities and authority levels were established and both the corporate and operating levels – key decisions were allocated to the Board

The governance framework looked, on paper, to be effective. However it broke down leading to the CEO operating outside his authority level and this created significant financial risk. The issues were as follows:

- Due to the "geographic divide" and the location of the Board, management found decisions were taking too long and as a result the CEO made decisions outside his approval limits – this occurred in the areas of contract approvals and the establishment of strategic partners
- It was discovered that contracts were being agreed with related parties without the required transparencies and disclosures
- These decisions were not being reported to the Board of Directors and they were also not reported to the local Board of Commissioners
- As a result significant financial commitments were assumed – financial commitments outside the approved plan and budget

Why did this situation occur?

- There was a lack of regular reporting of key commitments and contracts – the financial reports did not incorporate financial commitments and new contracts and the approval process within the enterprise system was not followed
- Board meetings were always conducted via a phone hookup – there were no in-person meetings – this limited the ability of the Board adequately to review and assess performance

- Board papers were always submitted in the meeting – not prior to the meeting
- The Internal Audit function reported to the CEO and did not provide any independent report to the Audit Committee

The issues could have been addressed by implementing the following:

- Enhancement of the Enterprise System to incorporate an improvement authorization structure – in particular, financial approval parameters
- Monthly Board meetings with Board papers submitted five days prior to the meeting – also, every second Board meeting being conducted in the country of operation
- Regular calls between the Chairman and the CEO and CFO to address any urgent management decisions – decisions that required Board approval
- Internal Audit reporting to the Audit Committee with reports communicated directly to the Committee
- Governance oversight allocated to a senior executive

It is interesting to note that the above initiatives were implemented by the Board. In addition the Company CEO was replaced. Governance has considerably improved.

Concluding Recommendations

As we stated, the establishment and operation of a "perfect" governance structure is possible. Successful companies have common characteristics. One of those characteristics is an effective governance structure. Companies that fail or have serious financial and operating issues will generally suffer from ineffective governance as one of the reasons for failure. The examples we have provided in this chapter all have common elements. These elements start with the shareholders and a clear understanding of the objectives and the governance framework within which the Board and Management must operate. In assessing the governance framework we recommend to complete a review and evaluate the framework against the features listed in this chapter. When reviewing the case studies, we recommend the identification of any similarities between your own framework and the case studies. We are confident you will discover some similarities and recommend, the Executive responsible for governance in your organization addresses the issues. In addition we recommend you develop case studies, based on your own organization's experiences, so as they can be incorporated into the goverance training curriculum.

Notes

1. Luo, Y., (2005), "Corporate governance and accountability in multinational enterprises: concepts and agenda", *Journal of International Management*, Vol. 11: 1–18; Huse, M., (2007), *Boards, Governance and Value Creation*, Cambridge; New York, Cambridge University Press; Charan, R., (2005), *Boards That Deliver. Advantages Corporate Governance from Compliance to Competitive Advantage*, San Francisco, Jossey-Bass.
2. Schleifer, A. & R. Vishny, (1997), "A survey of corporate governance", *Journal of Finance*, Vol. 52: 737–783.
3. Mallin, C.A., (2010), *Corporate Governance*, Oxford, Oxford University Press.
4. Carter, C.B. & J.W. Lorsch, (2004), *Back to the drawing board. Designing corporate boards for a complex world*, Cambridge MA, Harvard Business School Pres; Lorsch, J.W. & R.C. Clark, (2008), "Leading from the Boardroom", *Harvard Business Review*, April, pp. 104–111.
5. Leblanc, R. & J. Gillies, (2005), *Inside the boardroom. How boards really work and the coming revolution in corporate governance*, Ontario, John Wiley & Sons Ltd.
6. Jensen, M. & W.H. Meckling, (1976), "Theory of the Firm: Managerial Behavior, Agency Costs and Ownership Structure", Journal of Financial Economics, and reprinted in in Clarke, Th. (Ed), 2004, *Theories of Corporate Governance. The Philosophical Foundations of Corporate Governance*, London, Routledge, pp. 58–63; Jensen, M., (1986), "Agency cost of free cash flow, corporate finance, and takeovers", *American Economic Review*, 76: 323–329; Jensen, M., (2002), "Value Maximization, Stakeholder Theory, and the Corporate Objective Function", *Business Ethics Quarterly*, 12(2): 235–256.
7. Arguden, Y., (2009), *Boardroom secrets. Corporate governance for quality of life*, Hampshire, Palgrave.
8. For a good overview of best governance practices across borders, we recommend the following sources: Aguilera, R. & Jackson, G. (2003). A cross-national diversity of corporate governance: Dimensions and determinants, Academy of Management Review, 28(3), 447–465; Bainbridge, S.M. (2008). The new corporate governance in theory and practice, Oxford, Oxford University Press; Bennis, W., Goleman, D., & O'Toole, J. (2008). Transparency: How leaders create a culture of candor, San Fransisco, Jossey-Bass; Charan, R. (2005). Boards that deliver: Advantages corporate governance from compliance to competitive advantage, San Francisco, Jossey-Bass.; Clarke, T. (2007). International corporate governance, London, Routledge; Dimma, W. (2002). Excellence in the Boardroom: Best practices in corporate directorship, Ontario, Wiley & Sons Canada; Fama, E. & Jensen, M. (1983). Separation of ownership and control, Journal of Law and Economics,

26, 310–325; Ho, K.L. (Ed.) (2005). Reforming corporate governance in southeast Asia: Economics, politics and regulations, Singapore, ISEAS Publications; Huse, M. (2007). Boards, governance and value creation, New York, Cambridge University Press; Khatri, N., Johnson, J.P., & Ahmed, Z.U. (2003). A two-stage model of cronyism in organizations: A cultural view of governance, In Kidd, J.B. & Richter, F-J. (Eds.), Corruption and governance in Asia, London, Palgrave Macmillan, 61-85; La Porta, R., Lopez-De-Silanes, F. et al. (1999). Corporate ownership around the world, Journal of Finance, 54(2), 471–517; La Porta, R., Lopez-De-Silanes, F. et al. (2000). Investor protection and corporate governance, Journal of Financial Economics, 58, 3–27.

9. Charan, R.; D. Carey & M. Useem, (2014), *Boards that lead. When to take charge, when to partner, and when to stay out of the way*, Cambridge MA, Harvard Business School Press.

10. Verhezen, P., (2015), "Fear, Regret or Trust? Transparency to control or transparency to empower", *International Finance Corporation World Bank Paper*, No 38, Washington.

11. Arguden, Y., *o.c.*, p. XI.

12. Cheung, Y-L; J.T. Connelly; J.P. Estanislao; P. Limpaphayom; T. Lu & S. Utama, (2014),"Corporate Governance and Firm Valuation in Asian Emerging Markets", in Boubaker, S. & D.K. Nguyen (Eds), *Corporate Governance in emerging markets. Theories, Practices and Cases*, New York, Springer, pp. 27–53.

13. Heath, C. & D. Heath, (2013), *Decisive. How to make better decisions*, London, Randomhouse.

14. Meyer, E., (2014), *The Culture Map*, New York, PublicAffairs.

8

Institutions and Leadership Really Matter: The Interdependency of Public and Corporate Governance in Indonesia

Peter Verhezen, Natalia Soebagjo,
and Erry Riyana Hardjapamekas

Introduction

Corporate Governance can only thrive in an environment where the rule of law prevails over personal power and relationships. Although one may argue that relationship-based governance plays an important role in an environment where law enforcement is weak, over time with the increase of participants in the industry and with the globalization of the Indonesian economy, one will need to embrace rule-based governance "best" practices embedded within well-functioning institutions. These widely accepted generic principles of transparency, responsibility, fairness and accountability are forming the norms in international business, while relationships will continue to play an indisputable role in ASEAN to allow firms access to scarce resources and 'political' connections. There is no one codified solution for all, but even

P. Verhezen (✉)
Melbourne Business School, Carlton, VIC, Australia
e-mail: p.verhezen@mbs.edu

N. Soebagjo
UI Center for Governance & Administrative Reform, Jakarta, Indonesia

E.R. Hardjapamekas
Independent Board Member and Chair of Board of Trustees at University of Indonesia, Indonesia
e-mail: erryrh@cbn.net.id

© The Editor(s) (if applicable) and the Author(s) 2016
P. Verhezen et al. (eds.), *Doing Business in ASEAN Markets*,
DOI 10.1007/978-3-319-41790-5_8

Indonesia will need to implement those universal governance principles to attract investment and to remain competitive in a global context.

At the other more "public" side, the Asian crisis of 1997 has clearly revealed that any liberalization in the absence of properly-functioning [public] institutions can be quite devastating for its citizens and businesses.[1] In other words, the ability to formulate and carry out policies and enact laws, the strength to administer efficiently with a minimum of bureaucracy, to control graft and corruption, to maintain a high level of transparency and accountability in government institutions are crucial forsustainable development in any country. Most important is the ability to enforce laws. In the absence of that facility, it will be hard to thrive, either as a business or as country in general.

First, we provide some facts of the interplay of Indonesian politics and business over the last two decades since the "democratization process after Suharto's downfall in 1998", and why we believe that the current president "Jokowi" is making serious efforts to improve public leadership and governance which should cause positive ripples on the corporate governance front. Suharto used state-owned enterprises with loyal appointments on their boards to hold leverage over strategic economic industries, and was closely befriended by loyal tycoons who provided an additional lever to get returns when needed. This crony capitalism is a kind of rent-seeking behavior that is often legal but very unfair. As the *Economist* recently analyzed, this "dealing with murky moguls"[2] undermines trust in the state, misallocates resources and stops countries and true enterpreneurs from creating wealth. Healthy competition, accountability and transparency can transform such unhealthy cronyism.

Second, based on a conceptual framework of public governance that is accepted by most countries, we argue that some characteristics of good public governance function as a fertile ground for improving corporate governance. The opposite is equally true. Moreover, the goals of many public institutions remain ambiguous, embedded in often political and tactical priorities that limit rational goal-setting. In addition the incentives between the principals and agents in those public institutions are far from clear, complicating the governance objective of controlling these governmental agents or bureaucrats. Finally, as in corporate governance, the delegation of authority to employees or agents down the bureaucratic line would be ineffective due to the lack of good leadership qualities of those agents.

Third, when focusing on corporate governance in ASEAN and especially in Indonesia, we see two crucial characteristics – different from most Anglo-Saxon Western countries – that still influence the way corporate leadership uses corporate governance to its "own" advantage: (1) relationships still prevail in Asian business, and (2) most [listed] companies in Indonesia are either family-owned or state-owned resulting in very concentrated ownership.[3]

Corporate governance – in spite of its own merit for shareholders and stakeholders alike – only thrives in Asia and most other countries under the pressure of good public institutional reform and pressure. The philosophy to self-interest, often at the expense of minority or non-family shareholders, is deeply engrained in the Indonesian psyche. Piecemeal engineering, as in step-by-step improvements in public governance and regulatory reform, will be necessary positively to affect the corporate governance realm. And that will require more than just to fill boards with independent personnel.

A Framework to Improve Public Governance

Our main hypothesis is that public governance[4] will have a significant impact on how corporate board members will execute their fiduciary duties in the interest of all shareholders, both majority and minority, and ultimately that of the public at large.

Good public governance practices might teach the corporate elite to implement good corporate governance, such as manager-compensation policies, proper division of power within the organization, rules of succession to top positions, and institutionalized competition in core areas of governance (for instance, voting rights, competitive processes, and voting rules).[5] Unfortunately Indonesia's lack of institutional strength, rather than scope to supply certain functions that only state organizations can provide, is hampering business growth and implementation of satisfactory corporate governance.

Hence, a stewardship approach of public governance would allow a more holistic approach to improving both public and corporate governance. So let us turn our attention to some indicators that allow us to understand public governance better in Indonesia and how it is interconnected with corporate governance.

A Public Governance Framework

Governance is defined as how "the traditions and institutions by which authority in a country is exercised. This includes the process by which governments are selected, monitored and replaced; the capacity of the government to effectively formulate and implement sound policies; and the respect of citizens and the state for institutions that govern economic and social interactions among them".[6] Hence the ideal of good governance to establish a prosperous and just society emphasized both political and economic principles. The political principles of good governance are based on the establishment of a representative and accountable form of government which requires good institutions as in sets of rules governing the actions of individuals and organizations and the negotiation of differences between them.

Good governance in its political interpretation also requires a strong and pluralistic civil society, where there is freedom of expression and association on the one hand, and the rule of law, maintained through an impartial and effective legal system, on the other. Moreover, this interpretation requires a high degree of transparency and accountability in public and corporate processes. The economic governance principles refer to the policies required to promote broad-based economic growth, a dynamic private sector (and state-owned firms) and social policies that will lead to poverty-reduction. Effective institutions and good corporate governance are needed to support the development of a competitive and thriving economy with a deep respect for contracts and property rights.[7] Governance at a macro-level includes institutional reforms and the overall role of the government itself, whereas micro-level governance or corporate governance involves the supervision and control of State-Owned Enterprises (SOEs) and Privately-Owned Enterprises (POEs).

It seems that most definitions of governance agree on the importance of a well-functioning state that effectively operates under the *rule of law*, to be distinguished from the *rule by the law*. Where "public" governance is not strong or when the institutions in which organizations function are rather weak, one sometimes speaks of "institutional voids".[8]

Indeed, public bureaucracies and public governance in most developing and quite a number of emerging countries (like Indonesia and other ASEAN members) are riddled by patronage and corruption,[9] and cleaning them up through the implementation of "modern" civil service systems has been a central goal of most institutional reform.[10]

However, it may not be ignored that most solutions to public-administration problems, while having adapted certain features of "good institutional design", will not be clear-cut "best practices" because a great deal of highly contextual specific information will need to be incorporated in the design of administrative processes. In other words, there is no pre-codified answer to the question of how to control the government agents executing the principal's objectives – admittedly often ambiguous goals – and how much to delegate authority to lower level bureaucrats that is rooted in the "agency costs" as result of asymmetric information.[11] The April 2016 exposure of the Chairman of the Supreme Audit Agency in the Panama Papers is a clear example of challenging and challenged public governance.[12]

Analysis of Public Governance Variables in Indonesia

Recent research in Indonesia has analysed some 12 variables of [macro-] governance: (1) property rights, (2) intellectual property rights, (3) investor protection, which on aggregate are defined as *Legal Certainty*; (4) public trust of politicians, (5) judicial independence, and (6) reliability of police service, together labelled *Public Trustworthiness*; (7) wastefulness of government spending, (8) burden of government regulations, (9) legal framework efficiency, defined in aggregate as *Government Efficiency*; (10) favouritism in decisions made by government officials, (11) strength of auditing and reporting standard, and (12) firms' ethical behavior, defined together as *Transparency*.[13] The conclusion of this empirical study by Soekarni and Arifin (2011) – both research officials at the Central Bank of Indonesia – revealed as hypothesized that Indonesian governance is still rather weak in the four main cluster variables: legal certainty, public trustworthiness, government efficiency, and transparency, despite some slight relative improvement since the 1997 crisis. The establishment of the Eradication Corruption Commission (KPK) did help to improve the reputation of Indonesia in attempting to curb corruption.[14]

Moreover, the authors found a clear correlation between governance and competitiveness on the one hand, and governance and economic performance on the other. In other words, improving [macro-] governance would have a direct positive effect on the competitiveness, productivity and absorption capacity of Indonesia, as well as an amelioration of its economic macroeconomic performance.[15]

To understand better how public governance fares, we focus on the following six clusters of governance-related variables:[16]

1. *Voice and accountability* (VA) – that capture the perceptions of the extent to which a country's citizens are able to participate in selecting their government, as well as freedom of expression, freedom of association, and a free media.
2. *Political Stability and Absence of Violence* (PV) – capturing perceptions of the likelihood that the government will be destabilized or overthrown by unconstitutional or violent means, including politically-motivated violence and terrorism.
3. *Government Effectiveness* (GE) – that captures perceptions of the quality of public services, the quality of the civil service and the degree of its independence from political pressures, the quality of policy formulation and implementation, and the credibility of the government's commitment to such policies.

4. *Regulatory Quality* (RQ) – refers to the perceptions of the ability of the government to formulate and implement sound policies and regulations that permit and promote private sector development.
5. *Rule of Law* (RL) – capturing perceptions of the extent to which agents have confidence in, and abide by, the rules of society, and in particular the quality of contract enforcement, property rights, the police, and the courts, as well as the likelihood of crime and violence.
6. *Control of Corruption* (CC) – analyses the perceptions of the extent to which public power is exercised for private gain, including both petty and grand forms of corruption, as well as "capture" of the state by elites and private interests.

The first indicator,[17] *Voice and Accountability*, focuses on the democracy index, vested interests, accountability of public officials, human rights, and freedom of association. The second indicator, *Political Stability and Absence of Violence*, looks into orderly transfers, armed conflict, violent demonstrations, social unrest, and international tensions and the terrorist threat. The third measurement, *Government Effectiveness*, emphasizes the quality of bureaucracy and institutional effectiveness. The fourth governance measurement, *Regulatory Quality*, deciphers the extent of unfair competitive practices, price controls, discriminatory tariffs, excessive protections, and discriminatory taxes. The fifth governance indicator, i.e. the *Rule of Law*, refers to violent crime, organized crime, fairness of the judicial process, enforceability of contracts, speediness of judicial process, confiscation and expropriation, intellectual property rights protection, and private property protection. The authors strongly believe that law enforcement protection – under the Rule of Law – are economic. Finally the *Control of Corruption*, the sixth governance indicator, specifically analyses the extent to which the country combats corruption among public officials.

Indonesia falls in the category of those countries which were able slightly to improve their overall status in terms of *Accountability* and *Rule of Law* from 1996 (before the Asian crisis) to 2008 (after it). Moreover, there seems to be a direct correlation between weak governance structures and rather limited ability to express one's meaning as in "voice" on the one hand, and a rather dismal control of corruption on the other. Indonesia does not fare too well in terms of governance and *voice and accountability*, and fails to control or *reduce corruption* in the country.

The "Panama Papers", which revealed powerful elites to have taken advantage of tax havens to avoid Indonesian taxes, motivated Parliament and the executive office to introduce tax amnesty packages to lure back funds stashed overseas – curiously called "Bursanomics" – to be invested in the local stock market. Together with a pardon for past wrongdoing and a small penalty charge of between 1% to 6%, instead of the usual 25% to 35% tax rates, the government expects these elites to repatriate their funds to help boost the weak state budget. This non-tax compliance by the powerful elite and the incredibly low tax-to-GDP ratio of less than 10 % in Indonesia – among the lowest in the world versus 25 % in more mature markets – indicate weak institutional quality and governance[18] as well as ineffective government regulation and tax-extraction.

Kaufmann and his team at the World Bank argued that 'fighting corruption' cannot be done merely through another well published anticorruption campaign, or by just adding anticorruption offices or incessant redrafting of decrees (often not enforced in reality). Instead, corruption needs to be viewed within a broader governance context whereby other important dimensions, such as rule of law, protection of property rights, freedom of the press, political competition, transparent campaign finance and other matters [that in turn affect corruption] need to be addressed as well.[19] The role of participatory voice mechanisms afforded to the citizenry in curbing corruption is of particular importance in this context.

Although the accountability score did not improve dramatically, its positive trends should be seen as hopeful. At the other hand, one could argue that the post-Suharto era has been quite successful from a democratic and political stability perspective.

Another indicator of slightly improved governance in Indonesia is the increase in governmental effectiveness since 1996 till now, despite the global financial crisis in 2008. This improvement is probably attributable to the success of democratically-elected institutions in Indonesia, including the Presidency. With the exception of some heinous terrorist acts over the last decade and the rise of some Muslim fanatical splinter groups aiming at a new Islamic Caliphate, Indonesia has been characterized by relative peace and political stability.

However, despite the slight improvement of control of corruption over the last decade – probably attributable to the initiation of KPK – we still believe that much more can be achieved in terms of combatting corruption. This measurement of attempting to get corruption under control will have a significant and direct effect on corporate governance and its battle with corruption in firms, especially State-Owned Enterprises.

Corruption still remains (too) high in Indonesia[20] which has an immediate negative effect on corporate governance practices. Indeed, it is especially in this domain that Indonesia's governance could be dramatically improved and this, in turn,would have a positive effect on corporate governance in particular and the investment climate in general.[21]

Indonesia is characterized by a high level of 'pervasiveness' and a reasonable level of 'arbitrariness'. *Pervasiveness* is the average firm's likelihood of encountering corruption in its normal interactions with state officials. It captures the degree to which a firm is obliged to address corrupt behavior.[22] *Arbitrariness* defines the inherent degree of ambiguity associated with corrupt transactions in a given nation or state and is often the result of the ability and willingness of corrupt officials to vary the set of necessary approvals to extract maximal bribes or from the entry of bureaucrats into the market for extortion.[23] When corruption is highly arbitrary, transactions with government officials are usually characterized by a high level of uncertainty in terms of size, target and number of corrupt payments necessary to obtain an approval. Indonesia under the authoritarian regime of Suharto was characterized by a high level of pervasiveness in terms of corruption; in other words corruption was systemic and to a certain extent predictable.[24] Since the downfall of Suharto in 1998 corruption has become less "predicable" and more arbitrary. That will not necessarily reduce the country risk perception and might therefore deter multinational companies from investing in Indonesia. Government corruption is a serious impediment to economic development and stability.[25] About 35 % of business enterprises reported that they had not made any new investment lately due to the high cost of corruption.[26]

The overall consensus indicates that there is indeed a direct correlation between "good" [public] governance and "best" corporate governance practices – the main subject of this chapter. One of the very sensible and public perceptions about the relationship between public and corporate governance is the extent to which the government succeeds in reducing corruption by public officials while internationally-effective companies will attempt to reduce the tendency to bribe public officials for favourable treatment or cut corners to secure big governmental projects. The fact that there was no real significant improvement in the yearly Transparency International index for Indonesia – comparing the perception of the degree of corruption in a country relative to other countries – confirms the consensus among many scholars and activists that Indonesia's anti-corruption reform is stalling.[27]

Much still needs to be done to improve the government's effectiveness in the prevention and eradication of corruption and in particular in enhancing the integrity of Indonesia's law enforcement agencies and in dealing with political corruption. According to the *2013 Global Corruption Barometer,* Indonesians perceive the police force as being the most corrupt institution

(91 %), followed by parliament (89 %), with political parties and the judiciary being equally corrupt (86 %). It is clear that the uncertainty and the arbitrariness that occur due to institutional weaknesses are risks that investors have to consider when doing business in Indonesia.

The cosiness and close relationships between government officials and businesses can be brought back to the historical dependence on governmental protection or favouritism of some well protected "indigenous" business groups.[28] This "relationship-based" capitalism was quite useful in the early stage of the development of Indonesia as a way to protect those favoured groups from foreign competition. Sometimes this relationship-based capitalism is referred to as crony capitalism when favors and licenses are granted to befriended businessmen by the powerful political elite. However, this managed capitalism was not well equipped to deal with, or diligently oversee, foreign money invested in Indonesian firms in the 1990s. One could easily argue that such close relationships between government officials and business people became quite pernicious over time, allowing any limited form of governance to break down with the known results in the Asian crisis.

The Indonesian Legal & Societal Context

Since the fall of Suharto in 1998, Indonesia has indeed succeeded in transitioning away from authoritarian rule to a democracy in the making, attempting to shift from relations-based governance[29] to rules-based governance. During this transitional period, however, the challenge lies in deepening the democratization process and strengthening the institutions that have been established over the past decade which also entails strengthening governance reform.

Indonesian Institutional Reform Since 1998 Till 2014

Indonesia is now characterized by relative political stability; violent outbursts are relatively rare. Indonesians enjoy freedom of expression and association and a lively media, but there are concerns about backtracking. Unfortunately, the use of criminal defamation laws, the 2008 Information and Electronic Transfers, a vague state secrets bill, the ownership of media by business groups with political affiliations endanger freedom of expression and the work of journalists. Lately, Indonesia's stability has become more fragile due to the lack of protection for minorities, who are often threatened by armed thugs acting in the name of religion or ethnicity. This not only undermines freedom of association but also endangers that diversity in which Indonesia takes greatpride.

In the political arena, direct presidential elections were peacefully held for the first time in 2004 and again in 2009, leading to a legitimate government that provided the necessary stability to allow business to thrive again after the disastrous financial crisis of 1997 that led to the downfall of Suharto.

For the business community, political stability is only one of the many prerequisites for investing in Indonesia. Government effectiveness is just as essential. The 2008/2009 Global Competitiveness Index, which ranked Indonesia 55th in its assessment of 134 countries, cited the inefficient bureaucracy of the government as being the most problematic factor for doing business in Indonesia, followed by the inadequate supply of infrastructure, policy instability, and corruption. In its 2010/2011 Report, Indonesia moved up to the 44th position, and to 34th position (out of 144 countries) in 2014/2016. But the inefficient bureaucracy is still considered the most problematic factor, with corruption a very close second.

Aware of this, bureaucratic reform and governance, infrastructure, energy, the investment and business climate and environmental management are among the list of 11 national priorities which President Yudhoyono (SBY) had set for his second and last constitutional 2009–2014 term.[30]

Creating a more efficient, effective and accountable bureaucracy requires thorough reform and improved governance mechanisms, which seem to have stalled over the last year or two, despite the pledges of President Jokowi since 2014. Both are considered vital to the improvement of public services and this has been frequently emphasized since 1998. Changing mindsets of bureaucrats known for their culture of power rather than service delivery, patron-client relationships, and low level of competency is a daunting endeavour[31] However, bureaucratic reform is inevitable and has to be undertaken in three areas, namely the institution, the business process and human resources. Indonesia's bureaucracy is weighed down by its "fat" organization structure, uneven number of institutions at the national and regional level, and by the number of non-structural bodies whose functions often overlap with existing formal institutions. These characteristics make doing business in Indonesia challenging.[32]

Moreover, the *agency problem* in the public sector remains an enormous challenge.[33] Politicians are often described as self-interested individuals who are inclined to maximize their own personal interest rather than that of the public they are meant to represent. Unfortunately, crony capitalism or rent-seeking behavior ranging from string-pulling to bribery is still rampant in Indonesia and other ASEAN countries (except Singapore). Although quite a number of these activities may not be considered illegal, they remain very unfair. Crony capitalism undermines trust in the state, misallocates resources and prevents Indonesian entrepreneurs from thriving. Hence, anti-corruption activists are pushing for greater transparency at the agency level to enable greater public participation in policy-making and in monitoring the implementation of public policies so as to establish a more deliberative democratic system.

Law UU no.17/2007 regarding the Long term National Development Plan 2005–2025 highlighted the fact that improving the professionalism of state agencies and of governance in the central and local governments are key objectives of bureaucratic reform. Guidelines were issued in 2008 by the Ministry of Administrative Reforms which set a target for national level reforms to be completed by 2011 and at the sub-national level by 2025. Thus far only the Ministry of Finance, under the leadership of former Finance Minister Sri Mulyani, has been notable for its bold efforts in restructuring the ministry and improving its efficiency although the Supreme Audit Board, the Supreme Court, Ministry of Foreign Affairs, State Secretariat and the Attorney General's Office have also embarked on reforming their bureaucracies with limited success. A Grand Design and Road Map have since been drafted and is pending approval by the vice president who has been delegated the task of leading the effort. However, despite the need for a clean and effective bureaucracy, President Jokowi does not seem to view this reform as a priority.[34]

And in terms of the elephant in the room, corruption, Indonesia has made little progress.[35] President Yudhoyono (SBY) was elected partly because of his expressed determination to tackle the issue but under his watch, particularly during his second term, the fight against corruption faced serious setbacks. The anti-corruption committee KPK (the Anti-Corruption Agency) was established in 2002 based on Law no. 30/2002 and in its early years it succeeded in closing major corruption cases involving regional leaders and corruption by officials in the Election Commission, the Department of Oceans and Fisheries, the consulate in Penang (Malaysia) and the state radio station to name a few. In 2004, SBY issued a Presidential Instruction no. 5/2004 which called for a more aggressive drive in the fight against corruption and for an improvement in Indonesia's rating in the corruption perception index. In that same year a strategic plan was drafted; it was finalized in 2009, complete with an action plan for 2010–2015 detailing how to realize the missions to: (i) establish an integrated anti-corruption systems and mechanisms on a national scale; (ii) reform national laws and regulations that support corruption prevention and eradication in a consistent, consolidated, and systematic manner; (iii) build and consolidate a system and mechanisms for asset recovery gained by illicit means through effective national and international cooperation; (iv) build and internalize an anti-corruption culture in government and society; and (v) develop and publicize a system for reporting the implementation of anti-corruption measures[36]

Reform of these public institutions has beenmost difficult but it is essential if better corporate governance is to be supported. Needless to say, corporations are reluctant to become embroiled in legal cases in which the laws are unclear or inconsistently enforced, such as in the cases against TIME Warner, ManuLife, and Newmont.

Decentralization has added to the complications of improving public governance in Indonesia. Law no. 22/1999 gave local governments greater responsibilities in all areas except for security and defense, foreign policy, monetary and fiscal matters, justice and religious affairs. The main objectives of this policy were the improvement of public service delivery and government accountability. The policy has succeeded in stimulating local initiative but at the same time has often led to confusion between the authority of central and local governments and to inconsistent policies. This confusion has led to what some anti-corruption activists see as a decentralized system of corruption in which graft occurs in a fragmented manner, dispersed between the different levels of government.

The National Committee on Governance, established in 2004 by the Coordinating Minister of Economic Affairs has produced guidelines which explain the basic principles of good public governance and how state institutions in the executive, judicial and legislative branches, as well as various non-structural government agencies, should adopt these principles. A roadmap towards improved public governance is in planning although it has proved more challenging to design than the counterpart for corporate governance..

The guidelines also highlighted the importance of the involvement of stakeholders, including the corporate world in improving public governance. One tentative step in this direction is the cooperation between the Indonesian Chamber of Commerce and Industry and the National Committee on Governance in coordinating a movement known as KUPAS – acronym for the Community of Businessmen against Graft. The Community was established in January 2010 and has organized a series of meetings involving various business and professional associations. To create a culture of doing 'clean' business, it plans to give recognition to individuals and companies as anti-graft champions, to learn from their example, and to establish role models.

The continuing efforts and initiatives undertaken by the government to combat corruption are multi-pronged. Taking the principal-agent approach, strategies to curb corruption usually fall into three categories, namely by policy change to limit the scope of corruption; by strengthening external monitoring and sanctions so that the costs of corruption increases; and by creating systems to induce self-restraint within government organisations.

In September 2010, the IMF warned Indonesia that if it wants to remain as one of the world's fastest-growing economies, it must be able to defeat corruption and uphold the rule of law. Ironically, despite its poor record in this regard, Indonesia was elected co-Chair of the G20 Working Group on Anticorruption. Perhaps this new leadership role at the global level will give Indonesian political leaders greater incentive to 'walk the talk' and root out the evil with greater resolve and commitment.

A New Era Under President Jokowi Since 2014?

Enormous hope and excitement erupted when Joko Widodo – popularly known as Jokowi – got elected in 2014, but with a much smaller margin than expected. Jokowi won by a margin of 6.30 % against ex-General Prabowo Subianto in one of the most hotly-contested elections the country had ever witnessed. The campaigning split not just the nation but also families due to the very different backgrounds and styles of the candidates.[37] Unlike other local government leaders, Jokowi was elected not so much for his financial clout as for his social capital. He was considered a man of action and integrity, result-oriented and, most attractive to voters, a man of the people with empathy for the marginalized, bringing a breath of fresh air into Indonesian politics.

Given the daunting leap from mayor of a town of half a million[38] to president of Southeast Asia's largest economy and a population of more than 250 million, Joko Widodo's Presidency has so far not been easy. His popularity rating dipped slightly from 70.1 % in the first 100 days in office to 64.7 % in his first year but the people still had faith that he would bring change.[39] Public confidence in his leadership is needed to execute his transformational plans as outlined in his 'Nawa Cita' or the '9 Priorities' which addressed all the right concerns.[40]

Execution of these priorities, which are in favor of economic growth and encouraging private sector development, not only requires leadership and public confidence but unity of government. Despite the people's strong support for Joko Widodo (like SBY before him), early in his leadership he chose to prioritize consolidation of his political position. Being an outsider and never being part of the political elite, with little experience in the workings of national politics and with limited financial resources, Joko Widodo felt he had to calibrate his political power base, particularly when he was being undermined by his own political party, the PDI-P who often openly disagreed with his decisions. The shaping of his cabinet, which many had hoped would be based on merit, was influenced by political considerations to ensure a balance of power. This decision clearly did not reflect his intention to create an efficient and effective bureaucracy which would be capable of realizing his ambitious goals and transformational agenda. Instead, his cabinet has been mired by lack of coordination, friction, and public spats between his ministers. After just a few months in office, a cabinet reshuffle was necessary and, at the time of writing, another is imminent.

And Jokowi's fight against corruption in Indonesia has been mixed.[41] Moreover, the pressure on the Anti-Corruption Committee, KPK, is enormous because of its track record. Since its establishment in 2002, the number of cases being investigated by the KPK continues to increase. With its limited resources for a nation as big as Indonesia, within the 2004–2014 decade, the KPK has succeeded in finishing 321 cases and retrieved IDR 873 billion for the state. In its control of gratuities, IDR 24 billion has been retrieved.[42] The actors involved in corruption cases are mostly government officials (27.62 %), the private sector (24.67 %) and politicians (20.25 %) in cases mostly related to procurement and bribery.[43] The onus now lies on the shoulders of the new KPK leadership, appointed in December 2015, to continue being as tough on corruptors as their predecessors. When they were appointed there was a lot of public scepticism regarding the competency and backgrounds of the new anti-corruption leaders as they were relatively unknown figures but, at the time of writing, they have proved to be as relentless as their predecessors in their sting operations and in their corruption-prevention campaign albeit in a lower profile manner, and this despite the ever-present connections between businessmen and politicians.

"Relationship-Based" Versus Rules-Based Corporate Governance

In order to provide sustainable solutions to challenges, leaders need to be able to fall back on certain institutions. When corporate governance is defined as the power structures by which a corporation is governed to create sustainable value, it becomes obvious that the way power is (mis)used by the board and its top management plays a crucial role in creating a trustworthy and transparent environment.

The fact that ASEAN boards are mainly manned by insiders – and possibly complying with the legal minimum of one-third independent board members – makes it clear that governing and leading such organizations in the interest of all shareholders may be less straightforward than often thought. This is complicated by the fact that in economies like Indonesia and most ASEAN emerging markets with weak public institutions and high uncertainty, informal relationships within the board, as well as between the board and other powerful elites, still play an important role in securing success of the organization. Yet ironically, almost all regulators in ASEAN, and thus also in Indonesia, have underwritten the OECD corporate governance principles.[44]

How then to understand this emphasis on building informal relationships over formal governance structures and why they have played such a crucial role in Asian economies?

Relationships, Network and Gift Practices in Indonesia

Rather than merely relying on formal contractual structures, quite a number of 'overseas' Chinese and more recently indigenous (*pribumi* in Indonesia and Malaysia) businessmen and entrepreneurs use the strategy of utilizing or constructing informal social ties with individuals who can facilitate the process of investment or help secure favorable contracts. While such strategies relying primarily on social guarantees and relationships can dramatically speed up a process and may increase the odds of securing contracts, they usually come at the cost to traditionally negotiated legal guarantees or judicial boundaries. Nonetheless, these informal norms have their own mechanisms for monitoring and enforcement which are often more subtle and flexible than formal governance rules and regulations. And these norms, values, shared experiences and intense social relations actively shape the preferences or "utility functions" of both agents and principals.

It has been argued that such "bamboo network" strategies have led to amazingly quick economic growth in these countries in the 1970s and 1980s, but have also sown the seeds of their downfall[45] as the financial crisis of 1997–2001, afflicting most ASEAN countries demonstrated.

These relationships, *"guanxi"*, bamboo network or "social capital" constitute trust among the participants and function as substitutes for elaborate formal incentive systems. So instead of formal corporate governance monitoring system and rules that aim to regulate agents' behavior, Indonesian and most Asian organizational cultures rely on a complementary mixture of informal norms and formal mechanisms to resolve the traditional principal-agent problem. The agency cost is rooted in the existence of information asymmetry between majority owners and minority investors in Asia, whereas in the US, UK and Australia, the agency cost is mainly ascribable to the information gap between hired managers with a fiduciary duty and the firm (owners or beneficiaries of the fiduciary relationship).

Nonetheless, business networking is part of the "way business is done in Asia". Moreover, networking and bonding refer to a natural human tendency to relate to one another. Hence, giving gifts, as a form of establishing alliances, bonds and networks, is a prevalent practice in most traditional cultures.[46] Likewise, the jostling for an advantageous position in social relationships and networks is a predominant way for Asians to survive in their communities[47] aside from gaining a competitive advantage in business. One of the reasons why networks accompanied by gifts[48] still prevail in Asia (except Singapore,[49] Hong Kong and to a lesser extent Malaysia) is the fact that legal institutions do not fully function or protect individuals; in such a context, relationships substitutes the lack of rule of the law, Lee Kuan Yew allegedly said.

No three issues incite such heated debate as nepotism, collusion and bribery in the Asian media and business courses. Many seem to suggest that gifts,[50] networks and their less benevolent expressions are indeed cultural phenomena and are therefore acceptable. On the contrary, we emphasize that bribery and nepotism[51] should not be endorsed as "culturally acceptable".[52] As bribery connotes a wrongful transfer of resources between parties,[53] so nepotism implies a misuse of relationships between parties. If relationships are perceived to determine the success of companies, then it should not surprise us that boards vie for influential and well-connected members who can open doors to government officials, or banks or other useful people. Some may even label this type of "governance" relationship-based[54] in contrast to rules-based governance systems.

If informal norms continue to play a crucial monitoring role, despite increasing pressure from regulators and especially foreign institutional investors to abide by best governance practices, an organizational culture conducive to more appropriate behaviour would be better created by corporate leaders through the force of their own enlightened and exemplary personality rather than through the implementation of rules and regulations.

Insider Boards in Indonesia

Despite the prevailing governance paradigm in Anglo-Saxon markets that shareholder value-creation is the main – and, according to many, the only – objective of top management, we here (re)interpret the "fiduciary duties" of any board member as creating value for the organization. Obviously, this value-creation ultimately benefits its owners or shareholders, but this should be distinguished from the organization. It is the board which needs to be clear about how to interpret this real duty to create value: whether the focus needs to be on equity stock or whether other performance indicators need to be taken into account. Thus the board has a responsibility to determine and to identify which audiences are crucial for the organization's vitality and long-term success.[55] It is the (non-executive and executive) directors who will make the decision about the ultimate performance objective. In theory, the directors' duty to shareholders is separate from, and not necessarily superior to, their' duty to the corporation as a separate legal entity. In order to assess these duties, it is necessary briefly to analyze the generic profile of these powerful decision-makers, who often turn into power-brokers, both in State-Owned Enterprises (SOEs) and in Privately-Held Enterprises.

It may not be ignored, either, that the managed or relationship-based governance model, made up of *insider* board members (in Asia in general and in Indonesia in particular), is quite different from the arm's length or rules-based corporate governance structures in the Western developed world, with more *outside* board members, especially in the Anglo-Saxon business environment.[56] In the latter, transparency and easy enforceability of contracts through a well-functioning legal system characterize rule-based corporate governance, also referred to as "arm's length" systems. Although the "arm's length" governance system based on a transparent price market mechanism may claim to be quite effective and efficient in allocating capital to the most productive investments, it is also true that such allocation is much more short-term oriented. Moreover, such a short-term focus enhances the financial self-interest of the shareholders and investors on the one hand and the powerful top executives and advisors on the other. The principles of corporate governance did not aim, however, to endorse such short-termism.[57]

This is in contrast to a relationship-based governance system – that is more often controlled by a family patriarch or the state – that can endure a longer-term vision and strategies in making decisions that overall provides more social security than the profit-driven Anglo-Saxon system in the USA.

However, the financial system in Indonesia is not characterized by transparency. Public financial information is very limited while government and bank intervention were perceived as "useful" for a business to thrive in Indonesia. In other words, information is still closely guarded within a group of insiders who benefit from this managed capitalist system. Unfortunately, such a relationship-based system has proved to be inefficient in monitoring the responsibilities and accountabilities of those in charge – a primary role of governance.

Moreover, if public governance is in disarray, and if government officials are intervening in business process decisions (such as investment), itcannot be expected that businesses will adapt to "best" corporate governance practices of transparency, accountability and fairness. The more so because both governmental officials and favored business groups have a vested interest in such beneficial relationships. Macro-economically, the society at large may lose from these vested relationships in the longer term, unless the government and businesses acknowledge that efficiency and effectiveness may need to be taken into account in order to make more appropriate transparent investment decisions. Relationships should not be banned altogether, but features of minimum transparency and accountability[58] might be needed to reduce "un-economic" and unfair corruption.

Although the US/UK governance system has produced quite innovative companies, one should not dismiss relationship-based governance as always ineffective and corrupt. Relying on long-term relationships with suppliers, bankers, customers and employees might have some significant advantages as well – such as loyalty, incremental progress, and the willingness to share gain and pain among their associates – that are not easily found in an Anglo-Saxon system.

On the other hand, relationship-based governance that uses discretion to make decisions often leads to certain abuses as in 'KKN' (Korupsi, Kollusi, Nepotisme), especially when the power by the elite is not monitored or scrutinized through appropriate checks and balances, either publicly or within corporations. These institutional flaws often create additional pitfalls for foreign organizations doing business in Asia. Taking advantage of those voids[59] by engaging in specific networks, or by having inside access to specific non-public information – not necessarily legal or ethically appropriate – one can often obtain some competitive advantage. Moreover, well connected patriarchs, tycoons and their organizations will use networks to obtain business deals and to enforce contracts. Any business that can reduce these organizational risks in one way or another, will help to achieve a higher return or a better competitive advantage. It can only be hoped that responsible leadership will guide organizational behaviour towards adherence to best governance principles while continuing to build institutional capacity for reform.[60]

Concluding Remarks

Bureaucratic reform, strengthening anti-corruption agencies, improving law enforcement and greater public engagement need to be done simultaneously. The corporate world also needs to be encouraged to participate through active corporate citizenship as part of a collective action pushing for reforms, while at the same time adopting anti-corruption measures internally (although few companies have done this). Corporations in Southeast Asia in general, and in

Indonesia in particular, should also have anti-corruption programs in place which analyze the corruption risks in their context; adopt a training and communications program to ensure that business processes are in line with the anti-corruption program; that a sanctions system is in place; that a system exists for employees to seek advice when faced with ethical issues; and that there is constant monitoring and evaluation of the implementation of the anti-corruption program. Such a system not only helps to ensure the integrity of the company but is useful as a defense mechanism when having to deal with a corrupt public sector. Anti-corruption measures at both the corporate level and as collective corporate action can contribute to the integrity of the public sector.

This is all the more pressing because corruptors remain undeterred, despite the strategies implemented by the Indonesian government. Indonesia's scores in the 2011–2014 Corruption Index hardly showed a significant change, being still in the same league as Madagascar, Malawi, Benin, Burkina Faso, Argentina and Mexico to name a few, although still better than its neighbours Vietnam, the Philippines, Cambodia, Laos and Myanmar. In 2015, Indonesia slightly improved and is now in 88th position together with Morocco, Peru, Suriname, Egypt, Algeria and Albania.

Within the Indonesian public sector, citizens as principals have little control over the governing elites and the bureaucrats as their agents. Rarely do public office holders have the best interests of the public in mind. Entering the bureaucracy and politics is seen as employment for self-interest where the wielding of power takes precedence over serving the public. Moreover, the high cost of elections to win their public positions have to be recouped and being in office enables them to do so. Nevertheless, in terms of the six governance indicators mentioned above, Indonesia has improved, particularly in *voice and accountability,* as well as *government effectiveness.* Indonesia's rank in the World Bank's *Doing Business 2016* was up to 109th place and is 15th in the East Asia & Pacific region in the overall ease of doing business, far below Thailand and Malaysia which rank 5rd and 4th respectively.[61] Indonesia will need to acknowledge the need to promote good governance to ensure the inflow of capital and the outflow of products on the corporate level, and to position Indonesia as a creditworthy and trustworthy country in international politics and global economics on the public governmental level. Obviously, one will need to take into account the political and economic context and the social institutions that either facilitate or constrain the good functioning of governance mechanisms.

Although Indonesia as a typical Asian country has culturally embraced relationship-based "governance" rather than the usual transaction-oriented method, it will need to respect some international recognized "minimum" governance standards of transparency and accountability to position itself within an international context. Although we did not specify all the contextual details, it is clear that the reforms, cultural norms, the implementation of the rule of law, regulations and the role of history all play a significant role in understanding the "institutional context" in which governance in Indonesia will either thrive or be stifled. Such an institutional governance context has an immediate effect on corporate governance practices as pursued in Indonesia. The unfortunate example of rampant collusion between government officials and businesses is not exactly the best way to convince the outside world. On the other hand, it may also be argued that corporate businesses implementing internationally-recognized corporate governance standards could positively influence the way the public and government will stimulate reform through good public governance.

Notes

1. Basri, M.C., (2011), "The impact of Global Financial Crisis on the Indonesian Economy", in Swee-Hock, S. (Ed), *Managing Economic Crisis in Southeast Asia*, Singapore, ISEAS, pp. 292–325; and Kaufmann, D. (1999), "Research on corruption: critical empirical issues", in Jain, A. (Ed), *Economics of Corruption*, Norwell, Kluwer, pp. 129–176.
2. *The Economist*, May 7th 2016.
3. Claessens, S., S. Djankov & L.H.P. Lang, (2000), "The separation of ownership and control in East Asian Corporations", *Journal of Financial Economics*, Vol. 58: 81–112; Claessens, S., S. Djankov, S J.P.H. Fan & L.H.P. Lang, (2002), "Disentangling the incentive and entrenchment effects of large shareholders", *Journal of Finance*, Vol. 57: 2741–2771; Claessens, S. & B.B. Yurtoglu, (2013), "Corporate Governance in emerging markets: A survey", *Emerging Markets Review*, Vol. 15: 1–33; and Djankov, S., F. Lopez-de-Silanes; R.L. La Porta & A. Schleifer, (2008), "The Law and economics of self-dealing", *Journal of Financial Economics*, Vol. 88: 430–465.
4. The purpose of this chapter is not to engage in the debate of how a good state institution (and good public governance) is one that is able to transparently and efficiently service the needs of its clients, in this case the citizens of Indonesia, but will instead focus on some aspects of public governance, particularly legal enforcement that immediately affects the functioning and effectiveness of corporate governance reform and practices in Indonesia. Hence, the authors will forego the practical and academic debate on institutions design, reform and institutional management as in (1) organizational design and management of public administration; (2) political system design; (3) analysing the basis of legitimization; (4) the cultural and structural factors that affect the functioning of state institutions.

5. Benz, M. & B. Frey (2007), "Corporate governance: what can we learn from public governance?", *Academy of Management Review*, Vol. 32(1): 92–104.

6. World Bank 2007 & Kaufmann, D., A. Kraay & M. Mastruzzi, (2010), *Governance Matters. Aggregate and Individual Governance Indicators 1996–2008*, A World Bank Paper 4978; Washington DC.

7. Verhezen, P. (2011), "Opportunities and Pitfalls in emerging markets: Institutional Voids, Reputation and Economic context", Keynote Speech at *Seminar on Risk by ACE-Vlerick Management School*, 18 September 2011 at Vlerick Ghent-Belgium.

8. Khanna, Palepu, Sinha (2005), "Strategies that fit emerging markets", *Harvard Business Review*, June; Khanna, Palepu (2006), "Emerging Giants", *Harvard Business Review*, October.

9. Komar, M. (2006), "Challenging Corruption in Indonesia", *International Association of Women Judges 8th Biennial Conference* 3–7 May 2006, Sydney Australia; Prasojo, E. (2010), "Implementing Anti-Corruption Education in Universities: Creating National Integrity" in seminar in Jakarta in April (Faculty of Social and Political Sciences, University of Indonesia); Klitgaard, R. (1998), *Controlling Corruption*, Berkeley, University of California Press; and Banerjee, A. (1997), "A theory of misgovernance", *Quarterly Journal of Economics*, Vol. 112: 1289–1332.

10. Fukuyama, F. (2005), *State Building. Governance and World Order in the Twenty-First Century*, London, Profile Books – Cornell University Press: "[…] The hardest areas to reform are the low-specificity activities with high transaction volume like education and law. There is legal system in the world that can be "fixed" by ten technocrats, no matter how bright. These are also the areas of public administration that are likely to be the most idiosyncratic and subject to variance according to local conditions. These are areas where design and input from people immersed in local conditions will be the most critical…" (p. 115).

11. Fukuyama, F. (2005); and Jensen, M. (1998: 2), *Foundations of Organizational Strategy*, Cambridge MA, Harvard University Press: "Because all information cannot be moved to a central decision-maker, whether a central planner in an economy or the CEO in a firm, most decision rights must be delegated to those people who have the relevant information. The cost of moving information between people creates the necessity for decentralizing some decision-rights in organizations and the economy. This decentralization in turn leads to systems to mitigate the control problem that results from the fact that self-interested people (with their own self-control problems) who exercise decision rights as agents on behalf of others will not behave as perfect agents."

12. Since 2009, leadership positions in BPK (Supreme Audit Agency) have been filled by former members of parliament or are affiliated to them, triggering the need to revise the UU BPK to change the selection process in order to ensure an independent leadership and protect the integrity of the institution.

Several in the 2014-2019 leadership have had political affiliations. Its Chairman, formerly of the GOLKAR political party, was named in the Panama Papers with no sense of wrong-doing.

13. Soekarni, M. & S. Arifin (2011), "Governance and Economic Performance", in Ananta, A.; Soekarni, M. & S. Arifin (Eds), *The Indonesian Economy Entering a New Era*, Singapore, ISEAS.
14. Soekarni et al. 2011. In 2007 for example, KPK started about 29 investigations that increased to 53 cases the subsequent year 2008. Indonesia did not fare well in comparison with its ASEAN neighbours (till 2009). Only Philippines scored worse.
15. Soekarni et al. 2011.
16. Kaufmann, D., A. Kraay & M. Mastruzzi (2010), *Governance Matters. Aggregate and Individual Governance Indicators 1996–2008*, A World Bank Paper 4978; Washington DC.
17. Those six indicators can be elaborated by sub-indicators as measured by the World Bank which refers – to quote a few – to the Economist Intelligence Unit (EIU), EBR, Global E-Governance Index (EGV), Business Environment Risk Intelligence (BRI), Freedom House, Transparency International, Global Integrity Index, Gallup World Poll, Political Economic Risk Consultancy Corruption in Asia (PRC), and the Institute for Management Development World Competitiveness Yearbook (WCY). We specifically mention the EIU sub-categories as found on www.eiu.com.
18. Fukuyama (2005), *o.c.*, p. 27: "[...] countries that would like to be able to take in a higher portion of GDP in taxes but are unable to do so because they cannot monitor tax compliance and enforce tax laws. That a strong positive correlation exists between tax extraction and level of development suggests that overall, the negative effects of excessive state scope are in the long-run counterbalanced by the positive effects of greater administrative capacity."
19. Kaufmann, D. (2003), "Anti-Corruption within a Broader Developmental and Governance Perspective – Some Lessons from Empirics and Experience", Speech in Yucatan-Mexico, December 3; Kaufmann, D, A. Kraay & M. Mastruzzi (2006), "Measuring Corruption: myths and realities", Draft version at *World Bank*, Washington DC.
20. Olken, B. (2007), "Monitoring corruption: evidence from a field experiment in Indonesia", *Journal of Political Economy*, Vol. 15(2): 200–249.
21. Hamilton-Hart, Natasha (2001), "Anti-Corruption Strategies in Indonesia", *Bulletin of Indonesian Economic Studies*, Vol. 37, No. 1, pp. 65–82.
22. Rodriguez, P.; Kl. Uhlenbruck & L. Eden (2005), "Government Corruption and the Entry Strategies of Multinationals", *Academy of Management Review*, Vol. 30(2): 383–396.
23. Banerjee, A. (1997), "A theory of misgovernance", *Quarterly Journal of Economics*, Vol. 112: 1289–1332; and Shleifer, A. & R. Vishny (1993), "Corruption", *Quarterly Journal of Economics*, Vol. 108: 559–617.

24. Rodriguez, P., Kl. Uhlenbruck & L. Eden (2005), "Government Corruption and the Entry Strategies of Multinationals", *Academy of Management Review*, Vol. 30(2): 383–396.
25. Kaufmann, D. (1997), "Corruption: some myths and facts", *Foreign Policy*, Summer, pp. 114–13.
26. Soekarni, M. & S. Arifin (2011), "Governance and Economic Performance", in Ananta, A., M. Soekarni. & S. Arifin (Eds), *The Indonesian Economy Entering a New Era*, Singapore, ISEAS, p. 11.
27. Kid, J.B. & F-J. Richter (2003), *Corruption and Governance in Asia*, London, Palgrave Macmillan.
28. Rosser, A. (2004), "Coalitions, convergence and corporate governance reform in Indonesia", in Jayasuriya, K. (Ed), *Asian Regional Governance*, London, Routledge, pp. 106–126.
29. Li, J.S. (2003), "Relation-based v. rules-based governance: An explanation of the East Asian miracle & Asian crisis", *Review of International Economics*, 11(4), 651–662.
30. To ensure that the priorities and targets will be achieved, he established the President's Delivery Unit on Development Monitoring and Oversight headed by Kuntoro Mangkusubroto, known for his professionalism and success in leading the post-tsunami Aceh reconstruction program. Its mandate is to monitor the action plans of each government ministry and to eliminate bottlenecks within the bureaucracy. Using internet-based technology, the Delivery Unit presents a 'report card' at cabinet meetings clearly detailing the progress made by each ministry and marking targets with 'alerts', 'warnings', 'on track' and 'completed' status. Effective though this system might be for monitoring certain development projects, such as the construction of drinking water and sanitation facilities by the public works department, or the operations of port and customs services at Tanjung Priok by the Ministry of Finance, there are limitations to what the Delivery Unit can do. This is partly due to the fact that the Delivery Unit's functions are merely to monitor and verify progress whilst implementation remains the responsibility of each ministry. Nevertheless, the monitoring and evaluation process has encouraged government agencies to be more accountable for their performance.
31. Prasojo, E. (2010), "Implementing Anti-Corruption Education in Universities: Creating National Integrity", paper delivered at a seminar in Jakarta in April (Faculty of Social and Political Sciences, University of Indonesia); and Menteri BUMN: 118 Perusahaan KomitmenAntisuap, (2010), ANTARA News, 22 September downloaded from http://www.antaranews.com/berita/1285151623/menteri-bumn-118-perusahaan-komitmen-antisuap
32. According to *Doing Business 2010*, Indonesia, as represented by Jakarta, wasAsia's most active reformer of business regulations in 2008/2009. Starting a business, registering property and protecting investors had become relatively

easier and have improved the ease of doing business. In the 2009/2010 assessment, nonetheless, Indonesia's ranking fell 6 places down to 121 out of 183 countries. In six out of the nine categories rated, Indonesia's performance declined. Improvements have only been made in the ease of starting a business and in trans-border trade. In licensing for construction projects, Indonesia's performance remained the same.

33. Anwar, S. & Choon-Yin Sam (2006), "Singaporean style of public sector corporate governance: Can private sector corporations emulate public sector practices?", *New Zealand Journal of Asian Studies*, 8, 1 pp. 41–68.

34. An independent team of public administration experts and practitioners established by SBY's Vice-President.

35. There is yet little policy infrastructure for a collaboration between the private and public sectors in fighting corruption. This is potentially a grave oversight. The KPK originally intended to develop such a policy infrastructure, starting with informal meetings with chambers of commerce, but clearly there is room for improvement and creativity. Recently, the KPK announced that it will restart this endeavor in a more proactive fashion.

36. The *Perpres re Strategi Nasional Pencegahan dan Pemberantasan Korupsi* 2012–2014 and 2012–2025 was signed in 2012 by SBY. Prior to that there were *InPres no.9/2011 re Rencana Aksi Pencegahan dan Pemberantasan Korupsi tahun 2011* and *Inpress No.17/2011 re Aksi Pencegahan dan Pemberantasan Korupsi tahun 2012*. These presidential instructions are issued every year and implementation is monitored by Bappenas.

37. Character assassination featured heavily in the campaigning but in the end, the people made their choice. Unhappy with the results, with his pride hurt, Prabowo Subianto alleged widespread electoral fraud and challenged the outcome but the voters had spoken. Indonesians wanted a break from the past and Joko Widodo was seen as the right person. A man of humble background, who hailed from a small town in Central Java, he was able nevertheless through his industriousness to build up a successful furniture export business, and then went into public service in 2005 as mayor of his hometown, Surakarta.

38. As mayor of Surakarta in Central Java, prior to becoming governor of Jakarta, he focussed first on changing the mindset of the bureaucracy, orienting them towards service to the people rather than wielding power over them, and showing them how to adopt a more open and participatory approach to solving problems. With this approach and the major improvements he made in delivering public services, Joko Widodo was elected for a second term in 2010 garnering more than 90 % of the vote, until two years later, the PDI-P named him their candidate for the governorship of Jakarta. To the surprise of the incumbent, Joko Widodo won the elections with Basuki Tjahja Purnama – an ethnic Chinese – as Vice-Governor. In his two years in office as Governor of Jakarta, Joko Widodo maintained his humble, low-profile, problem-solving approach and the citizens of Jakarta were able to see change. Infrastructure

projects, which had languished in the desks of city planners, were implemented, roads were built, the perennial issue of flooding was tackled and greater transparency and accountability of the civil service were demanded. It was these qualities that endeared him to the citizens of Jakarta and, in the end, the people of the country. He was like a breath of fresh air in Indonesian politics, whose actors were still very closely linked to the previous regime. On October 20th 2014, Joko Widodo became Indonesia's seventh President, with Jusuf Kalla as his deputy.

39. Based on a national survey conducted by Populi Center during 15–22 October 2015 in 34 provinces.

40. http://www.thejakartapost.com/news/2014/05/21/jokowi-kalla-hawkish-economic-policies.html

41. Joko Widodo's commitment to eradicating corruption came into question over his choice of National Police Chief in January 2015, just a few months after his presidential inauguration. His sole candidate submitted to parliament was Komisaris Jendral Budi Gunawan who had been under investigation by the KPK for allegedly having illicit funds in his 'fat' bank accounts. Three days after the announcement, the KPK named Budi Gunawan as a suspect for corruption committed between 2003 and 2006. Despite being named a suspect, parliament accepted him as the President's candidate for police chief. This led to another bitter struggle between the Police Force and KPK, more intense than the 'Gecko vs Crocodile' case a few years earlier because of the involvement of politicians in parliament wanting to curb the authority of the KPK.

Budi Gunawan challenged the KPK's arrest in court and won, which emboldened the police force to arrest KPK Commissioners Abraham Samad and Bambang Widjojanto. Samad was arrested for entering political negotiations while in office and for falsifying documents, while Widjojanto was accused of witness tampering in a legal case prior to being a KPK commissioner. As tensions heightened between the KPK and the police force, the public had expected the President to take firm action to end the 'criminalization' of the commissioners and to name an alternative candidate for Police Chief but he did not. Only when remaining KPK commissioners were also being threatened with arrest for various alleged crimes, the President created an Independent Team to offer a way out. The Independent Team recommend that he should name an alternative candidate and that he should uphold his commitment to fight corruption.

42. Giri Ahmad Taufik. "Prolegnas Anti-korupsi" in *KOMPAS Daily*, May 3 2016.

43. Based on KPK statistics for the period between 2004 and March 31, 2016. In terms of numbers, 150 government officials, 134 private sector players and 110 politicians were involved.

44. The OECD set for Good Corporate Governance contains the following basic principles:

    1. *Ensuring the Basis for an Effective Corporate Governance Framework:* The corporate governance framework should promote transparent and efficient markets, be consistent with the rule of law and clearly articulate the division of responsibilities among different supervisory, regulatory and enforcement authorities.

    2. *The Rights of Shareholders and Key Ownership Functions:* The corporate governance framework should protect and facilitate the exercise of shareholders' rights. The basic shareholder rights should include the right to: (1) secure methods of ownership registration; (2) convey or transfer shares; (3) obtain relevant and material information on the corporation on a timely and regular basis; (4) participate and vote in general shareholder meetings; (5) elect and remove members of the board; and (6) share in the profits of the corporation.

    3. *The Equitable Treatment of Shareholders:* The corporate governance framework should ensure the equitable treatment of all shareholders, including minority and foreign shareholders. All shareholders should have the opportunity to obtain effective redress for violation of their rights.

    4. *The Role of Stakeholders in Corporate Governance:* The corporate governance framework should recognize the rights of stakeholders established by law or through mutual agreements and encourage active co-operation between corporations and stakeholders in creating wealth, jobs, and the sustainability of financially sound enterprises.

    5. *Disclosure and Transparency:* The corporate governance framework should ensure that timely and accurate disclosure is made on all material matters regarding the corporation, including the financial situation, performance, ownership, and governance of the company.

    6. *The Responsibilities of the Board:* The corporate governance framework should ensure the strategic guidance of the company, the effective monitoring of management by the board, and the board's accountability to the company and the shareholders.

45. See Pye, L.W. (2000), "Asian Values: from Dynamos to Dominoes?", in Harrison, L. & S. Huntington (Eds), *Culture Matters. How values shape human progress*, NY, Basic Books, pp. 244–255.

46. Verhezen, P. (2009), *Gifts, Corruption and Philanthropy. The Ambiguity of Gift Practices in Business,* Oxford; Bern, Peter Lang Publishing.

47. Verhezen, P. (2002), "Gift and Alliances in Java", *Ethical Perspectives*, Leuven, Vol.1: 56–65.

48. Our understanding of gratification is that a gift in any form is bribery if it is connected to a public officer's position and must be reported to the KPK within 30 days by the recipient; for anything above Rp10 million (about USD 800) the recipient must prove that it's *not* a bribe; for anything below that the

burden of proof rests with the prosecutor. This is in accordance with *UU No.20/2001 ttg Perubahan atas UU no.31/1999 ttg Pemberantasan Tindak Pidana Korupsi.*

49. Anwar, S. & Choon-Yin Sam (2006), "Singaporean style of public sector corporate governance: Can private sector corporations emulate public sector practices?", *New Zealand Journal of Asian Studies*, 8, 1 pp. 41–68.

50. Verhezen, P. (2009), *Gifts, Corruption and Philanthropy. The Ambiguity of Gift Practices in Business,* Oxford; Bern, Peter Lang Publishing. Gifts may not necessarily be considered bribes if they are understood as non-secret and integral to the relationship, unless it is a means to attain immediate instrumental goals.

51. Nepotism is defined as the practice among people with power or influence of favoring their own relatives and extended family members, especially by giving them jobs or promotion. *Clietelism* is interpreted somewhat more broadly and includes non-family members in the network of loyal members who are bound by valuable gifts and job opportunities in return for complete loyalty.

52. Despite specific differences, gifts and networks can certainly be found in most cultures. Some of those gifts are not bribes becoming president) openly and transparently would give an emotional small present - as a Kris (Javanese symbolic knife) - to another business person, this could be seen as an expression of gratitude and willingness to establish a relationship See Verhezen, P., (2009), Gift, corruption and philanthropy.Oxford, Peter Lang.

53. Wrongful because the gift-giver and receiver apparently strike a deal, which put their own interests above other parties or the principal, who have legitimate prior claims in the transaction on whose behalf the agents are acting. Such acts not only corrode trust between people and their agents but also undermine the legitimacy of social institutions or principals.

54. Li, J.S. (2003), "Relation-based v. rules-based governance: An explanation of the East Asian miracle & Asian crisis", *Review of International Economics,* 11(4), 651–662.

55. Eccles, R.G. & T. Youmans (2015), "The real duty of the board of directors", *Harvard Business School Working Papers*, September.

56. Towle, M.M. (2014), *Master of Finance. Interview with some of the greatest minds in investing and economics,* Colorado, IMCA – Henry Wurst Publ. Despite the fact that the US capital markets have been perceived as markets with dispersed ownership, we note that institutional investors increasingly own most of the shares, currently about 68 %; 25 companies own about 40 % of the total NYSE and NASDAQ capitalization. In other words, institutions become increasingly concentrated and this despite the alleged dispersed ownership structure in most US companies.

57. Taft, J.G. (Ed) (2015), *A force for good. How enlightened finance can restore faith in capitalism,* New York, Palgrave MacMillan; Charan, R. (1998), *Boards that work. How corporate boards create competitive advantage,* San Fransisco, Jossey Bass; and

Charan, R. (2005), *Boards that deliver. Advancing corporate governance – from compliance to competitive advantage*, San Fransisco, Jossey Bass.
58. Verhezen, P. (2015), "Fear, Regret or Trust? Transparency to control or transparency to empower", *International Finance Corporation World Bank Paper*, No 38, Washington http://www.ifc.org/wps/wcm/connect/topics_ext_content/ifc_external_corporate_site/corporate+governance/publications/private+sector+opinion/fear+and+regret_or+trust
59. Dealing with an uncertain and ambiguously risky context – which can be very different from what Westerners would experience at home – usually depends on how one deals with those idiosyncratic risks or pitfalls in those emerging Asian markets. Often these risks are related to institutional voids – one of the central themes of this book.
60. Although Institutional Reform goes beyond merely strengthening self-sustaining institutions, this chapter will not look into the other two generic aspects of Institutional Reform, how to promote good government and how to improve the democratic legitimacy of the institutions.
61. Even though the trajectory in improving public governance is upward, Indonesia still lags behind others in the region in important indices. Indonesia's ranking in the World Bank's *Doing Business* has indeed jumped from 129th in 2012 to 109th in 2016, but in the ASEAN 10, Indonesia fares better only against Cambodia, Lao PDR and Myanmar. The CPI score and ranking has also improved, from a score of 32 and ranking 118th in 2012 to a score of 36, ranking it 88th out of 168 countries taking part in the Transparency International survey. Although Indonesia still ranks below Singapore, Malaysia and Thailand within ASEAN in 2015, it has managed to overtake the Philippines and its score is higher than the ASEAN average of 40, mainly due to better public accountability.

9

Indonesian State-Owned Enterprises: Boards that Govern and Lead

Peter Verhezen and Tanri Abeng

Introductory Comments on Governance at Indonesian SOEs

What can and should we really expect from boards, be it in state-owned enterprises or privately held companies in ASEAN and more specifically in Indonesia? In its most generic expectations and definition, it is widely agreed among practitioners and scholars that boards in ASEAN and elsewhere are legally assumed to govern and lead organizations towards opportunities that create value and to reduce threatening risks, all on behalf of shareholders and stakeholders.

We here aim to answer the following question – *what should Indonesian listed organizations expect from their boards?* – within a context of state-owned enterprises in ASEAN, and more particularly applied to the case of PT Pertamina, chaired by one of the co-authors, Dr Tanri Abeng.

When analyzing State-Owned Enterprises (SOEs) in Indonesia, we need to contextualize our research. The establishment of Indonesian SOEs is the result of the nationalization of Dutch commodity firms after Indonesia achieved

P. Verhezen (✉)
Melbourne Business School, Carlton, VIC, Australia
e-mail: p.verhezen@mbs.edu

T. Abeng
Chairman ECGL, Chairman Pertamina
e-mail: tanri_a@ecgl.co.id

© The Editor(s) (if applicable) and the Author(s) 2016
P. Verhezen et al. (eds.), *Doing Business in ASEAN Markets*,
DOI 10.1007/978-3-319-41790-5_9

independence. The first president of Indonesia (Sukarno) had no clear strategic vision for those newly-nationalized companies beyond taking over the assets and management of colonial enterprises. The result was that most of the boards of these new Indonesian SOEs were manned by loyal military personnel put in place by the President. And although these boards had no entrepreneurial or management expertise, they were able to survive, mainly because of their monopolistic licenses to operate on behalf of the new state. When Suharto took over as the 2nd President of Indonesia, he recognized the need that these SOEs could and should contribute to the national development and budget. But despite this economic understanding, most boards of these SOEs remained supervised and managed by military and some bureaucrats from different influential Ministries – be it Plantation or Finance – and manned by technocrats. In other words, the officials put in charge at supervisory Board of Commissioners (BoC) of these SOEs were (a) expected to control the assets on behalf of their respective Ministry, or (b) being given a reward for long loyal service. It was only after the Asian crisis in 1998 that (the 2nd President) Suharto acknowledged the need to the country, be it with the objective could be either to enhance the fiscal policy and budget through dividend pay outs, or to enhance employment. In addition, the IMF pressed Indonesia to reform and restructure these ineffective but important and often huge companies, resulting in the establishment of a Ministry of State-Owned Enterprises, with Tanri Abeng as its first professional Minister overseeing 158 SOEs (that were previously overlooked by 17 different Ministries). When Habibie, the 3rd President took over after the overthrow of Suharto, Pak Tanri was reappointed in that same function, overseeing the reform and restructuring of these SOEs. These days, the SOEs are not mere bureaucracies anymore – but managed and monitored by presumed professionals – and are legal firms operating in a competitive market place. However, because all these SOEs started as monopolies, they had gathered a lion's share of the market, whether it was in telecommunications (Telkom-Telkomsel), or Banking (Mandiri, BNI, BRI), or gas-& oil (Pertamina), or plantations.

Previously, it was mainly a one-party system (Golkar), that "supervised" and influenced the appointments of boards at these influential and resource rich SOEs. Today, however, with much more splintered political parties, each vying for a piece of the cake, the political intervention – somehow seeking special rents – is quite widespread among all parties now. Indeed, through the more fragmented democratically-elected parliamentary system, allied collaborative parties are not just attempting to influence the choice at the cabinet level, they continuously seek to place their nominees on the boards of these SOEs. The political lobbying is intense, especially in strategically-important

SOEs such as PT Pertamina (gas- & oil), PT PLN (electricity provider), Telkom (telecommunication) and to a slightly lesser degree in banking.

This chapter will look into the functioning of the dual-tier board system in Indonesian listed companies, with a strong emphasis on State-Owned Enterprises. However, we also include listed privately-held companies in our analysis that are governed with slightly different objectives, but are legally embedded within the same corporate governance regulation and governance practices, ensuring control over assets and strategies.

Boards and their chairmen can be quite powerful, especially under single-tier boards where the function of chairman and CEO is often combined. In the USA, in about 68 % of the cases, the CEO combines this executive title with chairmanship of the board, making him or her extremely powerful. Cases such as Enron and Disney have indicated that it is very hard to challenge such powerful chairman-CEOs, and such entrenched boards may be too loyal decision-makers, without being critical enough after an initial effective leadership period to optimize the creation of sustainable value for the organization. In Indonesia and Malaysia, the law requires the separation between chairman (President Commissioner) and CEO (President Director) by having installed a dual-tier board structure. Nonetheless, dual-tier boards in Indonesia still face very daunting challenges. Despite the legal separation between those two functions, quite often (1) the founder entrepreneur of the company remains at the helm of the company, usually as President Commissioner or non-executive Chairman of the supervisory board (Board of Commissioners), or (2) the encroachment and power play by the political elite in SOEs can have disastrous consequences for the efficiency and effectiveness of long term value creation, both for their majority (the state) as well as minority owners. Obviously, majority owners can impose these final decisions, but that should not be at the expense of minority shareholders.[1]

How then to rein in this king-entrepreneur or hired mandarin? How to reduce the potential agency costs when family members of the majority owners are running the company, often headed by the patriarch. And how to assure that these Indonesian "mandarins" hired by the political elite have the proper incentives to effectively run and govern those SOEs. In other words, how to reduce potential entrenchment at Indonesian boards?

The first section analyzes what the tasks are of these SOEs' boards. We look at what actually is happening on Boards in some cases, and determine what is different from Western boards. We then briefly look at the distinction between dual-tier boards as legally imposed in Indonesia versus single-tier boards as practiced in Australia, the USA, the UK and a number of other Western countries. Our second section analyzes the common weaknesses at boards, both in a Western context, and especially in Indonesia. We question whether Indonesian boards can learn anything from mistakes encountered in the West and "best corporate governance practices". Our final section will formulate some recommendations and possible solutions for SOEs and other listed companies in an Indonesian context. Analyzing the weaknesses is one thing, providing solutions quite another matter. And more particularly, we will address the major leadership challenges and possible governance solutions at Indonesian SOEs and big conglomerates. We conclude with some high level suggestions for future research and implementation of improved governance practices.

Governance Practices Under Single-Tier and Dual-Tier Board Systems

Corporate governance refers to the system of checks and balances within an organization that takes optimal strategic decisions to create value. A board monitors and steers its executive directors. However, creating and sustaining organizational value requires trust and cooperation among its board members, not just mere (legal) compliance to rules and regulations. Chairmen and CEOs are also aware that they, and not just the regulators, might need to lead the way forward. Massive corporate governance[2] changes have swept through corporate boardrooms, affecting the way companies report earnings, pay executives, and manage board and societal expectations.

How relevant are those changes in global governance for firms in Indonesia? And how can boards of Indonesian organizations optimize a mandatory dual-tier legal structure with separated supervisory and executive boards? How to optimize the board's functioning with two interdependent boards versus boards with a single-board structure?

Generic Functions of a (Supervisory and Executive) Board

Executives make decisions on a daily basis that are supposed to serve the organization. However, quite often those decisions may better themselves at the expense of other parties related to the firm: those costs are known as *agency costs,* which are rooted in the separation of ownership and top management and the subsequent information asymmetry between them. A system of checks and balances – the basis of corporate governance – is assumed to lessen those agency costs by controlling and monitoring top management.

Governance will not prevent misconduct or misdeeds, but it can actually improve the way a corporation is run in Indonesia and for that matter in other Asian countries. One usually refers to successful companies that apply *"best"* (*international*) *corporate governance principles* as those which have diligently incorporated and integrated (1) the protection of basic shareholder rights, (2) the prohibition of insider trading, (3) disclosure of board and top-manager interests and adherence to international disclosure standards, (4) a respect for the legal rights of the main stakeholders of the company while acting responsibly within a wider community context, (5) an independent audit committee that regularly meets, (6) the norm that all shareholders should be treated fairly by the board, (7) the expected disclosure of capital structures that enabled certain shareholders to obtain disproportionate control, (8) providing good access to information by the board members, and (9) allowing fair and timely dissemination of information to all relevant parties.

Good corporate governance (GCG) should therefore provide proper incentives for a board and its management to pursue objectives that are in line with the interests of the company and its shareholders.

The Board of Commissioners' main task is to monitor and oversee the performance of the Board of Directors and the continuity of the organization. In addition, the non-executive directors or commissioners provide valuable advice and mentoring to top management. In this *advisory capacity*, the board pays attention to guide top management's decisions that balance risk and reward, whereas in its *oversight capacity*, the board aims to monitor management and ensure that it is acting in the best interests of the company's long term goals. The board is a governing body elected to represent the interests of shareholders and the company at large.

One of the main functions of a board is, indeed, to monitor whether top management effectively executes its fiduciary duty to optimize the interests – usually summarized in the return on investment or profitability – of the organization and thus its owners. The *fiduciary duty* of a board usually includes a *duty of care* that requires directors to make decisions with due deliberation, a *duty of loyalty* that addresses conflicts of interest whereby the interest of shareholders should prevail over the interest of a director, and a *duty of candor* that requires that management and the board inform shareholders of all information that is important in their evaluation of the company and its management. These fiduciary duties are often translated in the legal requirement of having at least two or three professionally run subcommittees at the board: (1) a committee of internal audit and internal control to contain accounting and other specific risks, (2) a nomination committee that explicitly ensures that the best professional CEO will be chosen, and (3) a remuneration committee that decides on an appropriate and fair remuneration package for its top managers, and sometimes (4) a subcommittee to assess the risks associated with the suggested strategy. Governance systems are influenced and affected by the firm's owners, their managers, creditors, labor unions, customers, suppliers, investment analysts, the media, and regulators; in other words, by relevant stakeholders and all those who could significantly affect (the value of) the company.

In practice, non-executive directors – i.e. the Board of Commissioners (BoC) in Indonesia – spend most of their time on supervising audit reports and on the determination of executive compensation according to monitored performances. Moreover, the BoC should also assure that activities are conducted according to, and compliant with, existing regulatory norms. Unfortunately, a BoC spends less time on advising management on strategic planning, as well as on preparing for leadership succession planning.

We distinguish five primary elements to ensure the implementation of corporate governance: (1) proven "best" board practices, (2) Disclosure and Transparency, (3) appropriate Control processes, (4) Shareholder Rights, and (5) Commitment to Corporate Governance.[3]

It is important to note, however, that the typical "agent" problem – as it is defined in a Western context – in Indonesia and other Asian countries need to be interpreted differently. Although it is obvious that the top executives might use their privileged position and access to asymmetric information as ways to optimize their own objectives as in remuneration optimization instead of "maximizing shareholder value", it is exactly the task of a (supervisory) board to monitor the performances of the top executives. Within an ASEAN context, one major governance challenge is the prevailing potential of abuse of power by the controlling family or state, the ultimate owners of a public listed company, at the expense of minority shareholders, be it local or international / foreign shareholders. However, in SOEs, the political intervention in appointments to the Executive Board of Directors, complicates to run, to govern and to lead those organizations. Those directors are expected to show loyalty to their benefactors – often politicians from fractured but powerful political parties. They may work within their own field of authority and responsibility, creating powerful silos, but somehow undermining a cohesive and strategic interlinked approach in the benefit of the company and thus of the owners.

In an Anglo-Saxon context – as practiced in the US, UK, Canada, and Australia -, boards are usually manned by outsiders or independent non-executive directors. These Anglo-Saxon listed companies are characterized by dispersed ownership. Moreover, disclosure is quite stringent on the capital markets in New York and London. These markets are characterized by an active IPO searching for public investment to finance growth objectives, and by an active take-over market of companies that would be deemed to be undervalued because of underperforming top executives.

Most capital markets in Asia are characterized by very concentrated ownership: be it by a controlling family or a mighty state, which may squash minority shareholders' rights. However, the tendency is to increase the number of independent non-executive directors at Boards in ASEAN markets: because Indonesia adopts a two-tier board system, with boards of commissioners fully composed of non-executive directors and boards of directors composed of top executives, the size of its boards of commissioners is on average smaller, with a median of six commissioners. In Singapore and Malaysia, independent directors constitute the majority of the board of directors. The median percentage of independent directors in Singapore (67 %) is the highest, followed by Malaysia (63 %), Indonesia (50 %) and Thailand (46 %).[4]

Most of the board members of these companies are consequently insiders, and not independent of the controlling shareholders. It is therefore of the utmost importance to safeguard equal shareholders' rights, proper accountability, transparency, and proper disclosure of information.[5] In Asian markets minority rights are often not adequately protected. Moreover, in Indonesia (and in Asia in general), there is a hardly an active take-over market, and new market capitalization is underdeveloped compared to their Western counterparts.

We therefore argue that boards have two if not three main generic functions to fulfill: (1) guiding, assisting or coaching top management to achieve the objectives and the direction the company wants to obtain; (2) guaranteeing proper oversight and monitoring to secure that performance objectives are met and rules and regulations are properly observed, and finally (3) succession planning by developing the potential leaders and prepare them to becoming the new leaders in the foreseeable future. Interpreting this in an Indonesian context, we believe that Boards should not just supervise, but under certain circumstances should *lead and govern*.

Advantages and Disadvantages of Dual-Tier Versus Single-Tier Board Systems

There is a huge difference between dual-tier and single-tier boards. The major difference is that dual-tier boards have legally engrained a supervisory board in the board structure of an organization whereas single-tier boards do not have that separated supervisory board. Indeed, the main tasks of a supervisory board or "board of commissioners" (BoC) – derived from the Dutch system of "*board van commissarissen*" – are (a) to monitor the members of the management or executive board or "board of directors" (BoD) and (b) to appoint or dismiss them. In addition, the supervisory board must approve the annual accounts and can intervene in cases where the company's interests or reputation are seriously affected. In addition, members of the BoC are also expected to be involved with networking with stakeholders. It is also important to note that the BoC not only advises and supervises the BoD in the management of the company, but that the commissioners must also be involved in decisions of fundamental importance to the enterprise.

What are advantages and disadvantages of dual-tier boards versus single-tier boards,[6] and how can SOEs in Indonesia improve their board functioning? The key advantage of a two-tier system – in which the supervisory board is independent of the executive or management board – is at the same time also one of its structural weaknesses. Traditionally, the commissioners, by definition, do not take strategic management decisions on their own, and are most often not involved in the decision-making process at all. Consequently, the way in which the commissioners exercise their monitoring is almost always reactive and never pro-active. This necessarily results in a reduction of the quality of control since the supervisory board seems to be restricted to comment on the chosen solutions in hindsight. The commissioners may criticize the choice and in extreme cases may even suggest the dismissal of executives. But, structurally-speaking, the commissioners do not seem to have an opportunity to exert influence on (strategic) decisions *ex ante*.

Under a single-tier system, decisions might be faster because of a unified board where both executives and non-executives jointly debate and make decisions, but the monitoring function under such a system can theoretically only be absorbed by emphasizing the importance of the independency[7] of the non-executives, who then assumedly focus on the monitoring control function. Moreover, the effectiveness of the monitoring control function under a single-tier board system depends not only on the independency and personality of the non-executive directors, but foremost on the personality of the chairman.

Another weak point of a dual-tier control system is the asymmetry of information. Since the commissioners are not involved in the decision-making process, and since they may not be present in the meetings when those strategic decisions are made, commissioners receive the (requested)information filtered from the executive BoD. And because of the strong information asymmetry between the BoD and BoC, the information concerning questions of strategy, future projects, business opportunities, budgetary questions and others lies in the hands of the BoD who provide that (filtered and interpreted) information to the BoC. That also limits access to sensitive information by the BoC. Theoretically and notionally, the BoD must not withhold information from commissioners, which in reality is deemed to be delicate. In other words, in a two-tier board system, with its typical flow of information from the executives to the supervising commissioners, there is a real danger that the BoC cannot discover deficiencies due to a lack of information. Moreover, in evaluating the BoD, the commissioners may make the same mistake as the executives because there has been no supply of independent information available. Here a single-tier board system has an enormous advantage since the decision-making process is much swifter due to the presence of both executive and non-executive directors in one board meeting. Nonetheless, as it is true that there is information asymmetry between a supervisory and executive board under a dual-tier system, there remains information asymmetry within a single-tier board system between executives and non-executives who never can be privy to all the information on a daily basis.

Furthermore, the meeting frequency of about four times a year confines a BoC to its traditional but weak position, in which it exercises a mere *ex post* monitoring control function. More continuous monitoring and more frequent meetings could be suggested in order adequately to process the high amount of data.

Common Weaknesses at SOEs' Boards in Indonesia (and ASEAN Countries)

Leading a company requires a lot of dedication and commitment by a professional board. Obviously, most organizations can improve and would benefit from avoiding the following weaknesses, be it boards that act as "paper" boards, be it "insider boards" only, a lack of financial literacy or focus on financial information only, be it no effective or non-existent subcommittees, be it an uninformed board and poor information, be it "informal" working procedures that would not stand any scrutiny, or no clear distinction between the function of management and the supervisory board undermining the effective functioning of both executives and or non-executives.

More broadly, when we apply those board challenges to companies in Indonesia, and especially to state-owned enterprises like PT Telkom and PT Pertamina (which were and are chaired by one of the co-authors), the following issues should be addressed: (1) how to unify the supervisory and executive team–each fulfilling their specific function–with the aim to achieve joint objectives; (2) how to reduce the continuous lobbying by self-interested political parties to put their appointees in place, which undermines the objective of creating value for the company and not to provide special rents to the political parties which had lobbied for these appointments; (3) how to improve the lack of proper skills, especially at the supervisory board where the enormous challenging job of the chair require professional understanding of the business and diplomacy skills; (4) how to improve the indecisiveness between the two boards since all individual members – especially at the executive board – have different objectives and allegedly serve different patrons; and (5) how to reduce the avoidance of accountability and responsibility at both the supervisory and executive boards since no cohesive objectives are openly addressed or pursued, and rent-seeking goals are often hidden in "discrete and stalling behavior".

The Lack of Commitment by Supervisory Board (BoC) to Assist the Management Board (BoD)

A primary task of a supervisory board – the board of commissioners – is to monitor the performance of the board of executive directors.

How can the chairman ensure that the supervisory board (BoC) *collaborates* with the executive board (BoD) to ensure optimization of organizational value-creation and preservation, while at the same time, walking that fine line of supervisor/collaborator to secure the necessary *checks and balances*?

Since the stakes in SOEs can be extremely high, both in terms of absolute cash flow (and the danger of rent-seeking behavior by the board members who may tacitly serve two masters – the company and their shareholders, and the political patron who put him or her in that position) and strategic risk. When one looks at a company like PT Telkom, the national telecommunications company with a net profit of IDR15.489 trillion (USD1.17 billion) in 2015 – from IDR14.471 trillion in 2014 – on Revenues IDR102.470 trillion (USD 7.88 billion) in 2015 (an increase of 14.2 % compared to 2014), the strategic stakes could not be higher. In order to reduce potential conflicts of interest, and to enhance the functioning of the boards, the Chair pushed through some reform and institutionalized a system in which the BoC was directly involved in supporting and supervising the executive BoD. For instance, for any investment decision about IDR 100 billion (i.e. USD 10 million in 2004–2005 when the new "unifying" decision-process was initiated). In addition, to reduce possible internal fighting at the executive board level, the Chair subtly installed a system in which the supervisory board would be "consulted" for any new top appointment – which till then was the prerogative of the CEO only.

By getting the BoC more involved in key appointments, the chair was mimicking some of the advantages of the single-tier board system under a dual-tier board system, preparing for a more coherent and consistent policy and decision-making process where it really matters: key personnel and key investments.

Patronage at the Board Appointments by the Majority Owner (the State) and Other Vested Political Parties

We all have heard of stories where friends or acquaintances are appointed at boards to "look after" the interests of their respective patrons who put them on that board. Such practices often result in blatant nepostism or even corruption where the interest of the particular boss or party will prevail over the generic interest of the organization.

How can boards avoid unnecessary and often harmful political intervention in appointments of board members at SOEs?

Political influence in the appointment of key board members at strategic companies is nothing new. However, such a patronage system deliberately installs loyal silo thinking in which each (executive) board member exercises his or her power to its fullest, and is detrimental to long-term value-creation by the company. Unless you have a strong chair who can accommodate the different demands, and is able to unify the executive board, advised and monitored by the supervisory board, those strategic organizations might continue to perform suboptimally and fail to achieve their full potential..

One of the first typical attempts to "professionalize" SOEs was the appointment of the late Robby Djohan, a seasoned banker, to turn around the biggest Indonesian bank, the state-owned Bank Mandiri, that was itself the result of a merger of a number of state-owned banks. He repeated such a surprising turnaround again by becoming the CEO of the flagging national airline Garuda in the late 1990s to turn the company around "from a one dollar company into a thriving billion dollar company", focusing on competitive high standards of service and quality. And quite unusually, Robby Djohan got a free hand from Tanri Abeng at the Ministry of State-Owned Enterprises to appoint his own team at the Executive board, allowing him to take full responsibility and being accountable for his management without interference from political parties.

Admittedly, it was much easier to implement such a policy without party meddling because in those days, Golkar was the only serious political organization. Today, a number of parties are continuously vying for positioning and getting the upper hand in appointing their "man" at influential strategic companies.

Lack of Board Skills to Properly Govern and Lead the Organization

Like in any profession, board members need to have the necessary skills to govern and to lead an organization or a board. Indonesian boards are often stacked with "friendly" members whose task is to protect the interests of the one who put them there, and not genuinely to provide guidance to management to enhance opportunities and to reduce risks.

What kind of leadership skill set is expected from board members, both commissioners and executive directors?

Because of the historical context in which SOEs evolved, boards were filled for many decades by non-business-savvy military personnel and inexperienced bureaucrats who were unable to protect either the national interest or the assets of the country. Unfortunately, they were not necessarily well-prepared to make organizations thrive and add financial value in an increasingly competitive market after the 1998 deregulations. Finding professional board members remains a challenge. And even finding professional outsiders – like attracting a seasoned banker to turn around Telkom in 2005 – does not guarantee success, since the organizational culture within those SOEs is based on security for employees in return for loyal behavior. Pushing through changes in such an organization is extremely difficult and professionalism alone does not suffice. To unify a team, diplomatic skills and emotional intelligence are extremely important, especially in such "politicized" environments. Not every professional is such an unassuming team player. Hence the important role of the chair of the board – the "*commissaris utama*" or president commissioner – whose diplomatic and business skills are needed not only to make the supervisory board (BoC) collaborate with the executive board (BoD), but also to mold a unified team at the supervisory and executive level to direct the organization into one clear direction to optimize long-term value-creation.

In Decisiveness of the Board (BoC and BoD)

When boards make decisions, its members need to be decisive and take responsibility for their decisions, as well to be accountable for the consequences those decisions carry with them. Historically and culturally, one often sees that the members of the board of directors will postpone decisions by pushing the buck to the supervisory board for "approval" because of the increased fear for "doing something wrong". So boards – especially at state-owned enterprises – have become very ineffective and indecisive, undermining the ultimate task of a board.

How can the functioning of the board (BoC + BoD) be improved to ensure real collaboration and joint responsibility?

At Pertamina, a USD 43 billion SOE, and one of the biggest companies in Indonesia, the decision-making process can be quite slow and the executive board even drags its feet to avoid "mistakes". That is where the Chair of the BoC and its supervisory board members need to be able to subtly push the executive board to take the necessary decisions to move forward. As mentioned earlier, in SOEs it is not uncommon that boards are run like silos with each board member protecting their respective fiefdoms. Overcoming such destructive behavior and minimizing this silo-management style requires (1) a genuine dialogue between all the board members, which concretely means that the supervisory and executive boards agree on the strategy and the main operational plans of the company, (2) more frequent meetings to create such a collaboration – driven by enabled and empowered professionals – aiming to optimize long-term value, and (3) to adapt the board structure where needed. Pertamina's growing complexity therefore requires more expertise. Hence why the current Chair of the BoC has prepared to expand the executive board from seven to nine members – to be approved by the Minister of SOEs – aiming to blend a more professional team able to face the daunting challenges.

For instance, till very recently, Pertamina never made the decision – during the last 25 years – to invest in a profitable refinery business. Making such bold decisions requires the credibility of the board to be pushed through. It is crucial, therefore, that the chair and CEO collaborate in a spirit of helping and leading the company, and not serving their presumed patrons. The only objective that really counts should be the long-term value-creation of the company, benefiting its ultimate shareholders, in this case, the state.

How to Implement Real Accountability at the Board

When a board hides out of fear of "wrongdoing", hardly any substantial decision will be made, aggravating the ineffectiveness of boards. Being collegial at a board does not preclude taking tough decisions, or to disagree. In the end, a board makes a "unified" decision, though individual disagreement could be noted in the board notules/notes, and all board members should be jointly responsible for the decisions made.

How to improve the accountability of a collegial board while improving (incentivized) performances? How to avoid the silo-mentality of individual board members?

As result of a clear separation of functions between the supervisory and executive boards, enterprises still need to be properly governed, managed and led by a team held to account, which implies a high level of integrity and transparency. Whether at Pertamina, Telkom, PLN or any other SOE, or by extension, any listed company, achieving certain financial and non-financial objectives that secure the sustainability of the organization is only possible when measurement and evaluation systems are put in place, and when all board members without exception are accountable for those (non)performances. Only by applying minimal international standards – notwithstanding the unique legal and cultural context in Indonesia and other ASEAN countries – will boards be able properly to govern and lead.

Recommendations for Boards to Better Lead and to Govern

Keeping in mind the limitations of any recommendation due to the path dependence of the enterprise, its legal background, the socio-political and cultural context, any endeavor should be made to enhance the systems by implementing features for each of the above weaknesses analyzed.

As often, *ineffective boards* hardly spend time on understanding the overall impact on long-term value-creation through well thought strategies. These ineffective boards do not align with the executive team on how to manage company risk. They mainly focus on basic compliance issues and on monitoring whether executives perform according to the objectives set. BoCs hardly seek out information on their own, and blindly rely on their BoD for information gathering. *Complacent boards* do slightly better because of the fact that there is more trust and respect between the BoC and the BoD, and more time is spent on building a cohesive team. However, *striving boards* effectively help to develop and implement strategies on a continuous basis, and also focus on the performance of the management. Moreover, such boards report an exceptionally strong culture of trust and respect where executives and non-executives constructively challenge each other; while a seasoned chair is efficiently running board meetings. Striving-board directors are more than twice as likely as complacent-board directors to conduct regular evaluations, and more than three times likelier to ask for input after each meeting.[8]

For two-tier board systems, as in Indonesia, we suggest the following generic recommendations to improve the functioning of the board: (1) strengthening the position of the chairman of the BoC, (2) professionalizing the role of the other members of the BoC, and (3) more involvement of the BoC in strategic management decisions which practically means that a single-board 'system' is exercised within a legal dual-tier structure.

In the case of Pertamina and Telkom, the chairman is convinced that the two following elements should be given priority:

1. **Openness** and *transparency in decision-making.* Such openness implies some "trustful conversations"[9] between the board members allowing constructive feedback and improvement.
2. Agree on **objectives** that are specific and which can *be accounted for,* reducing the burdensome silo-mentality that prevails at many boards of SOEs.
   Concretely, it means that the Chairman who chairs the board meetings (a) stimulates collaboration between BoC and BoD in developing and providing a strategy. Once a decision on the strategy is jointly made by the BoC and BoD, the BoD is responsible for the execution, and (b) ensures that the BoC will **overlook/supervise** the execution but won't and shouldn't be involved in the actual *execution* of the strategy (which is the BoD's task).
   Boards take the final and ultimate responsibility for the performance of an organization, be it a state-owned enterprise such as PT Pertamina, or a family company, or a listed company with many different shareholders, or a privately-held company, or a NGO, all are bound by evaluating the performance of the board and its executives to the agreed objectives and goals of the organization.

Strengthening the Position of the Chair: Boards that Govern and Lead

As established above, the key principle of good corporate governance is ensuring that consistency, responsibility, accountability, fairness, transparency, and effectiveness are deployed throughout an organization. Governance is much more than compliance. Good corporate governance is a question of culture and a climate to apply these best principles, which is the foundation of trust. Boards need to create trustworthy relationships, providing guidance and oversight to the directors and management in order to ensure that the company creates value on a sustainable basis while protecting the interests of all stakeholders.

One could easily argue that good corporate governance is established through a combination of: the right *people*, the right *team*, the right *processes*, the right *culture*, the right *information*, the right *guidance*, and the right *oversight*.

Boards could be significantly improved by specifying (1) the board roles and director/commissioner duties – i.e. defining the specific duties and roles of each of the board members, specific board authorities and responsibilities; (2) wisely deciding on the board composition and committee structure – i.e. determining how many board members and what are the terms of those members; qualifications required, board independency, structure of subcommittees, nomination and remuneration process; and (3) improving the board working procedures and other board practices – i.e. preparing an annual plan, meeting frequency, and agendas; securing and arranging information to board members, meeting venue, minutes of meeting, attendance, proxies and undue absence, presiding role, board decision-making procedures, written consent, BoC and BoD interaction, provision of information, responsibility for securing information, access to records and use of experts.

As argued above, one of the primary fiduciary duties of any board member is to secure that shareholder or organizational value is created by the management and employees. The second primary function (to advise the executive board) implies that the experienced non-executives will partner with the directors to prepare the overall strategy, the capital allocation for this strategy and discuss how it will be executed. The two boards will also join forces to discuss the financial goals, and jointly decide how to deal with the stakeholders' concerns, balancing the shareholders' interest with the stakeholders' interests. It is also the task of both boards to debate the risk appetite that will provide constraints for the decisions to be taken. Both need to collaborate to optimize resource allocation, and any M&A will need to be discussed by both the non-executives and executives. It is also crucial that the dual board is jointly engaged with talent development and improving a culture where a board dares to make the necessary decisions.

It is also widely agreed that a supervisory board will stay out of the way of the executives in execution the strategy, its operations, non-strategic decisions and any activity that is explicitly excluded by the board charter. However, it is also clear that a supervisory board should take charge in the modus operandi and competence of the board functioning itself, to set the tone at the top in terms of ethics and integrity, to prepare the compensation architecture for top management, and they should also be clearly involved in the "central strategic idea" that guides the whole organization.[10]

Professionalizing the Board which is More Entrepreneurial and Accountable

More specifically, we suggest that there is a relationship between **governance** and its generic principles (especially transparency, accountability, responsibility and fairness) on the one hand, and entrepreneurial innovation or *managerial entrepreneurship* on the other. We believe that some simple rules can "institutionalize" that causal relationship and significantly improve the performance of the firm in the process.

Big companies like Pertamina face the danger of being so big that innovative entrepreneurship or managerial entrepreneurship become impossible, and governance is reduced to mere compliance with rules and regulations. Boards should help to induce innovation – the necessary oxygen for any company – by the avoiding group-thinking or status-quo and by improving sound decision-making.

By becoming more open to a changed context and to accommodate such changes, big companies may avoid to become ineffective. Although Boards may have the ultimate legal power in any organization, Boards do not necessarily have a monopoly of truth, and will need to induce "managerial entrepreneurship" throughout the organization, learning from a number of international cases such as *Polaroid* (the now defunct inventor of instant pictures), IBM ("the elephant that learned to dance") and *Bridgewater* (a very successful international investment company, handling over USD 170 billion in investments for governments, pension funds, universities and charities).

In our approach, we see a causal correlation between accountability and openness, between well governing boards and improved innovative entrepreneurship within the company. How do we explain why Petronas – roughly the same size as Pertamina – was many times more profitable than Pertamina?

So one of the first exercises counterintuitive is for a board to question *how completely to undermine or kill PT Pertamina?* Such Thinking – which may sound counter-intuitive – about "how to kill Pertamina" would help the board to engage in increased accountability while at the same time avoid group-thinking and to become better "managerial entrepreneurs" for the company. And an improved decision-making process could partially help to achieve this. Indeed, once we have gone through that thought process exercise, we suggest drawing attention to **some simple rules** that will make the boardroom more effective and help to make managers ***become more accountable*** for their actions, and to ***engage in more entrepreneurial innovations*** that create value for the organization beyond mere "preserving of assets".

Improve Efficiency by Making Better Decisions Based on Simple Rules

Simple rules possibly add discipline to the thinking process to increase efficiency and increase the odds that the resulting innovations will create value, simple rules also increase accountability. The current fascination with disruptive innovation obscures an important reality. For many established companies, incremental product improvements, advances in existing business models and moves into adjacent markets remain critical sources of value-creating innovation.

Too much constraint can stifle innovation, but too little is just as bad. A blank sheet of paper sounds nice in theory. In practice, pursuing novelty without guidelines can overwhelm people with options, engender waste, and prevent the coordination required for collective innovation. While it is appealing that simple rules arise from clever and innovative thinking, they usually are based on long experience of trial and error.

As mentioned earlier, a board needs to set clear corporate objectives in terms of profitability, growth, innovation, social good and others. Subsequently, the dual board will attempt to identify the potential bottlenecks that keep the organization from achieving those set objectives, by looking where opportunities most exceed organizational resources (be it time, money, or people and talent), and to question which improved processes would help to manage that bottleneck problem. Once that has been cleared, one can develop simple rules for managing these bottlenecks.[11] Simple rules can inject discipline into the process by providing a threshold level of guidance, while leaving ample room for creativity and initiative.[12]

What are the advantages of simple rules? First they make it easier to seize outside opportunities. Both flexibility and consistency have their advantages, but increasing one often reduces the other. Detailed rules are especially useful for avoiding catastrophic errors, such as plane crashes, mishaps in nuclear power plants and surgical deaths that result from known causes.

However, simple rules allow management to seize opportunities where flexibility is crucial. Flexibility, based on simple rules, makes it easier for management to embrace changing contexts and circumstances and seize fleeting opportunities.

Second, simple rules often produce better decisions. Simple rules or heuristics (rules of thumb) are powerful decision-making tools, often matching or even outperforming more sophisticated approaches, especially in situations – such as stock markets – where the underlying causal relationships among variables are not well understood. Simple rules focus on only the most critical variables.

Decision rules provide a framework for making better decisions center on what to do, what is most important to do and what to stop doing.[13] These decision rules – boundary, prioritizing and stopping – provide clear guidance for making better decisions in difficult and sometimes very tempting contexts. These rules aim to answer the question of *what to do – what is acceptable to do, what is more important to do* and *what to stop doing*. By asking these strategic important questions, one forces both the supervisory and executive boards at SOEs (but similarly at other listed companies as well) to think through and make joint decisions of what direction to go or not.

However, process rules provide guidance on how to do things better. For instance, investments above USD 10 million at PT Telkom need to be discussed and agreed upon by both the supervisory and executive boards, allowing a more unified and accountable board to govern and lead the company. One therefore can argue that simple rules also promote collective behavior, not to be confused with herding behavior. Finally, simple rules impose a minimal level of coordination, while leaving ample room for individuals to pursue their own objectives. The cases of Pertamina and Telkom have shown how the actual decision-processes and management and governance at these companies under the guidance and steering of a unified board.

This level of constructive collaboration between the BoC and the BoD is crucial to improve strategic decision-making. Having agreed on some simple rules by the dual board helps the chair and the BoC to improve its collaboration with the BoD. Failing to take decisions can be very harmful for a firm and is contrary to the fiduciary duties that board members have undertaken when accepting that function.

Concluding Remarks: Governing & Leadership in the Boardroom

A well-functioning board is about **good leadership**, about securing that organizations sustain over a longer period Good leaders at boards should steer and assist with preparing and executing appropriate strategies, securing that no excessive risks are taken and that executives remain with the risk boundaries as agreed at the board, that enough liberty is given to executives to take reasonable risks to create value and that all board members and executives can be accounted for their performances according to the objectives in a transparent and fair manner.

Well-functioning boards – "boards that lead" or "striving-boards" – are aware that the increasing global complexities and interdependencies require an engaged and well-informed board to discharge the fiduciary duties of their respective board members. First of all, it means that non-executive board members at SOEs like Pertamina or Telkom might need to focus even more on attending to their tasks. On average, board members (BoC) spend two or three days a month, or 33 days per year, for board meetings. Internationally, many board members are spending 50 days or more annually on board work, either due to regulatory pressure or simply to the fact that the time required to perform fiduciary duties is usually more than non-executive directors initially expect. Secondly, there should be a balance between trust and challenging discourse. Internationally the boards that are most effective and well-rounded also have the strongest board dynamics. It can easily be argued that in a healthy boardroom, a culture of trust and respect is vital, while at the same time it is an environment where BoC members and BoD company leaders challenge each other. This could be quite a challenge in a hierarchical culture like we face in most Asian cultures. However, we also suggest that regular evaluations of BoC and BoD should be conducted, which seems to be exceptional these days. Finally, and most significantly, the appointment of a good ambitious chair is crucial. Experience and case studies have overwhelmingly proved that one of the most important ingredients of improved board dynamics – and thus an improved board – is an effective chairperson, who runs meetings well, establishes a culture of trust and constructive discourse, and invests in training, development and feedback. Good leadership sets the tone for the board and the top management as a whole, and is one of the primary factors that can set the stage for a more effective value-enhancing board. Telkom, Pertamina and other SOEs are no exception. A company needs to be run and led by a well-oiled team, chaired by an experienced, trusted and ambitious chair, while executed by the best managers one can get. Leadership – the Chair or CEO – wil continue to play a crucial in preparing for the future of the company. Both need to collaborate closely while at the same time, some subtle hierarchy, accountability and responsibility should be acknowledged.

Notes

1. The Bakrie group for instance had incorporated Bakrie Investindo as the holding Bakrie company or entrepreneur-owners' vehicle above the Bakrie Brothers company. During the Asian crisis, it was the same Bakrie Investindo which was not disciplined enough and encroached on the assets of the Bakrie Brothers by collateralizing those assets for the family's benefit, endangering the whole company.
2. Tricker, B., (2009; 2012), *Corporate Governance. Principles, Policies and Practices*, Oxford, Oxford University Press.
3. The International Finance Corporation of the World Bank Group distinguishes five main priorities to establish good corporate governance (GCG): (1) Good board practices: clearly defined roles and responsibilities of board members; clear understanding of the Directors' responsibilities; appropriate board composition (independent and qualified); Director remuneration in line with leading CG codes; Board self-evaluation and training conducted

periodically. (2) Disclosure and transparency: Timely and adequate disclosure of financial and non-financial information by the firm according to IFRS/GAPP; Board composition, openness about related party lending and potential conflict of interest needs to be disclosed. (3) Control environment and processes: Independent audit committee, Risk representation on the Board, independent membership of nomination & remuneration committees. (4) Shareholder rights: Formalized minority shareholder rights, Policy on related party transactions in place, Policy on extraordinary transactions in place, Clearly defined and explicit dividend policy. (5) Commitment to Corporate Governance: Presence of Governance committee at firm. Active involvement of Board in CG discussions, Resources earmarked for the CG program, Formalized policies and procedures published in public domain for all shareholders, Periodic review of the CG program, policies and procedures, training of Board members.

4. Hay Group, 2012, Non-Executive Directors in ASEAN. Pay Practices, regulations and policies.

5. Cheung, Y-L; J.T. Connelly; J.P. Estanislao; P. Limpaphayom.; T. Lu & S. Utama, (2014), "Corporate governance and Firm Valuation in Asian Emerging Markets" in Boubaker, S. & D.K. Nguyen (eds), *Corporate Governance in Emerging Markets*, Berlin, Springer; and Claessens, S.; S. Djankov; J.P.H. Fan & L.H.P. Lang, (2002), "Disentangling the incentive and entrenchment effects of large shareholders", *Journal of Finance*, Vol. 57: 2741–2771; and Claessens, S. & B.B. Yurtoglu, (2013), "Corporate Governance in Emerging Markets: A Survey", *Emerging Markets Review*, Vol. 15: 1–33.

6. This summary of pros and cons of dual-tier board systems is based on an excellent summary by Jungmann, C., (2006), "The ffectiveness of Corporate Governance in One-Tier and Two-Tier Board Systems", *European Company and Financial Law Review*, Vol. 3; no 426.

7. Jungmann refers to the UK definition of a director's independency – under the influence of the Cadbury Report and the amended Combined Code for corporate governance 2008 – which can be seen as one of the most strict definitions of independency. A Non-executive director is not indepedent anymore "(1) if the director has been an employee of the company or group within the last five years; (2) if the director has, or has had within the last three years, a material business relationship with the company either directly, or as a partner, shareholder, director or senior employee of a body that has such a relationship with the company; (3) if the director has received or receives additional remuneration from the company apart from a director's fee, participates in the company's share option or a performance-related pay scheme, or is a member of the company's pension scheme; (4) if the director has close family ties with any of the company's advisers, directors, or senior employees; (5) if the director holds cross-directorships or has significant links with other

directors through involvement in other companies or bodies; (6) if the director represents a significant shareholder; and (7) if the director has served on the board for more than nine years from the date of his first election."

8. Kehoe, C; F. Lund & N. Spielmann, (2016), "Towards a value-creating Board", *McKinsey&Company.*

9. Thomas, R.J.; M. Schrage; J.B. Bellin & G. Marcotte, (2009), "How Boards Can be Better – A Manifesto", *MIT Sloan Management Review*, Winter, Vol. 50(2): 68–74.

10. Sharam, R. (2014), *Boards that lead*, Boston, Harvard Business School Press.

11. Sull, D. & K.M. Eisenhardt, (2012), Simple Rules for a Complex World, *Harvard Business World*, September, p. 71.

12. Sull, D. & K.M. Eisenhardt, (2015), *Simple Rules. How to thrive in a complex world*, Hachette UK, John Murray Publications.

13. Sull and Eisenhardt (2015 & 2016) distinguish three main decision rules under the label of Simple Rules: (1) Boundary Rules that guide the choice of what to do (and not do) without requiring a lot of time, analysis or information. (2) Prioritizing Rules that help rank a group of alternatives competing for scarce resources (money, time, or attention). (3) Stopping Rules that provide guidance on the decision to call it quits. Noble Price winner Herbert Simon labeled it "satisficing". Escalating commitment to a failed course of action is a well-documented error.

10

The Power of Human Corporate Narratives Across Borders: Narratives Constituting Corporate Reputation and Success

Warren Weeks and Peter Verhezen

Introduction

It takes years for an organization to build a good reputation. Yet a crisis that diminishes the trust that has been established between that organization and its various stakeholders, can not only quickly cripple or destroy all that reputational hard work, but also deliver significant and persistent financial damage in a matter of seconds.

Being in the headlines for all the wrong reasons, the erosion of trust by customers or investors can be sudden and dramatic. Corporate leaders are expected to function as good stewards for shareholders and other societal stakeholders, and they are more frequently being held to account for lapses in that stewardship, including reputational damage. But after the dust settles on each successive high-profile reputational crisis, it becomes clearer that there is often a disconnection between societal and regulatory expectations and the increasingly common reality of market-driven short-termism, and a culture of self-interest that leads to the majority of these situations.

W. Weeks
Cubit Media Research P/L, Melbourne, VIC, Australia
e-mail: warrenw@cubitresearch.com

P. Verhezen (⌧)
Melbourne Business School, Carlton, VIC, Australia
e-mail: p.verhezen@mbs.edu

© The Editor(s) (if applicable) and the Author(s) 2016   **159**
P. Verhezen et al. (eds.), *Doing Business in ASEAN Markets*,
DOI 10.1007/978-3-319-41790-5_10

Trust – often expressed in traditional and social media as an *organizational narrative* – is the glue that holds together any society, community-of-interest or organization. Trust binds that symbiotic coalition of key stakeholders that makes success possible. Reputation and its accounting representation as "goodwill" may be seen as the aggregation of trust, and therefore always remains at risk. By analogy, reputation may be seen as something like coastal sand dunes, a protective barrier built up over time but always at risk of rapid erosion by external factors such as storms and tides – and equally at risk from the destructive actions of those who dwell behind them. To extend the analogy, the ocean is public opinion – which is increasingly displayed as either positive or negative narratives through both social and traditional media channels.

Losing the battle for a positive public perception can have dire consequences. Bad corporate behavior – whether real or perceived – potentially blackens the reputation of the firm, undermining the relationships and trust on which that organization is established. Nike's corporate reputation, for instance, took a full decade to recover from the 1993 customer boycott over allegations about its employment practices in Asia. BP's Deepwater Horizon debacle in 2010 has had a dramatic effect on its share price and resulted in a significant leadership reshuffle. And banks in Europe and the USA have lost so much trust that they can hardly fill outstanding ICT jobs; new IT graduates prefer to work at more "cool" places than banks. Volkswagen is a battling preserve its reputational capital after its scamming of various nations' emissions testing programs came to light. Born of the need to meet ever stricter environmental standards while also delivering higher profitability, VW's inclusion of an engine management code to give false readings during emissions testing, stands to erode not only its financial performance, but that of all Diesel car manufacturers. As regulators across the planet scramble to tighten compliance-testing regimes, the flow-on effect is likely to be an increase in compliance costs. But in this case there are also signs that Volkswagen's actions have already led to the more rapid adoption of disruptive technologies such as electric and hydrogen fuel-cell-powered vehicles.

Short-term profit maximization strategies almost inevitably make *organizations more vulnerable to sudden loss of reputation,* because the interests of managers and shareholders are privileged over employees, suppliers, customers, and society at large. These matters should all be addressed by a sound, sustainable strategy that positions an organization in a dynamic and changing environment over a longer time-horizon. The pressure of day-to-day expectations of financial markets, combined with the lure of performance pay for senior executives that is linked to the share price, have generated an epidemic of myopia. In consequence, employees work on the knife-edge of dismissal through cost cutting, suppliers are put under pressure from longer and longer payment cycles, customers are exploited, and communication with the various publics served by the corporation is reduced to slogans and spin – all of which further damages the corporate reputational narrative.

Yet at the same time there has been a countervailing expectation, with some sanctions, for greater social accountability. And those CEOs that have realized how reputational narratives are increasingly linked to sustainable financial success, are giving attention not just to the usual economic costs, but also to the often-hidden social and environmental costs that their operations might generate. But whether or not it is recognized in the C-Suite or boardroom, today's reality is that organizations do not live in a social vacuum and therefore, decisions in corporations are not just dealing with economic choices, but will probably have social consequences. This it the reason why an understanding of the corporate narrative and reputation-management has become so crucial.[1]

Organizations that succeed in this increasingly-open environment are those whose operations are founded on the premise of a clearly-expressed, societally-endorsed purpose, enabled and supported by a set of values that is in the very DNA of the organization. Such a purpose informs "righteous" strategic planning and tactical response to situations, and is in turn reflected in an enhanced organizational reputation among shareholders and stakeholders alike.

A well-regarded reputation is one component of what marketers often refer to as "brand identity". However we have found it more useful to think of this identity in terms of the *narrative* that stakeholders of all kinds use to describe the organization in a range of contexts.

In terms of human interactions, narratives are ubiquitous. They are the expressions of what we know, what we've seen, and what we believe. They are the stories we tell each other and to which we refer when making assessments about all things. Narratives inform our own decisions, shape our behavior … and influence those of others.

Traditionally, a strong, positive reputational narrative would be seen as encompassing tangible elements like the quality of its products, its service ethic, its financial solidity, as well as the soundness of its strategic decision-making. But we are increasingly seeing corporate narratives expand to incorporate the less concrete aspects of organizational thinking – such as what a company stands for in terms of values and concern for its broader environment. In other words, as organizations constitute a larger and more integral part of their global communities, being respected by their employees, customers, suppliers and investors becomes a more important success factor.

Looking again at Volkswagen's recent emissions scandal, we might ask to what extent – beyond the probable regulatory retaliations – this situation might erode its profits, and for how long? Some already argue that it might represent a profit "hit" of USD 10 billion. But the bigger question is, could it also become such an entrenched part of the company's reputational narrative that it damages the long-term value of the Volkswagen empire?

Corporate crises such as this serve to highlight the extent to which managers are now caught between the expectations of financial markets for ever-increasing shareholder value and the relentless scrutiny of globally-networked media for socially-responsible behavior.[2] Somehow a compromise must be struck. The path of least resistance, most commonly followed, is to respond to the most pressing stakeholders, namely shareholders, while seeking to soothe and placate other external stakeholders – often through communication campaigns that might not reflect the reality of the company's real commitment to corporate social responsibility. This approach can work quite well for a time but it increases reputational risk and therefore is an unreliable long-term strategy. If anything goes seriously wrong after assurances to the contrary, public expectations are dashed, the poor behavior is exposed to the glare of public scrutiny ... and the organization might lose what little credibility it previously enjoyed. This might be a corporate Ground Zero – if not for the company, then most certainly for the executive team running the organization at the time.

When such a crisis strikes, an organization has a limited number of options in terms of its reaction: transparency and remedy, intransigent denial, obfuscation and 'spin'. Volkswagen found itself facing just such a situation. What could it have done to reduce its brand erosion as a result of this reputational crisis? In order to answer that question, we will provide a brief overview of what reputation is, how it is communicated, and how it is currently quantified. We will explore why many such current quantification techniques can never fully capture or express reputation in ways that allow for comparative analysis or genuine improvement – especially in an increasingly interlinked global world stories cross between traditional and social media to potentially smash the reputation of an organization, brand or individual.[3]

Subsequently, we will describe a new narrative analysis framework – based on two decades of work in the field by Cubit Research. This lays out a structured approach to identifying, quantifying, and improving reputational narratives, and tying this endeavor back to tangible organizational outcomes.

And finally, we will present a model showing how predictive analytics can be applied to corporate narrative tracking to predict and prevent reputational crises – whether self-inflicted or resulting from sabotage by rumor ("rumortage"). And for this we will examine a previous crisis involving Volkswagen – one that surrounded the recall of vehicles for inexplicably losing power.

What Is Reputation and How Can We Measure It?

The Cambridge dictionary defines reputation as: *the opinion that people in general have about someone or something, or how much respect or admiration someone or something receives, based on past behavior or character.*

The Merriam-Webster defines it as: *the overall quality or character as seen or judged by people in general, recognition by other people of some characteristic or ability, a place in public esteem or regard, and having a good name*

While these definitions of reputation may suffice in day-to-day life, they are largely unhelpful in quantifying corporate reputations to the extent that they can be compared, benchmarked, or deconstructed in ways that inform remedial action on the part of management teams. That is because the notions of character, respect, and admiration listed in the definitions can all be described as highly subjective, multivariate or aggregative elements. They simply lack the requisite precision for our purposes.

In order to enable the true management of reputation, we need to: (1) quantify it in the most objective, unambiguous terms possible; (2) recognize how different cultures think about reputation, (3) understand how people actually go about attaching a reputation to an organization, and (4) know how we all communicate and spread an organization's reputation.

Reputations are constructed in our minds and communicated to those with whom we engage, in the form of narratives. Those narratives comprise lists of things we like and do not like about products, services, governments, people, and organizations, and form the basis of many of our conversations.

Reputational narratives are also cumulative, reflecting (1) what we know about things – our long-term experiential and educational frameworks, (2) what we've seen in terms of recent experiences, and (3) what we believe. They are ubiquitous in the human communication process, and you will hear them emerge as part of every dialogue, on any street, and in practically any situation. If someone asks "Did you buy that new smartphone you were looking at?", the answer is likely to be in the form of a narrative, describing the features that ultimately sealed the deal … or those characteristics that made it a non-starter.

But rather than collecting narratives through a formal interview process, we have found the richest and most consistently representative source of narratives relating to organizational reputation to be the media – both traditional and social. Between stories of personal experiences related on Twitter or in blogs, on companies' Facebook pages, through expert commentary, and from product or service reviews, the media make it possible to "listen in" on a huge number of narratives, encompassing practically every stakeholder's perspective.

In order to quantify those reputational narratives, we first deconstruct each article, post or Tweet, to isolate the individual messages that comprise a communiqué. We then identify the target of each message and assess every individual message according to the level of satisfaction it expresses about how well the narrator believes the "target" (typically a product, company, government, or person) delivered against her expectations. Messages can then be reassembled into strings of narrative elements that together build the complete narrative for any organization.

An example of a narrative about a particular auto company might contain references to the price of its vehicles, their safety, and comfort, as well as to the kind of after-sales service most narrators experienced. Narratives regarding smart-phones might include references to battery life, ease of use, screen size, screen clarity, and price. But they might also incorporate rumors that the manufacturer builds "time bombs" into its software updates that degrades the performance of older models, thus forcing customers constantly to upgrade to the latest and most expensive offering.

An individual's narrative in respect of an organization can include any element of that organization's products, services, strategies, behaviors, or apparent values that are significant to that individual. And by assembling and aligning all the narratives extracted from the material studied, it is possible to determine the dominant narrative for any organization, among virtually any stakeholder group or segment thereof.

Narrative analysis allows us to identify areas of organizational strength or weakness in respect of any facet of its operations, from product or service offerings, to its business outlook, sustainability credentials, or its citizenship activities. And because quantified narratives can be compared across time and between competing organizations, insights derived from them can provide strong benchmarking both within and between companies.

If for example, 100 % of all narrators that identify as clients of Company A, communicate messages about their dissatisfaction with its service levels, while 100 % of the clients of Company B communicate their extreme satisfaction with its service levels, its pretty clear that the service level gap between the two organizations is extreme. But what's key from a management perspective is that the gap between the two companies has now been quantified, and can be monitored as Company A works to improve its performance.

Further, because people's narratives typically involve descriptions of exactly why the target company has variously delighted or disappointed them, reputational narrative analysis actually tells executives where they should focus their attention in order to change their stakeholders' perceptions. The combination of knowing exactly what's wrong, how bad it is, and why it is wrong, makes reputational analytics a powerful enabler of positive change.

Managing for Reduced Reputational Risk

When a company faces a reputational crisis,[4] the public and other spectators will not only pay attention to what is happening now, but to what has gone before and what has or has not been done to prevent it. And thanks to the internet's long memory, practically everything an organization has done is right there for the searching. More than at any time in our history, there is nowhere to hide. So, in the words of Doug Evelyn: "Institutions are becoming naked, and if you're going to be naked, fitness is no longer optional, If you're going to be naked, you better get buff."

What we do today prepares our future. But organizations' visible actions also contribute to the cumulative corporate narratives that we're all developing as we either experience companies first-hand, or we read, hear, or see reports of their actions.

In general, prevention and preparation are the two main components of reputational management strategies (as distinct from crisis and reputational response strategies). This is based on the recognition that when – mid- or post-crisis – people find that neither prevention nor preparation had been done, their view of the organization can deteriorate rapidly.

When Toyota had to recall its cars in 2009 and 2010, critics quickly concluded that its aggressive growth strategy had sacrificed quality and safety. Toyota's complaints had been significantly increasing since 2001 but were ignored by its management, or they misinterpreted these warning signs because they were blinded by cognitive biases.

Management either took these "near misses" as indications that systems were working well – or did not notice them at all. Either way this was seen as a breach of trust through poor management. Hence the need for strategies that can help managers recognize and learn from "near misses".

In order to avoid or to prevent catastrophes, managers should: (1) be on alert when time or cost pressures are high; (2) watch for deviations from the norm; (3) uncover the deviations' root causes; (4) hold themselves accountable for near misses; (5) envision worst-case scenarios; (6) look for near misses masquerading as successes; and (7) reward individuals for exposing near misses.[5] These strategies aim at reducing the likelihood that such an adverse event will occur. In the inevitable case that external risks cannot be prevented, organizations need to prepare themselves diligently.

Assessing reputational risk requires that top management not just maintain their awareness of their organizations' narratives among various stakeholder groups, but also anticipate and take proactive steps to *prevent* and to *prepare* for situations that could possibly threaten their companies' reputations. In addition to good preparation, successful reputation-management almost always requires the ability to react swiftly to unfortunate events, and to execute the prepared (crisis or disaster) plan quickly and effectively. But our work suggests that any reaction must also be consistent with the reputational narrative the organization wishes to foster.

Prudent reputational risk-management[6] must take into consideration that during a crisis, an organization might lose its ability adequately toengage with, and influence, customer perceptions. But there is strong evidence that consistency of purpose and genuineness of approach can minimize the impact of that loss.

Mercedes for instance introduced the smart A-Class model as the new city car in 1997 with a massive advertising campaign to lure young and female customers. Unfortunately, this newly launched A-car had rolled over during testing somewhere in Sweden during a "Moose-test" presentation. Mercedes – with its long-held reputation for quality and safety – was more dismissive of this roll-over incident than it should have been. So rather than living up to its own narrative, that had grown around its founding father Gottlieb Daimler's motto 'the best or nothing', the company simply released expert assessments that explained how the incident came about. However, Mercedes underestimated its customers' reaction: rather than quickly rebuilding trust, the less-than-expected reaction worsened the crisis. This was a situation in which expert assessments can become a dangerous public relations trap, because they risk becoming too dispassionately expert and insufficiently "human". While obviously not fully prepared for such a backlash, Mercedes swiftly got back on its feet, by using a more balanced pitch to the public. This time the company aired a far more personable presentation from highly-credible former F1 driver, Niki Lauda who lauded the A-class model as very safe.[7]

Preparation strategies typically attempt to mitigate the impact of possible crises.[8] This often involves establishing in advance relationships with trusted third parties, upon which the company can fall back in a crisis. Hence the growing number of big organizations that are choosing to collaborate with reputable, trusted NGOs – to "bank" goodwill to mitigate reputational damage should a crisis arise. Anticipating possible *strategic* or *external* risks through scenario building for instance allows management to become more prudent and to develop tactical steps needed in case a negative (non-preventable) risk materializes.[9]

Thinking about risks in a strategic sense requires the ability to assume an outside perspective and integrate it into the decision-making of the organization. The reputational impact of a business decision must be assessed before that decision is effectively made and implemented. And this is where having a keen sense of the organization's current external narrative can prove invaluable. Today's reputational narratives express not just how well the company is performing in the eyes of stakeholders, but also the areas of performance that are valued by those stakeholders. Such a perspective can be invaluable in assessing any decision by simply asking: 'How will this decision and the resulting actions fit with the narrative that is, and the narrative as we want it to be?'.

In contrast to a crisis situation, during that process of decision-making the risks are low and the control is high, allowing management to be proactively prudent and showing necessary foresight. Through decisions today, leaders are preparing the future of the organization. Being caught in a corruption scandal almost always hurts reputation. Corruption is a *preventable* risk that can be avoided by implementing proper standard operating procedures, processes and codes of conduct. When advising boards about the necessity of avoiding corrupt behavior, we often refer to an easy "front-page" heuristic[10] that is perhaps more easily related to that talking about narratives. We ask: "how would you feel about any of your decisions if they were to be accurately reported on the front page of the *Wall Street Journal, Financial Times*, or your leading local newspaper?" How might that kind of high-profile attention affect you or your family ... and what would that say about the decision in question?

For many the real value of corporate or individual reputation and trust is only apparent when its lost. In 2006, Siemens was accused of bribing foreign officials to secure contracts abroad. The bribery scandals caused uproar in Germany and beyond and has seriously tainted Siemens' international reputation. Ultimately, Siemens lost its CEO and Chairman in the process, and was shut out from World Bank-financed projects for two years. In addition, Siemens was to forced to pay more than USD 2.6 billion – from which USD 1.6 billion were fines and fees to regulators and government officials, and the remaining USD 1 billion were to fund internal investigation and reforms.

Leaders and boards are held responsible and accountable not only for their own behavior, but also for that of their subordinates. Leaders represent their companies, and in some special cases, like Apple's Steve Jobs, they become the very embodiment of its values – as it embodies theirs. But even when the concept of leadership does not extend to that extreme, it invariably comes with an expectation of impeccable behavior in every country and market in which that organization operates. The notions of leadership, responsibility for protecting the interests of all stakeholders everywhere, and stewardship of the company's best efforts and culture, have become inseparable. And this explains why CEOs, MDs and company directors across the globe are facing increasingly harsh penalties when they fail to live up to expectations.

In such an environment, it is important that boards and executives look at appropriate metrics that help them proactively to manage or assess their reputational risks. Some companies base their entire reputation management program on the yearly "beauty contests" of the *Fortune* "Most Admired" study. But as appealing as these rankings might seem, they remain an imprecise snapshot of reputation in the industries surveyed. And, as described earlier in this piece, they are often based on research involving the collection and interpretation of largely subjective, multivariate descriptors, such as admiration, character and respect. And because of the limited precision that can be reasonably applied to such semantic analysis, these rankings are ill-equipped to provide the kind of quantified comparative data sets needed to derive the insights necessary to manage and improve reputation. To inform effective reputational management, one needs to understand quite precisely the extent to which an organization is delivering against the expectations of different stakeholders, across all the "touch-points at which it interacts with or affects those stakeholders.

A somewhat more useful and quantitatively accurate approach to understanding some aspects of reputation is Bain & Co's Net Promoter Score system. Fred Reichheld and his colleagues at Bain & Company created a feedback system to connect loyalty and growth, that resulted in the *Net Promoter Score* (NPS) System.[11] Asking one simple, and as they describe it, "ultimate" question, "how likely is it that you would recommend this company to a friend or a colleague", resulted in the Net Promoter Score system.[12] In a way, the NPS is fine-tuning traditional reputation measurements by explaining how building relationships worthy of loyalty, translated into superior profits and growth. Those companies with the most efficient growth engines operate at NPS efficiency ratings of 50–80 %. But the average firm splutters along at an NPS efficiency of only 5–10 % where promoters barely outnumber detractors. Many firms and industries have negative NPS, which means that they continuously create more detractors than promoters by discouraging their customers.[13] However, regardless of whether they score well or poorly, an effective implementation of the Net Promoter Score system can still help companies to identify the proportion of customers likely to actively help their business, those likely to harm it, and the causes of each group's satisfaction or otherwise.

If there is a weakness to the Net Promoter Score system, it is that it typically focuses on just the most recent interaction between an organization and a client. But existing clients do not represent the entire reputational universe, and even in respect of those existing customers, the most recent interaction is rarely the only or greatest influencing factor in the development of positive or negative reputational narrative. So the question arises: how can organizations gain an understanding of the likely perceptions and predispositions of all those who are not yet clients?

We believe the answer lies in identifying the broader organizational narratives that are in circulation, and that are likely to have at least some effect on the perceptions of those who come in contact with them. Narratives form and change over time through a combination of personal experiences, the reported experiences of others (formerly by word of mouth, now increasingly by *word of mouse* via social media), and through exposure to reports appearing in traditional media. And these influences have the potential to affect a far broader range of stakeholders then exiting clients.

These reputational narratives – while often quite long and complex – can be thought of in simple terms as a series of expressions describing the extent to which any organization or person has delivered against the expectations of the narrator. A narrative is likely to comprise descriptions of delivery (versus expectations) across areas such as: product quality, price, customer service, returns to shareholders, environmental credentials, and good citizenship.

As we argued above, corporate reputation is the aggregate of those different perspectives based on these main pillars of corporate performance, expressed as cumulative and enduring narratives.

Delving further, the aggregate for measuring reputation can be visualized as a reversed Gauss curve – roughly indicating the frequency, impact and probability of reputation risks/opportunities occurring – in which leadership aims to optimize positive opportunities and minimize negative risk situations. As visualized in Fig. 10.1, reputational risks should be avoided, and genuine efforts should be made to enhance reputation.[14] Good corporate social performance, embedded within a philosophy of responsibility may be interpreted as an "insurance policy" against particular reputation risks. Corporate reputation is at stake when trust is eroded.

Too late, leaders often regret having made decisions aimed to maximizing profits while ignoring the "soft" side of values and trust within the organization. Internal drivers of values, beliefs, purpose and organizational culture provide an effective counter-force to behavior that seeks short-term profitability at all costs. But we would argue that good corporate behavior will be driven increasingly by the ability of the society in general – so called citizen journalists, and their attendant communities of interest – to share and spread the kinds of corporate narratives that can literally 'make of break' an organization.

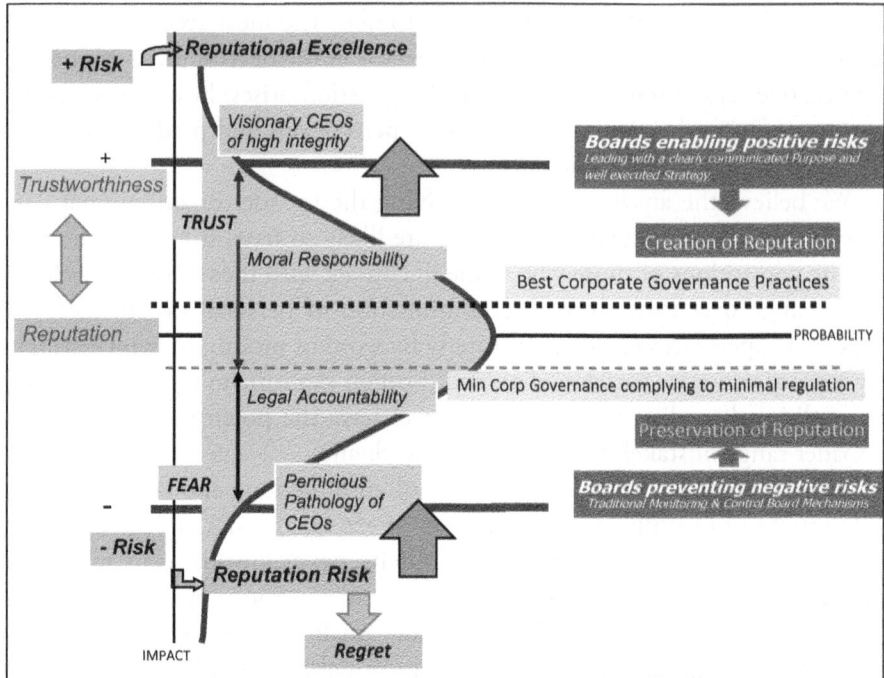

Fig. 10.1 The upside opportunity and downside threat on reputation (*Source*: A revised interpretation of a framework developed by Verhezen, P. 2009, *Giving Voice in a Culture of Silence,* Journal of Business Ethics, and Verhezen, P. 2015, "The Vulnerability of Corporate Reputation", Palgrave, London)

Applying an Understanding of Narratives to Dealing with Crises in an Increasingly Uncertain and "Social" World

At the start of this chapter we described narratives as those ubiquitous stories we tell ourselves and others: those expressions of what we know, what we've seen, and what we believe. We refer to them when making assessments about all things. Our narratives are always evolving because they grow out of our own experiences and those of others who share their narratives with us. And they inform our own decisions, shape our behavior ... and influence those of others.

But what does "sharing" your narrative mean in these days of social media? For many years, businesses and governments have recognized the power of word of *mouth*. However in the world of social media, where it is possible instantly to share your thoughts with a few million of your closest friends, word of mouth pales into insignificance against word of *mouse*. The good news from a reputational and risk management perspective is that the same basic principles apply to this new environment as to those in which managers have operated in the past. The big difference is the speed with which news of organizational missteps can spread, and the potential for those stories to reach a far wider audience than before.

However even without the added complexity delivered by the social media phenomenon, history has taught us that it is simply not possible for an organization to control every risk factor that could lead to a reputational crisis. Yet experiences such as those of Johnson and Johnson during its Tylenol crisis, show that the high trust levels associated with a solid reputational narrative that has grown from transparency and consistently-positive intent, constitute formidable intangible assets for firms and other entities. This is especially so for those organizations that rely on brand equity and on providing "an emotional experience" that is often related to a broader product or service eco-system. How then, are directors and senior executives to develop and protect their organizations' reputations when many risk factors are beyond their control?

In other areas of business, the answer to managing risk is often to dilute it to non-lethal levels. In the case of a production environment this may mean ensuring that there is always more than one supplier of critical components, or take the form of decentralized manufacturing, having multiple factories in different parts of the world … or by insuring against potential losses with third parties.

But whereas the direct costs and revenue impact of most crises associated with day-to-day business activities can be quantified to some level of precision, the value of longer-term reputational loss – and even the very nature of the shift in an organization's reputation can be difficult to quantify.

This quantification dilemma raises questions in respect of how much an organization should invest in maintaining a healthy reputational narrative. For instance, if a serious equipment failure in a factory would likely represent an opportunity cost of USD 1 million dollars per day for the month it would take to effect repairs, management has at least a ballpark figure attached to the risk of that failure occurring: USD 31 million. But what might be the cost in lost revenue if customers simply decide they have lost faith in an airline to keep them safe, or a bank to protect their wealth? And what additional ongoing costs might be associated with tighter regulatory controls applied should a government come to believe an organization is no longer operating in a way that is acceptable in the eyes of its constituents?

With narrative analysis – applied to traditional and social media channels – the views being expressed and shared by stakeholders about an organization can be more easily and precisely identified and quantified. And the results are then comparable against pre-crisis and competitive norms.

For instance when one US car-maker released a vehicle that performed exceptionally poorly in safety tests, some of the company's Australian sales outlets claimed 30 % of their orders for its small cars were cancelled by concerned customers in just one week. Confidence in the brand only returned after it made substantial changes to its product lineup. But this took many months to roll out.

This real-world experience highlights how perceived breaches in trust – in this case the duty to keep its customers safe – can result in swift and substantial punishment by customers and other stakeholder groups. Applying narrative/outcome correlative analysis to such situations allows senior executives and boards of directors to understand the magnitude in tangible terms of the effect a breach of trust in any key reputational area has had on organizations similar to theirs.

So what about organizations that have never "put a foot wrong", or where there are no relevant historical cases with which to work in quantifying the potential damage that can result from a reputation narrative crisis? Our work suggests that consistency of positive behavior is "king" in terms of the development and maintenance of an enduring, positive public narrative.

What should be kept in mind though, is that the verdict in regard to what represents positive behavior is increasingly being delivered by an organization's customers and other stakeholders. Every day through the sharing of narratives via myriad communication channels, they subconsciously analyze and compare what has been delivered versus their expectations; they calculate reality versus hope.[15] The higher the denominator over nominator, the better the organizational brand will perform in all circumstances , including crises.

However while the power to determine what is good and right is no longer the exclusive province of the executive team or the board of directors, organizations can protect or at least strengthen themselves by focusing on communicating consistent, credible narratives that align organizational imperatives with societal values. Such communication stems from a combination of executive intent, strong strategy, a healthy outward-looking core culture, and appropriate transparency. But it also requires the organization to have a clear understanding of what its narrative is "in the wild" – that is among its stakeholders and beyond its immediate influence.

One of the co-authors, the Australian ICT entrepreneur Warren Weeks, has developed a suite of narrative-centric analytical tools through his firm, CUBIT Media Research, based on human cognitive modeling. These enable organizations to gather and analyze traditional and social media content containing the narratives being shared by their stakeholders.

The insights that flow from his approach provide concrete data and rich insights that enable senior executives and boards of directors more effectively to understand their organizations' competitive narrative positions, and to seek reputational excellence and to minimize reputation risks.

Determining and analyzing an organization's narrative involves three stages:

1. collection of as much material as possible that contains its narrative elements,
2. identification of the various narrative elements potentially affecting stakeholder attitudes and behavior
3. application of an analysis framework in order to understand what the narrative is telling us.

Collection of as Much Material as Possible That Contains an Organization's Narrative Elements

When it comes to understanding the stories or narratives that are being shared by its stakeholders, one of the challenges facing organizations today is the vastness of the media landscape within which these narratives exist. The other is the almost incredible growth rate of the global data set. In January 2009, online news stories were being published at the rate of three million items per month – not including social media posts. Fast forward to 2015, and that figure had risen to three llion per day … a 31-fold increase. And as at 2016, the number was up to four million per day – again not including the millions of posts each hour to social media behemoths like Twitter and Facebook.

The "solution" adopted by many organizations in respect of keeping up with what's being said about them in this deluge of material, is to focus on an ever smaller proportion of the media universe. However the resulting narrative myopia almost guarantees that senior executives and boards will be blind-sided by emerging situations – only becoming aware of a reputational or commercial threat when it grows to be substantial enough to hit the major media outlets. And by that time it might simply be too late to avert a crisis.

A more sustainable approach is to harness the latest in affordable Big Data technologies to collect and analyze the world's media output in near-real time. By capturing the largest possible data set, and utilizing smart search and alert systems constantly to spot potential issues or opportunities, organizations can maintain an effective 360 degree view – a metaphoric reputational radar that delivers sufficient warning to enable considered action rather than panicked response.

Identification of the Various Narrative Elements Potentially Affecting Stakeholder Attitudes and Behavior

The narratives or stories we share comprise elements that we may think of as snippets of experience and opinion about the topic of conversation at hand. For example, if the discussion turns to which new smart phone one should buy, the narrative elements likely to emerge are around facets such as: price, battery life, available apps, ease of use, build quality, and views of the companies behind their manufacture.

By identifying the incidence of these various elements across large numbers of media pieces (both social and traditional), organizations can not only identify the various narratives that are being shared about them, but also determine the degree of representativeness of each of those narratives.

We recommend that organizations study both traditional and social media narratives, but that they do not aggregate the findings. That is because, while they are increasingly interdependent channels (traditional media often pick up stories from the social media universe, and vice versa), the approaches to many subjects are often dramatically different between the channels. Social media commentators tend to come from, and write for, more polarized communities of interest.[16] They are therefore likely to adopt a less objective position than their mainstream media counterparts.

Our long-term analysis of the differences between narratives appearing in social and mainstream media suggests that in a broad range of topic areas, social media narratives are often significantly left or right of centre, and are unlikely to be represent the views of "everyman": our largely silent majority. By extension, making important organizational decisions based purely or predominantly on social media narratives can prove counterproductive.

We have also found great benefit in studying separately an organization's narratives that pertain to the various countries and regions in which it operates. That is because our narrative responses to things, are influenced by what we know, what we have seen, and what we believe. And our knowledge, experience and beliefs are inherently shaped by the culture into which we were born, and in which we grow and develop as people. Any attempt to aggregate narratives across different cultures and geographies tends to obscure the very trends and elements that allow executives to make the best decisions.

The quantification of narrative elements is accomplished as follows:

- Identify each media item that contains mention of: the organization, its products or services, an issue of interest.

- Assess each mention, identifying the snippet (narrative element) that best describes the meaning of the statement.
- Categorize the level of satisfaction associated with the statement.
- Normalize all the narrative elements, grouping them into categories to facilitate quantitative analysis.
- Arrange these data so they show the relative importance of each of the elements or facets discussed across the entire media population studied.
- Score each element in terms of the satisfaction expressed by narrators.

Put another way, narrative quantification takes the form[17]:

$$\text{Narrative} = \Sigma\left(\left(\frac{D_1}{E_1}\right) \times W_1, \quad \ldots \left(\frac{D_n}{E_n}\right) \times W_n\right)$$

Where: D = Perceived quality of delivery in respect of each important attribute, E = The narrators' Expectation of delivery in respect of that attribute, and W = The relative importance or weighting of each attribute.

Once we have quantified a narrative, it can be described in tabular form, where each narrative element is shown next to one score indicating its relative prominence among stakeholders, and another score indicating the extent to which stakeholders and other commentators have described how well we delivered on their expectations. The benefit of this kind of description is that our narrative can be objectively compared against those of others in our industry, or even with those in other industries from whom we believe we can learn positive lessons. However because tabular data can be difficult to quickly interpret and absorb, it is often useful to describe our narrative – as a narrative of its own, or meta-narrative.

Here is a short example of a narrative explanation of the results of an analysis regarding the entirely fictitious AnyCo Inc. – a company operating throughout the Asia-Pacific Region.

Our dominant narrative in Singapore comprises five main elements. These are: quality of service, reliability of products, safety of our products, solidness of our company, and value for money represented by our offerings. We perform strongest in terms of our product quality, where stakeholders rate us as substantially exceeding their expectations (we score 150 of 100). Our weakest narrative element concerns our quality of service, where we failed to meet our clients expectations (we score 84 of 100). The most common snippet in regard to our quality of service is not that our people are unfriendly and unhelpful, but that there are too few on duty at peak times and customers are having to wait too long. In all other areas we are meeting our stakeholders' expectations (100 of 100).

Application of an Analysis Framework in Order to Understand What the Narrative Is Telling Us

From this AnyCo example, it is clear what the organization needs to do in order better to meet its customers' expectations. Most of its narrative elements are rated good to exemplary, with just one area requiring attention.

And this is the greatest benefit of narrative analysis: through their own exchanges in respect of the organization, stakeholders have not just found fault, but told the company exactly what needs to be done. In this case, it is to arrange staff rosters differently so there are more staff on hand at times of peak demand.

But what about using narrative analysis as a predictive tool to spot potentially damaging situations ahead of time?

So far we have broadly defined narratives as the stories we hold and share, that reflect our experiences, and that influence our attitudes and behavior. But what are the characteristics of a narrative that make it more or less likely to affect the way a person thinks about another person, an organization or an issue? In short, what specific trigger or combination of triggers makes one narrative more dangerous than others in terms of reputation?

Cubit's research revealed the presence of five success-indicators in the communications profiles of brands that stand out in terms of market share, stock market performance and customer satisfaction as found in attitudinal surveys.[18] In studying the nature of numerous media crises, Weeks and his company identified five indicators that appeared in advance of every communication disaster.

By tracking the narratives that swirl around an organization, and keeping a constant eye on those indicators, organizations can predict and prevent the kind of media storm that often accompanies a real reputational crisis.

The five factors that determine the extent to which organizational narratives are indicative of significant problems ahead:

1. Profile, or how prominent the narrative becomes.
2. Proportional engagement, the extent to which an organization engages with stakeholders in respect of an issue.
3. Message/Content, or the context in which the narrative snippets are framed.
4. Sentiment, or the ratio of positive versus damaging messages.
5. Emotional Representation, or the level of perceived personal risk associated with the issue.

Depending on whether the situation is a flash-event or more of a slow-burn, applying this five-factor analysis framework, will buy an organization varying amounts of time to prepare for the storm. But no matter what the nature of the crisis, it will deliver a far clearer understanding of the environment in which executives must act, and the narratives they must seek to influence if they are to mitigate the damage to their organization.

How Narrative Analytics can Prevent or at Least Mitigate Corporate Reputational Damage: The Volkswagen Case

Many cases have taught us that the potent combination of attention from traditional and social media can destroy or enhance the corporate reputation with equal ease. In recent years, Volkswagen's reputation in Australia has been hit twice, in two unrelated crises. The first related to the death of a young woman on the Melbourne highway in 2013 when her VW suddenly and inexplicably lost power. Suffering from rapid deceleration, her Golf was struck from behind by a heavy vehicle that was unable to avoid the collision. The second crisis concerns Volkswagen's more recent Diesel-software manipulation case (2015–2016). Let us have a brief look at the first from 2013.

Following the fatal collision, and despite stories of this mysterious power-loss phenomenon having been reported in media around the world, the local VW organization denied that there was any such fault with its vehicles. It did however promise to investigate the situation and offered its full cooperation with the investigating authorities.

But despite having proceeded, "by the book" in terms of its handling of the situation, the company found itself battered by a combination of traditional and social media commentary. Customers, and commentators simply refused to let go of the story, and eventually regulators became involved.

Over the following year, it was reported that that Volkswagen's sales dropped by more than 25 % in Australia. A full recall of affected vehicles was ordered, and this was said to have cost the company a further AUD 170 million. Clearly the established global corporate crisis management program was not working. But why did it fail? By applying narrative analysis and the five factors model, this becomes more obvious.

1. *Profile*, or how prominent the narrative becomes

As is the case in many multinational organizations after the GFC, Volkswagen had undergone a significant contraction and re-centralization of its market analysis functions. The resulting diminution in the scope and depth of its local media reporting, meant the company's local executives had a limited view of what was happening around them.

To illustrate how this affected their view of the profile of the approaching crisis, we present the chart below, which overlays three different views of the coverage that resulted from the power-loss incident.

The small dark grey area shows the view most likely seen by VW's international and local management. This represents the coverage, measured in numbers of relevant stories appearing in traditional media channels, pertaining to the release of new products (VW was not monitoring social media at the time). This is traditionally the most important view for auto companies involved in the constant roll out of new models to stay competitive in a crowded market (Fig. 10.2).

The two lighter areas above it show the volume of items appearing across traditional *and* social media channels in respect of the fatal accident, VW's response, and news that VW had recalled vehicles elsewhere in the world

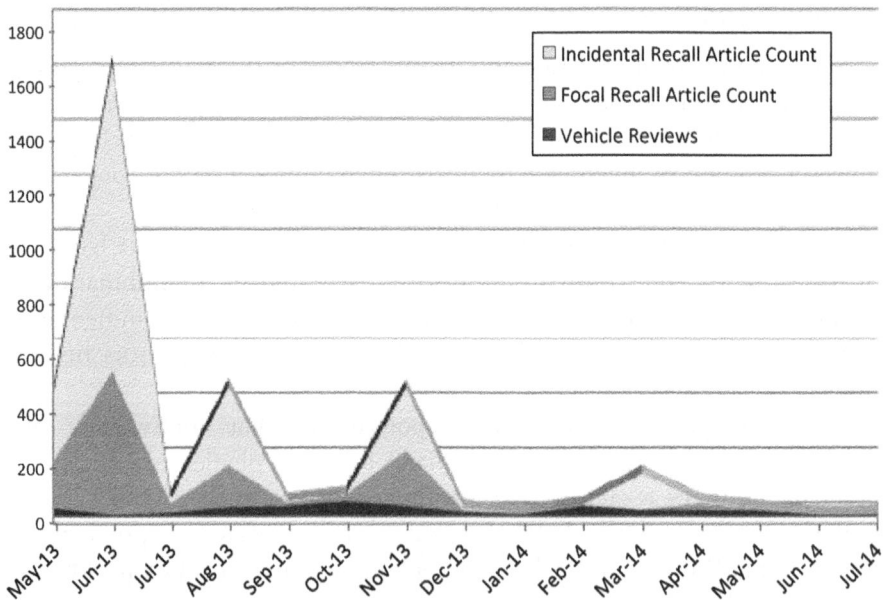

Fig. 10.2 Three perspectives in the media
(*Source*: Based on the data run in 2014 through Cubit Media Research's analysis systems (1995–2016))

in response to similar mysterious power-loss incidents. Even this simple volumetric assessment should have alerted the local management team that a potentially damaging storm was brewing.

2. ***Proportional engagement***, the extent to which an organization engages with stakeholders in respect of an issue.

    Without adequate systems in place to warn of impending trouble, Volkswagen proceeded in a business-as-usual manner. As a result, it failed to engage proportionally with its customers and other significant actors. The chart below, shows the substantial number of media pieces published by the media and public, that addressed the various issues surrounding the whole power-loss situation, and the far lesser response from Volkswagen.

While it is a common mistake to over-react and cave in to noisy but unrepresentative special interest groups that seek to harness the power of social media to force organizations to pander to their desires, that was certainly not the situation here. Volkswagen's own customers were venting in regard to the situation and respected journalists expressed their frustration at VW's lack of willingness even to discuss the matter in any meaningful way (Fig. 10.3).

3. ***Message/Content***, or the context in which the narrative snippets are framed.

    The narrative surrounding the entire loss-of-power situation, predictably related to the safety and reliability of Volkswagen's vehicles, and frustration at the way VW seemed not to share the concerns of its customers. Some even expressed their feelings in terms of betrayal by a once-trusted friend.

At a time in history when the societal expectation in many of Volkswagen's most profitable markets was that auto-makers would strive to design and produce cars with a five-star safety rating, any prominent narrative that cast doubt on an organization's ability to meet that key expectation represented a significant threat to reputation and prosperity.

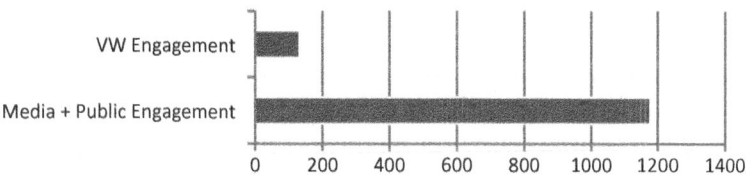

Fig. 10.3 VW perspective versus social media view
(*Source*: Based on the data run in 2014 through Cubit Media Research's analysis systems (1995–2016))

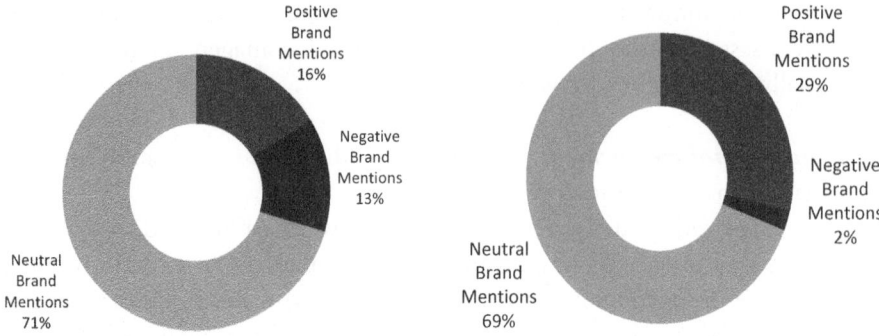

Fig. 10.4 Perspective on sentiments
(*Source*: Based on the data run in 2014 through Cubit Media Research's analysis systems (1995–2016))

4. *Sentiment*, or the ratio of positive versus damaging messages.

   The pie charts and bar chart below, show three different views of the narrative sentiment attached to the Volkswagen brand name and certain of its products, as the 2013–14 crisis unfolded. The pie chart to the right shows the picture most likely being painted by Volkswagen's product-launch analysis efforts. And it is this picture that VW's management team would have seen throughout the crisis (Fig. 10.4).

   The pie chart to the left however, shows a somewhat more realistic picture of the situation, although it still focuses primarily on traditional media sources. Even so, the appearance of such a large proportion of negative commentary may have prompted a re-evaluation of the seriousness of the situation. In contrast to compares the message sentiment levels between new-product-review oriented media and re-call/power-loss pieces – shows the full extent of the unfolding crisis. The story it tells is dire. Essentially, all crisis-related messages were negative (represented by the darker grey areas) (Fig. 10.5).

   It goes without saying that any time a company sees message sentiment approach or reach the 100 % mark in respect of any aspect of its operations, there is need for immediate and significant remedial action.

5. *Emotional Representation*, or the level of perceived personal risk associated with the issue.

   While not as immediately alarming in appearance as the previous sentiment chart, this emotional representation radar chart is actually the key to understanding why the VW crisis was so costly, both in terms of sales and recall costs. And it points to why some potential crises simply evaporate while others become devastating reputational typhoons.

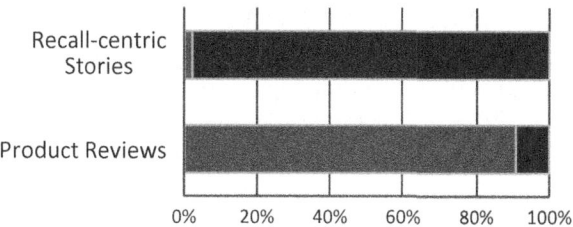

Fig. 10.5   Recall versus product reviews
(*Source*: Based on the data run in 2014 through Cubit Media Research's analysis systems (1995–2016))

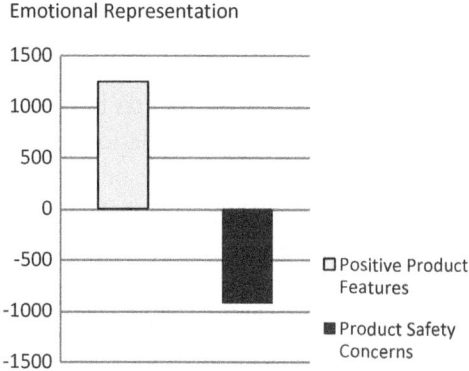

Fig. 10.6   Emotional representation
(*Source*: Based on the data run in 2014 through Cubit Media Research's analysis systems (1995–2016))

Here we see a mix of conflicting representations of the Volkswagen brand and product. On the one hand, the vehicles perform well during journalists' reviews, but on the other, it is recognized that this company produced a car that through some unknown mechanical fault, caused the death of an innocent customer. And the result is product outcome anxiety.

So whereas the high profile of the story captured stakeholder attention, and the lack of organizational interest was unhelpful because (whether accurate or not) it suggested that VW cared little about their concerns, it was the combination of *context, sentiment* and *emotional representation* – or associated personal risk – that determined the magnitude of the crisis (Fig. 10.6).

In this case the context in which the narratives were framed was: *someone died in this car because it was faulty*. The understandably negative sentiment came not just from the accident itself, but from the apparent subsequent lack of genuine concern from the manufacturer. But it was the emotional representation of this situation that was most devastating for VW. It was: "*this could happen to you or your family*".

Earlier in this chapter we observed that any prominent narrative that casts doubt on an organization's ability to meet key stakeholder expectations, could represent a significant threat to that organization's reputation and prosperity. And at the time of the power-loss crisis, the expectation of the majority of Volkswagen's customers and stakeholders was that auto-makers would produce cars with a five-star safety rating.

This same underlying logic can be applied to any organization, and to any crisis situation. Reputational and commercial risks are invariably proportional to the extent to which any organization fails to deliver against the expectations of its stakeholders. However the scale of this potential reputational and/ or commercial damage jumps disproportionally when that failure threatens the physical, social or financial well-being of those stakeholders.

To illustrate this, let us compare the power-loss crisis with a more recent and perhaps more widespread crisis for VW, that began in October 2015.

This situation involved the company's installation of a secret software module in the engine management units of a range of its diesel-powered vehicles. When activated, this module changed the engine's settings, allowing it appear "cleaner" than it was in normal operation. This successfully fooled the emissions testing equipment used by regulatory testing bodies, allowing Volkswagen to sell cars that would ordinarily would not have been passed as fit for sale.

Like the engine power-failure crisis before it, this painted VW in a bad light.[19] But whereas the previous situation dealt with a potential "life and death" fault in VW's vehicles, the *emissions-gate* crisis, as it came to be known in the USA, was seen as being all about maximizing profits by reducing the cost of vehicle production. Audiences read that it was cheaper to cheat than to employ the kinds of technologies – used by companies like Mercedes Benz and BMW – that could have made VW's diesel engines genuinely "cleaner". But what did that really mean in terms of the broader societal impact?

Testing authorities expressed their determination to implement new, more rigorous ways to test vehicles, and regulators in many countries vowed to fine the company heavily for its dishonesty. Automotive authorities speculated that, after the implementation of a "fix", affected vehicles would either be somewhat less fuel-efficient or a little less powerful. But ultimately no-one lost their life as a result of Volkswagen's emissions test cheat module. And that goes to the issue of how the combination of context, sentiment and emotional representation can serve as useful indicators of how serious a crisis could be.

We believe the lack of lethality in the emissions crisis, in concert with the company's superior handling of the situation, means that, while Volkswagen will undoubtedly suffer very significant financial penalties for its deception, its reputational narrative should remain in far better health than if it was facing another life-and-death issue.

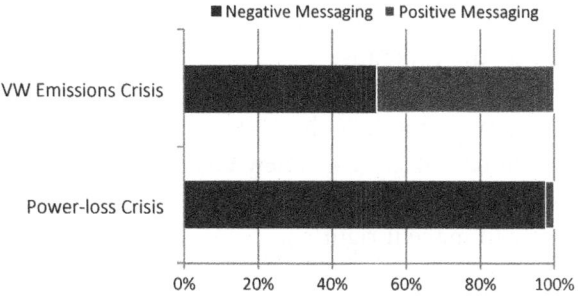

Fig. 10.7 Comparison between VW Emission cost versus power-loss crisis (*Source*: Based on the data run in 2014 and 2015 through Cubit Media Research's analysis systems (1995–2016))

This is evidenced by the significant difference between the negative sentiment levels and emotive representation of the narrative elements surrounding the power-loss issue, versus those from the emissions situation. Both are taken from the same Australian media set (Fig. 10.7).

Almost all of the traditional and social media commentary appearing in respect of the engine power-loss crisis centred around personal risk, the proportion of negative commentary represented ~98 % of the coverage tracked. However the proportion of narrative snippets associated with the non-lethal emissions situation was only 52 %.

In terms of the broader regional response to the emissions scandal, we saw very different negative messages levels in Singapore and China, that reflected the different levels of personal financial impact suffered by customers in those countries. In Singapore, where purchasers of affected VW vehicles faced the prospect of having to repay the Government subsidies for cleaner vehicles, negative messaging reached 40 %. However in China, where the media reported no affected vehicles had been sold, and therefore no citizens had been negatively impacted, negative messaging only reached 17 %.

To understand why we assert that Volkswagen dealt with this crisis far better than the previous one studied, we have reconstructed the early life-cycle of the emissions situation on a timeline below.

This time, rather than failing to engage with stakeholders, VW used the same global media channels that had brought its behavior to light, to reach out – following an historically successful crisis-management approach.

Stepping through the media timeline below, we can identify six stages in the early life-cycle of this crisis (Fig. 10.8):

1. Revelation of the wrongdoing,
2. Admission by the company,
3. Apology and purge (often this involves the removal of a senior officer of the company, in this case the CEO),
4. Appointment of a 'fixer' (e.g. a new CEO),
5. Promises of a thorough investigation,
6. The promise to make it right.

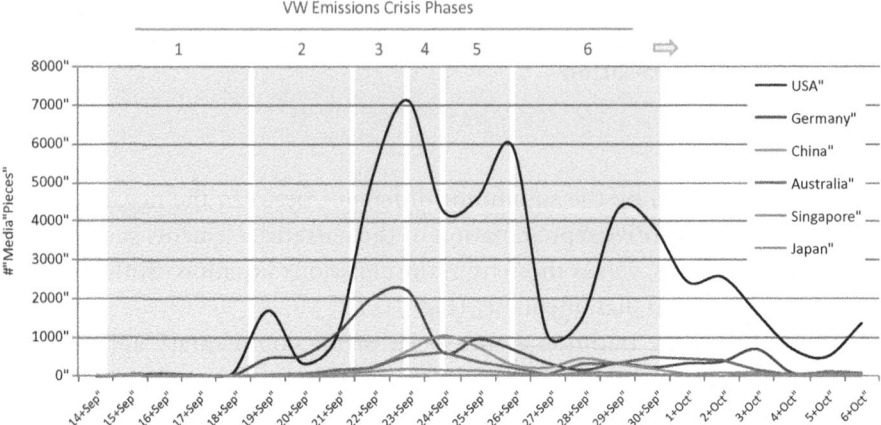

Fig. 10.8 Different phases in VW Emissions crisis
(*Source*: Based on the data run in 2015 through Cubit Media Research's analysis systems (1995–2016))

As a result of this, coverage levels had already fallen dramatically, just four weeks after the story broke in the mainstream media. This reinforces the proposition that the success with which an offending organization is able quickly to identify, understand, and respond to the negative narratives developing around it, is a direct determinant of the extent to which it can mitigate the damage it suffers. And on this occasion VW was highly successful.

Concluding Remarks: Some Preliminary Recommendations

How people perceive a corporations actions shapes the narratives that become associated with and personify that corporation. These narratives can significantly affect corporate financials preformance-either positively or negatively. The way a board and its top executives deal with potential crises situations affects the corporate narratives that permeate into the future. In Asia where branding and reputation increasingly becoming competitive forces to gain market share and to enhance the profitability of the corporation, the media is increasingly play a role in the evolution and communication of these influential narratives.

Moreover, in Asian societies where authorities and their messages are not necessarily perceived as authentic, rumors and mouth-to-mouth communication play a very important role. Increasingly in Asia, social media is becoming the digital proxy for the mouth-to-mouth communication of the past and traditional media is serving to disseminate the romours and narratives that originate in the social media sphere. Corporations will need to take the potential impact of this new media landscape more seriously if they are to avoid or to reduce reputational risks among stakeholders exposed to the increasingly ubiquitous influence. Understanding and acknowledging the way narratives unfold can and put a "shadow in the future", prepares boards and top executives to improve the way they handle potential or actual crises, and how they communicate their values and what they stand for. Any event that could undermine those foundations should be handled in a professional and appropriate manner. Engagging in "Corporate Spin" is becoming increasingly counterproductive.

Genuine analyzing and acknowledging the facts is a start. And success in addressing reputational and commercial risks is directly related to the extent to which any organization succeeds in delivering against the expectations of its stakeholders; and this rule seems to apply across borders. Business is ultimately about delivering according to, or beyond, expectations. Anything short of delivering these expectations and narratives could be very detrimental to the company. Understanding, analyzing and communicating these expectations and narratives implies proper board management and governance.

Notes

1. Walker, K. (2009), "A Systematic Review of the Corporate Reputation Literature: Definition, Measurement, and Theory", *Corporate Reputation Review*, Vol. 12 (4): 357-367; Walker, K. (2010), "A systematic review of the corporate reputation literature", *Corporate Reputation Review*; Walter, I. (2006), "Reputational Risk and Conflicts of Interest in Banking and Finance: The Evidence So Far", Working Paper Stern Business School NY, downloaded from Internet; and Wartick, S.L. (2002), "Measuring Corporate Reputation", *Business and Society*, Vol. 4(4): 371–392.
2. Williams, R.J., M.E. Schnake & W. Fredenberger (2005), "The impact of Corporate Strategy on a Firm's Reputation", *Corporate Reputation Review*, Vol. 8(3): 187–197; and Zabala, I., Panadero, L.M. Gallardo; C.M. Amate, M. Sanchez-Galindo, I. Tena & I. Villalba (2005), "Corporate Reputation in

Professional Services Firms: Reputation Management based on Intellectual Capital Management", *Corporate Reputation Review*, Vol. 8 (1): 59–71.

3. Ang, S.H. & A.M Wight (2009), "Building Intangible Resources: The Stickiness of Reputation", *Corporate Reputation Review*, Vol. 12 (1): 21–32; Barnett, M.L, J.M. Jermier & B.A. Lafferty (2006), "Corporate Reputation: The Definitional Landscape", *Corporate Reputation Review*, Vol. 9 (1): 26–38; Fombrun, C. & M. Shanley (1990),"What's in the Name? Reputation building and Corporate Strategy", *Academy of Management Review*, 33(2): 233–258; Fombrun, C.J. (1996), *Reputation: Realizing Value from the Corporate Image*, Cambridge, Harvard Business School Press; Fombrun, C.J. (2006), "Corporate Governance", *Corporate Reputation Review*, Vol. 8 (4): 267–271.

4. Eccles, R.G., S.C. Newquist & R. Schatz (2007), "Reputation and its Risks", *Harvard Business Review*, February: 104–114; Larkin, J. (2003), *Strategic Reputation Risk Management*, New York, Palgrave MacMillan; and Kaplan, R.S. & A. Mikes (2012), "Managing Risks. A New Framework", *Harvard Business Review*, June: 48–60.

5. Tinsley, C.H.; Dillon, L. & P.M. Madsen (2011), "How to avoid a catastrophe?", *Harvard Business Review*, April: 90–97. The authors argue that "Cognitive biases make these near misses hard to see, and, even when they are visible, leaders tend not to grasp their significance. Thus, organizations often fail to expose and correct latent errors even when the cost of doing so is small – and so they miss opportunities for organizational improvement before disaster strikes. This tendency is itself a type of organizational failure – a failure to learn from "cheap" data. Surfacing near misses and correcting root causes is one the soundest investments an organization can make".

6. Livingston, J.A. (2005), "How valuable is a good reputation? A sample selection model of internet auctions", *The Review of Economics and Statistics*, Vol. 87 (3): 453–465; Neef, D. (2005), "Managing Corporate Reputation and Risk", *Corporate Reputation Review*, Vol. 8 (2): 164–168; and Obloj, T. & K. Obloj (2006), "Diminishing Returns from Reputation: Do Followers Have a Competitive Advantage", *Corporate Reputation Review*, Vol. 9 (4): 213–224.

7. Diermeier, D. (2011), *Reputation Rules. Strategies for building your company's most valuable asset*, New York, McGrawHill; and Schreiber, E.S. (2011), "A Holistic Approach to Stakeholder Relations to Build Reputation Investment Strategies", in in Hiles, A. (Ed), *Reputation Management. Building and protecting your company's profile in a digital world*, London, Bloomsbury, pp. 69–80.

8. Wartick, S.L. (2002), "Measuring Corporate Reputation", *Business and Society*, Vol. 4(4): 371–392.

9. Kaplan, R.S. & A. Mikes (2012), "Managing Risks. A New Framework", *Harvard Business Review*, June: 48–60.

10. Verhezen, P. (2015), *The Vulnerability of Corporate Reputation*, London, Palgrave.

11. According to Wikipedia, the *Net Promoter* or *Net Promoter Score* (*NPS*) is a management tool that can be used to gauge the loyalty of a firm's customer relationships. It serves as an alternative to traditional customer satisfaction research and claims to be correlated with revenue growth. "Net Promoter Score" is a customer loyalty metric developed by (and a registered trademark of) Fred Reichheld, Bain & Company, and Satmetrix. It was introduced by Professor Reichheld in his 2003 *Harvard Business Review* article "One Number You Need to Grow". NPS can be as low as –100 (everybody is a detractor) or as high as +100 (everybody is a promoter). An NPS that is positive (i.e., higher than zero) is felt to be good, and an NPS of +50 is excellent. Net Promoter Score measures the loyalty that exists between a provider and a consumer. The provider can be a company, employer or any other entity. The provider is the entity that is asking the questions on the NPS survey. The consumer is the customer, employee, or respondent to an NPS survey.

    Reichheld, F. (2006a), *The Ultimate Question. Driving Good Profits and True Growth*, Cambridge MA, Harvard Business School Press: 15; Reichheld, F. (2006b), "The Microeconomics of Customer Relationships", *MIT Sloan Management Review*, Winter, Vo. 47(2): 72–78.

12. Reichheld 2006a: 17–20. The NPS is based on the fundamental perspective that every company's customers can be divided into three categories. Promoters are loyal enthusiasts who keep buying from a company and urge their friends to do the same. Passives are satisfied but unenthusiastic customers who can be easily wooed by the competition. And detractors are unhappy customers trapped in a bad relationship. Customers can be categorized according to their answer to the (ultimate) question. Those who answer nine or ten on a zero-to-ten-scale, for instance, are promoters, and so on.

13. Reichheld 2006b: 20.

14. As we search for meaning in our careers and yes, a good guide to use is to face and accept reality that is usually complex and rather ambiguous, use Occam's razor and simplify. Einstein told us to make things as simple as possible, but not simpler. We cannot change who we are and what we are given nor can we change the past. But we can always act and live in the present to shape our future.

15. Dowling, G.R. & W. Weeks (2008), "What the media is really telling you about your brand", *MIT Sloan Management Review*, Spring, Vol. 49(3): 27–34.

16. See Smith M.M, 6/29/2015, Mapping Twitter Topic Networks: From Polarized Crowds to Community Clusters | Pew Research Center.

17. Dowling & Weeks 2008.

18. Weeks 2014. Cubit's original Dimension-8 framework analyses the following critical success factors: "(1) Experiential Ecosystem focus: understanding that these days, it is about more than just the product or services; (2) Profile: generating a comparative 'critical mass' of volume and consistency of media attention;

(3) Broad-based Regard: the favorability of commentary surrounding all the various aspects of a brand in line with a Reputation Narrative; (4) Messaging: clarity, concentration and consistency; (5) IEMFC: crafting communiqués that match the various stages of a buying cycle, i.e. interest, educate, motivate, facilitate, and cultivate behavior; (6) Media Mix: recognizing that different audiences will prefer different channels and will respond best when addressed through their channel of choice; (7) Broad-spectrum Modality: the ability to use the right communication mode to connect with key communities-of-interest in a balanced effort; and (8) the Halo effect: where it is present, this typically comes from a strong personality associated with the organization, some historical aspect of the brand, or some uniqueness that sets it apart. Few brands carry a genuine halo effect – either positive or negative. But when they do, it can be a powerful influencer: think of Apple or Rolls Royce versus Enron."

19. As at the time of writing this snapshot (October 2015), it has been just four weeks since the first mainstream media reports emerged, describing Volkswagen's successful scamming of US emissions tests via the use of a sophisticated software module in the engine management systems of certain VW, Audi and Skoda models. Since then, more than 50,000 online global media items have been published, with >4500 of these appearing in Australia. Even without considering the frequent broadcast updates and social media commentary that has been produced, it is reasonable to believe there is not a car -owner, regulator, or prospective auto-buyer in the developed world that is unaware of VW's actions. The questions now being asked, centre not on whether there will be an impact on VW, but the nature of the impact, the commercial significance of any actions, and the broader ramifications for the auto industry as a whole. Cubit's conclusion is the following (only after four weeks and based on their own internal analysis): VW has responded to this crisis better than it did to the loss-of-power issue in Melbourne, back in 2013/14 – from which there is clear evidence that the company's Australian sales were negatively impacted. The big difference this time, is that there have been no fatalities from this emissions test scam. And despite various law firms' and academics' attempts to claim otherwise, there is general recognition that there is virtually no likelihood that VW owners' health could be affected. This situation also does not involve all models, so the company still has emissions-compliant vehicles to sell.

In terms of its management of the crisis, the Company has promised to make things right within a reasonable timeframe, which is likely to satisfy regulators. And an investigation has been launched into the affair - which will probably satisfy the needs of regulators, Governments, and the public to find someone to prosecute. It is our view that VW will suffer significant financial damage from this situation, but it will survive and rebuild. Historically, its share price and revenue have both been in worse situations than they are today, and yet the organisation survived. And with the company and its supply ecosystem estimated to account for ~11% of the German GDP it is simply too big to fail from an economic perspective. Logically the German government is likely to take whatever steps are necessary to prop up the company. Depending on the strength of the lobbying efforts by large automakers, we see the potential for a range of changes to the regulatory environments in the USA or EU - especially but not limited to diesel engine vehicles. This situation could be leveraged by the makers of hybrid, plug-in electric, and fuel-cell vehicles. Any significant changes could severely disadvantage auto-makers that have invested heavily in diesel technology.

11

Global Leaders in ASEAN: Lessons from the Region

Ernie Antoine

This chapter speaks to leaders who work in a borderless world. The term 'global leader' means many things to many people. However, attempts are being made to clarify the concept, and there is growing agreement among scholars in this new and fast-expanding field.[1]

In essence, global leaders are expatriates deployed to senior positions in organizations around the world. The focus in this chapter is on global leaders working in the region covered by the Association of Southeast Asian Nations (ASEAN). Interviews with these leaders tap into their rich experiences to draw lessons for current and emerging global leaders.

The chapter is not an academic discourse on global leadership in the ASEAN region. Rather it is an analysis and a synthesis of the experiences of global leaders in the region. It is guided by theory and research, although these are not its primary focus. Instead, the lived experiences of global leaders speak directly to other global leaders, engaging them as readers and stimulating reflection about their global leadership work. The intention is to provoke discussion between global leaders about what is working and what is not. Finally, although it does not focus on service, the chapter is intended to encourage learning and self-development of new global leadership capabilities in the service of the people they lead.[2]

E. Antoine (✉)
Senior Consultant MBS
e-mail: Antoine@mbs.edu

© The Editor(s) (if applicable) and the Author(s) 2016
P. Verhezen et al. (eds.), *Doing Business in ASEAN Markets*,
DOI 10.1007/978-3-319-41790-5_11

This chapter has three objectives. It will (1) Synthesize experiences of global leaders in ASEAN and develop a deeper understanding of their challenges and successes using Hofstede's framework; (2) Identify capabilities global leaders need to work ASEAN, and (3) Discuss a model for leading across cultures.

Stories from the Field: How Do Global Leaders Lead?

Seeking to understand the work of global leaders in ASEAN is best served by understanding the cultural landscape in which they work. The territory often appears foreign to them, and most begin with a tentative understanding. The leaders we spoke to have been working in the region for many years, sometimes for up to a quarter of a century. But they were all thrown in at the deep end when they first started. And even though some organizations are making an effort – sometimes quite sophisticated efforts – to prepare their executives for deployment, it is not clear that these programs are effective.

Usually, global leaders land in the region and learn how to navigate the cultural landscape by simply joining in. Their experiences can make for very interesting reading. But we need to get beyond the anecdotes if we are to learn lessons from them and develop principles to guide future action. So in this section we first listen to the stories of global leaders in ASEAN and then look for what makes them successful and why sometimes they fail. Hofstede's model is then used to explain those successes and challenges.

Hofstede took an international approach to the consequences of cultural differences between people's values as they related to work.[3] This provided an impetus for understanding culturally-based behavior. His interest in this field was aroused when he saw that sociology, psychology and management sciences did not offer adequate explanations, because they began with the assumption that universal laws governed human behavior – an assumption he recognized to be deeply flawed. Although Hofstede only used data from IBM employees from 40 countries in 1980 – but was able to get 50 countries and three regions for the second 2001 edition – , he discovered that variations in cultural values provided a better explanation for how people think, feel and act. In fact, cultural values are powerful predictors of human behavior. Hofstede refers to culture as 'mental programming'. This model has generated debate, and Hofstede's work, while very widely cited, has also attracted the inevitable critics.[4]

For the purposes of the discussion in this chapter, Hofstede's model is used as a roadmap for understanding the experiences of global leaders in ASEAN. The dimensions are broadly based insights that aid understanding, and they do not deny that anywhere in the world, individuals can differ.

Leading: Top-Down or Egalitarian?

How should global leaders lead in the ASEAN region? In general, people from ASEAN countries accept inequalities in society as normal and natural. This is reflected in the way relationships are conducted at home between parents and children; at school between teachers and students; and in organizations between bosses and direct reports. In ASEAN organizational power is usually centralized and concentrated, and subordinates expect to be told what to do. Most global leaders who come to the region will immediately notice the power differential between themselves and their direct reports. One South Asian senior executive working in the region said,

> Hierarchy is important in Malaysia. So the attitude that the boss is always right is prevalent. They are expected to give directions. Subordinates owe them respect, defer to their views and acquiesce to their wishes.

He went on to say,

> [...] global leaders working in this region must be prepared to coax direct reports to express dissenting views without fear of repercussions.

Another senior executive who had worked as an expatriate in South Africa, North America and Europe for more than 17 years before coming to Malaysia said,

> Malaysian staff need detailed instructions to carry out tasks. I have refused to respond to this expectation, so many have left the organization or moved to other departments.

A senior executive – a CFO, global business, based in Kuala Lumpur – who had worked in Europe and Africa for more than 16 years before coming to Malaysia said,

> People (in Malaysia) are committed and willing to go the extra mile. But they can't think outside the box, don't have a sense of the bigger picture and prefer to work within their comfort zone. I am not able to stretch them to think more innovatively. The most challenging aspect of my work is encouraging them to think outside the box.

A South Asian senior executive with ten years of global experience felt her organization has become embedded in the local Malaysian culture. Even though the global business had European roots, the behavior of bosses and subordinates was sometimes more Malaysian than European. In Malaysia, patronage defines the relationship between these two groups. So, to avoid embarrassment, issues – especially those involving bosses – are rarely brought up by direct reports. She said that in her business a European senior executive in the supply chain had made a wrong call that cost the business millions of dollars. Even though his Malaysian direct reports could see the impending calamity they did not feel they could say anything to him – with disastrous consequences. His services were terminated and he was sent home. Western readers might feel incensed by the behavior of his subordinates. They would probably say that his direct reports were disingenuous and disloyal. Yet many from the ASEAN region would disagree. For them, respect means not embarrassing the boss in public, and believing that the boss will eventually find the right solution. That is the appropriate behavior of loyal subordinates.

Why are there such diverse reactions to this story? There are valuable lessons here, if we consider the responses in a structured way. Hofstede and his son thought their research could provide a deeper understanding of the behavior of global leaders and their direct reports in ASEAN.[5] The authors identified five cultural values that can be used to understand the ASEAN cultures: *power distance, individualism, masculinity, uncertainty avoidance* and *long-term orientation*. And it turns out that power distance, calibrated as the power distance index (PDI), provides the best explanation of this story and the similar experiences of other global leaders.

PDI describes the attitude in a society about inequalities between individuals. PDI is defined as the extent to which the less-powerful members of a society expect and accept that power is distributed unequally.[6] This is a symbiotic expectation, in that it is shared by both the more and less powerful members of a society. In some societies, bosses and their direct reports will accept a large gap as the natural order of things. But in other societies, group members will not tolerate a large gap. For them, a much smaller gap will feel more natural.

So, how do ASEAN countries fare on PDI scores? These authors' research results show that ASEAN countries have higher PDI scores than Australia, Germany, the UK and the USA. Malaysia has the highest PDI score in the world. In the ASEAN region, the Philippines is second highest followed by Indonesia, Thailand, Singapore and Vietnam. On the other end of the spectrum, Australia, Germany, the UK and the USA have low PDI scores: Indonesia (78), Malaysia (100), Philippines (94), Singapore (74), Thailand (64), Vietnam (70), Australia (36), Germany (35), UK (37) and USA (40).[7]

So, with the help of the PDI scale, what can global leaders expect to see when they are deployed to organizations in ASEAN? Although there are small variations in the PDI scores between the ASEAN nations, they are generally regarded as hierarchical societies. They are certainly more hierarchical than many western nations such as Australia, Germany, the UK and the USA. However, even though, in this discussion, the ASEAN countries are clustered together, global leaders deployed to these countries are urged to explore country specific variations.

Global leaders in an ASEAN environment are likely to find marked inequalities between themselves and their direct reports. Several social and organizational markers are used to indicate these differences. Big salary differences and occupational classifications are obvious indicators of inequalities. Less-obvious indicators are terms of address, body language and other forms of culturally-relevant behavior. Global leaders should attempt to identify and understand the markers of inequality in the people they work with.

Unequal relationships between global leaders and direct reports inevitably result in global leaders taking a more directive role. Direct reports will expect to be told what to do. They are less likely to take initiatives or proffer new ideas and solutions to problems. In their view, these are best left to their leaders, who are in a position of power and thought to possess greater wisdom. It would feel impertinent to offer solutions before their leader had thought of one.

Even when asked to participate in a problem-solving discussion, direct reports are less likely to think outside the box. They may be inclined to explore solutions that are safe and perceived to be acceptable to their leader. So they would steer away from solutions that are innovative, in the belief that these may upset their relationship with their leader. Disruptions to the relationship between themselves and their leader are unwelcome: they create uncertainty and might possibly result in reprisals.

Motivating: Through Achievement or Relationship?

How should global leaders in ASEAN motivate people with whom they work? Understanding people's motivation for work is critical for success in the region. If global leaders can understand what motivates people in their organizations, they can focus on providing the right impetus for work. People are motivated by a wide variety of factors depending on context. Some are motivated by financial rewards, others by achievement and yet others by social relationships they form at work. Or people could be inspired by a combination of these motives. A common mistake new global leaders can make is to assume that people in the ASEAN region are motivated by the same things as they are themselves. Indeed, the data from Hofstede seem to suggest there is not much variation between the ASEAN countries and some of the western nations.[8] But when we take a more fine-grained view, the experiences of current global leaders in the region paint a more nuanced picture.

A global leader who works for a global business in the resources sector in Malaysia said that her staff is not usually motivated by 'job achievement and there is a lack of competitive spirit.'

However, with some notable exceptions, like Singapore, low achievement motivation is compounded by a lower skill base in the regional workforce. Global leaders are not likely to find out about this, as direct reports are unlikely to ask questions about matters they don't understand, for fear that it could lead to a loss of face. Various country-specific factors present barriers to achievement motivation: one example is the ethnically-based affirmative action policy of the Malaysian government. Originally conceived as a poverty-reduction strategy, the National Development Policy provides for preferential treatment of people who are ethnically classified as *bumiputra*.[9] Global leaders believe that affirmative action based on ethnicity reduces achievement-based motivations. Being aware of country-specific policies like these enables global leaders to calibrate their motivation strategies for their direct reports.

So, what motivates employees of organizations in ASEAN? The answer is simple: relationships. In ASEAN organizations, employees work better if they can maintain contact with colleagues and work collaboratively. Although money is important, it is rarely the sole driving force. Money is a means to support workers and their families. Even the way conflict is managed in ASEAN organizations underscores the importance of relationships. In many ASEAN organizations, conflict between colleagues is resolved by compromise and negotiations. However, negotiations can be conducted differently in different countries, even within the ASEAN community, and also perhaps between generations.[10] In countries like Indonesia, Malaysia, Singapore, Thailand and Vietnam, negotiations are often conducted subtly and indirectly. Sometimes they are conducted through third parties, without any direct communication between people who are in conflict. Even if global leaders find this odd, it makes perfect sense to their direct reports who live in these countries. The underpinning value and priority here is maintaining relationships. Direct negotiations put this relationship in jeopardy. But negotiations through a third party can protect the relationship while allowing the negotiations to continue.

Hofstede's dimension of masculinity throws light on the nature of motivations of people who work in ASEAN organizations. The authors characterize employee motivations of as

"masculine" or "feminine". In this dimension, competition, achievement and a desire to win are designated masculine. They also found traditional gender roles in societies in which masculine motivations were prevalent. In a traditional mindset, men are understood to be assertive, tough and focused on material success; women, on the other hand, are understood to be modest, tender and concerned about the quality of life.

Societies where feminine motivations were more salient tended to prioritize caring for others, liking what one does, and quality of life. Indeed, quality of life is a sign of success. Also the roles of men and women are blurred, as both are supposed to be humble, tender and concerned about the quality of life.

At first glance, the labels *masculine* and *feminine* can be misleading, and Hofstede has attracted a great deal of criticism on this account. Clearly, it would have been better to signify this dimension according to 'task oriented motivation' and 'relationship oriented motivation'. After all, *task* and *relationship* orientations are more apt labels to describe motivations because they accurately reflect the behavior found in each category. The gender labels, on the other hand, tend to reinforce gender stereotypes and detract from understanding the differences in behavior.

Here, the GLOBE study offers useful alternatives. The terms *assertiveness*, *performance orientation* and *gender egalitarianism* to describe characteristics[11] similar to the Hofstede terms *masculine* and *feminine*, with a rather feminine Indonesia (46), Malaysia (50), Singapore (48), and Vietnam (30), to a more masculine Australia (61), Philippines (64), Thailand (64), Germany (66), UK (66) and USA (62).[12] So, with the help of the masculinity scale, what can global leaders expect to see in their organizations in ASEAN? How does the masculinity scale help to understand the experiences of global leaders in the region?

On the masculinity dimension, there are similarities between the scores of ASEAN countries and those of Australia, Germany, UK and the USA. This suggests that working in places like the Philippines and Thailand should be similar to working in many western countries with high masculinity scores.

Again, however, finer-grained differences show up in what global leaders currently working in the region tell us:

"There is a difference in the way you communicate. In some places it is more materialistically based. So there is a strong emphasis on financial incentives that is the way you move people. But in this part of the world financial incentives are important but you also have to win the hearts and minds of people. This is very important. Here you must lead with compassion, you lead with empathy, you lead with understanding. You make an effort to understand the cultural differences", according to a CEO of a global business in ASEAN.

People working in ASEAN organizations are not generally motivated by achievement, at least not as much as their counterparts in the west.

Other motivations, like maintaining good relationships with colleagues, bosses, associates and partners are more important. So global leaders should be mindful of which motivational lever they should pull. An obvious strategy will be to assign tasks to small project teams rather than assigning individual tasks. Team members are likely to work harder because of their connection to each, other and not wanting to let their colleagues down. Inviting peers to work together is preferable for the same reason.

Low skill levels and government policies in many ASEAN countries can also adversely impact achievement motivation. If direct reports do not have the required skill levels, it is understandable if they are not motivated by achievement, because the skills gap lowers their chances of achieving their objectives. Instead, relationships or relying on each other, is a better way of achieving results. However, this cooperation does not compensate for a lack of overall skills in the group. This is a real issue for global leaders across the ASEAN region. In places like Malaysia, government policies and other country-specific issues have dampened achievement motivations even further.

Working: By Individuals or in Groups

How should global leaders work with direct reports? In some cultures, employees would prefer to work on their projects on their own and be recognized for their achievements. In the other cultures the opposite is true – employees generally prefer to work in groups. This is somewhat akin to experiences of global leaders described in the previous section. While in the previous section global leaders reflected on motivations of employees, this section considers their reflection about employees' preferred way of working.

Global leaders have reported that group membership has a strong influence on employee behavior. One senior executive, CFO, a European from the financial services sector responsible for Singapore, Negara Brunei Darussalam and Malaysia, said,

> I found that in Malaysia there is a lack of openness or curiosity for differences. Although Malaysia is a culturally complex place people tend to stick to themselves. I don't get invited to go out socially with Malaysians.

In varying degrees this will also be true for other ASEAN countries. There could be several reasons for this lack of curiosity. This global leader attributes it to the region's education system, which is content-centred as opposed to project-centred. In content-centred learning, a successful student can recall and reproduce facts from a text book during examinations. In project-centred learning, a successful student masters *how* to learn rather than *what* to learn. In adult life, employees coming through a system that uses content-centred learning are less curious about differences, have strong loyalty to their group, and are reluctant to admit people who are different from themselves. Group membership is also important in later life because it enables group members to rely on each other to solve problems. Admitting someone who does not have similar characteristics would dilute group loyalty and mutual support.

Another executive, an HR Director of a global business based in Kuala Lumpur from the same sector said,

> In this organization it seems we emphasize group membership above all else and sometimes we don't address important business issues directly.

For this organization, working relationships are primary group relationships, much like one's family. These relationships are important and must be carefully nurtured. They serve the purpose of heightening employees' sense of loyalty to the business. But the downside is that the business might not address mission-critical issues that could upset relationships. Bottom-up feedback and asking questions are difficult, whilst asking for help is a sign of weakness. Arguably, a system that discourages honest examination of business issues will eventually become uncompetitive. How ASEAN organizations can examine business issues while maintaining important cultural values like relationships is a major challenge for global and local leaders. Numerous businesses are rendered less flexible in a fast-changing world because priority is given to maintaining relationships, at the expense of open and frank discussion of issues.

Can Hofstede's research give a deeper appreciation of the global leaders' experiences described above? Perhaps *individualism* can shed some light. This dimension describes the degree of interdependence between individuals in a society. In individualistic societies everyone is expected to look after themselves and their own immediate family. The employer–employee relationship is largely contractual, and parties stay in a contract only as long as it is mutually beneficial.

In a collectivist society, on the other hand, people belong to a group from birth, and it remains unchanged for life. The group nourishes and cares for its members in return for unquestioning loyalty. Employer–employee relationships approximate family relationships, so negative feedback is taken very personally. In-group customers get better treatment, which means deliveries can be fast-tracked if the supplier and purchaser know each other. Collectivist values also underscore the importance of relationships over task: starting with low *Individualism* scores for Indonesia (14), Malaysia (26), Philippines (32), Singapore (20), Thailand (20), Vietnam (20), versus high Individualism scores in Australia (90), Germany (67), the UK (89), and the USA (91).[13] Obviously, there are stark differences between individualism scores for ASEAN countries and Australia, Germany, the UK and the USA, where many global businesses in the region originate. If global leaders come from one of these countries, or other states with similar values, what can they expect to see?

A CEO of a global business unit, based in Kuala Lumpur, mentioned that:

> The situation in business is much more complex than it used to be. You need the joint power of the team because (leaders) can't actually manage on their own any more. We need people to be leaders in their own right be quite autonomous, react on their own and quickly.... To encourage people to do this we send our future leaders all around the world to give them exposure to different cultures. We send them on placements to Germany, China, Switzerland and many other places. We take them out of their comfort zone and they discover what worked for them in Malaysia does not work for them anywhere outside this country. They mature from these experiences and can stand up for themselves.

Robust discussions about business issues between peers and when direct reports are speaking to their bosses are not common. Expression of one's opinion is not a comfortable way to behave, especially if those opinions might be controversial – discussions between peers about controversial issues are usually subdued. Very rarely, if ever, will a direct report express an opinion that may appear to contradict their boss' views. In the case of a conversation between bosses and their direct reports, low individualism value and hierarchy are mutually reinforcing, which result in even more subdued behavior on the part of direct reports. Even when the issue is mission-critical, direct reports are not likely to speak up to express a contrary view lest they appear impertinent to the people around them.

In one example, a European senior leader in food manufacturing was dealing with supply chain issues in the ASEAN region. But he was not able to get his direct reports to participate in resolving the issue, and that failure resulted in millions of dollars being lost to the business. It would be easy to blame the direct reports. But in a collectivist society, their behavior is normal. It may change in time and some groups may behave differently, but the behavior of this group is what leaders should expect.

A more skillful leader might have approached this situation differently, posing the business challenge to the group and asking them to work it out among themselves while the leader stepped out of the room for a while.

Or arranging their direct reports into two groups and setting up the task as a challenge between them. ASEAN groups are more likely to express controversial ideas in the 'safety' of their peer group while the boss is not in the room. When the boss returns they will feel more comfortable in expressing the ideas of the group – even those that may be a little risky.

Global leaders will find that relationship is at the heart of almost all business transactions in ASEAN. If they don't know people it is very hard to do business with them. Everything from the most complex negotiations for multimillion contracts to paying the electricity bill at a post office works better if there is a pre-existing relationship. Tasks take less time, problems are resolved quickly, and discounts are easily given. Of course this is a reciprocal arrangement when a local leader approaches a global leader about a business project. Global leaders are expected to give a similar priority to their business projects because of pre-existing relationships. Of course this is a delicate balance between running a profitable business and being a good corporate citizen. There are numerous cases of global leaders tipping the balance in favor of profitability and compromise on principles of corporate governance, as with Leighton's behavior in Malaysia and Indonesia.[14] Walking this tight rope is an important leadership capability for global leaders in ASEAN.

Creativity and innovation are major issues for businesses in the ASEAN region. There is a long history of research on creativity, and the 'standard' definition incorporates two criteria: originality and effectiveness.[15] However, for the purposes of this chapter, *creativity* can be defined as unconventional thought processes, thinking outside the box or thinking that does not fit into the dominant paradigm. The concept of innovation is also interdisciplinary and has evolved.[16] Again, it is sufficient for our purposes to think of innovation as applying creative ability to business problems.

Broadly speaking, collectivism, reinforced by other cultural values such as hierarchy and uncertainty avoidance (discussed below), does not encourage creativity or innovation. In fact, these values encourage conventional thinking and the application of tried and tested principles to problem solving. There is now growing awareness among local and global businesses that creativity and innovation are needed to be competitive in the twenty-first century. Singapore has formally adopted creativity and innovation as part of its education policy to ensure the nation stays at the cutting edge of economic development. Many leaders in business generally are asking for development programs that will build a workforce with skills for creativity and innovation.

Global leaders coming to the region will have to be prepared to engage with a workforce that is less creative and innovative than they are used to finding in organizations with more western cultural values. But innovation plays an important role in economic development,[17] and it is an important dimension for global leaders to consider, since they will need to establish workplace conditions that reduce the complexity of internal rules and processes and encourage employees to speak about new ideas in ways that are culturally safe. This will enable their ASEAN work force to rise to the challenge posed by the need to innovate.

Control the Future or Go with the Flow

Research indicates that different cultures had different ways of dealing with the fact that the future is uncertain.[18] They call this value "uncertainty avoidance". Some societies do not mind that the future is unknown and unknowable and they are prepared to let it unfold. For other societies, even though the future cannot be predicted, it is important to control it to prevent events that would adversely affect one's life. Purchasing life insurance or health insurance are examples of controlling the financial future to minimize the impact of unforeseen negative events.

Global leaders interviewed for this chapter had not been made aware of uncertainty avoidance as an issue in their daily work. However, this does not mean that uncertainty avoidance is not relevant for global leaders in ASEAN countries – clearly it does have relevance, as the statistics supporting the Hofstede research demonstrate. It might not be brought forcibly to global leaders' attention, but because it influences the lives of people and businesses in the region, future global leaders should think about its possible impact.

In societies with strong uncertainty avoidance scores the future is unknown, unknowable and must therefore be controlled. In these societies rules are regarded as important, people possess a strong urge to work, time is seen as money, and precision and formal processes in work are important, as are beliefs in experts and technical solutions that they can produce. Managers usually concern themselves with daily operations, innovation is limited and, when making decisions, facts and figures supporting the decision are important. Innovation is somehow rather limited in this region because of the complex requirements to observe internal processes. Hence invention is not prolific. However, the very same organizations are better at implementation thanks to the same complex processes. Staff from cultures with high Uncertainty Avoidance Index (UAI) scores are usually motivated by security, self-esteem and belonging.

In other societies with weak uncertainty avoidance scores, the future is an opportunity to seek out interesting adventures and new knowledge.

They subscribe to rules only when needed and only working hard when needed. "Time is certainly not money", it is a framework for guiding one's activities through the day. They are not unsettled by ambiguity and chaos in society; and they rely on common sense to solve problems. Top managers concern themselves with strategy and allow their direct reports to worry about implementation. There is usually a strong tradition of innovation and invention but less-good implementation. Staff is usually motivated by achievement, belonging and self-esteem. The *UAI scores* are: Indonesia (48), Malaysia (36), Philippines (44), Singapore (28), Thailand (64), Vietnam (30), Australia (51), Germany (65), the UK (35), and the USA (46),[19] according to Hofstede Centre (2016).

These Uncertainty Avoidance Index scores for the ASEAN countries and the UK, the USA, Australia and Germany might explain why global leaders interviewed for this chapter did not find uncertainty avoidance salient to their businesses. With the exception of UAI scores for Singapore and Vietnam, there is a great deal of overlap between the remaining countries. The UK and Malaysia are almost the same; the USA and the Philippines are close; Australia and Indonesia are also very close. When the profiles of global leaders are similar to the cultural values of ASEAN employees they are said to be in synergy and are unlikely to cause any challenges. It is possible that the profiles of global leaders interviewed for this chapter are similar to those of their direct reports, hence no issues emerged from their daily interactions.

Planning: Short Term or Long Term?

Short- and long-term orientation refer to the degree to which a society maintains links with the past while dealing with the challenges of the present and future.

Countries with a short-term orientation emphasize the past and the present, especially respect for tradition and social obligations. In business they prioritize the rights of workers, importance of leisure, focus on bottom line outcomes and annual profits. In this society managers and workers are psychologically in two camps, rewards are based on merit, personal loyalties are contingent upon business needs, and personal savings are low.

Countries with a long-term orientation prioritize future rewards achieved through the practice of virtues such as thrift and perseverance in the present. In business, work is shaped by personal values such as honesty, accountability and self-discipline. Managers and workers share the same aspirations for the business. The relational art of maintaining personal networks or *guanxi* (pronounced "kuangzi"), as it is referred to in many East Asian cultures, is highly valued and preserves lifelong commitments that can have positive or negative effects on business.[20] Living frugally and saving for a rainy day are also very important characteristics of societies that have a long-term orientation towards work and life. Businesses in these societies are more focused on market shares, and have a more pragmatic approach to life. They are frugal and encourage education as a way of securing the future. The Long Term Orientation scores are: Indonesia (62), Malaysia (41), Philippines (27), Singapore (72) Thailand (32), Vietnam (57), Australia (27), Germany (83), the UK (51), and the USA (26), according to the same source.[21]

These LTO scores disclose significant differences, yet tensions between short- and long-term outlooks were not explicitly expressed by global leaders interviewed for this contribution. However, they could be seen at work in the background, in subtle form. A consistent theme was *timeliness* with respect to meeting deadlines. Global leaders from places like Australia and the US were more comfortable with short time frames for task completion with fixed deadlines. Direct reports from Indonesian, Malaysia, Thailand and Vietnam would be more comfortable with longer time frames and flexible deadlines.

Indeed, in some of these countries certain playful terms capture the essence of long-term values. In Indonesia we find '*jam karet*' or rubber time, and in Malaysia, 'Malaysian standard time'. Both mean flexible deadlines. The short-time orientation has its equivalents (e.g. in Australia and the USA, "time is money", so wasting time is like throwing money away). But if direct reports in countries with long-term outlooks are pressed hard by their global leaders from short-term outlook countries, they may well feel stressed. However, many global leaders from short-term outlook countries have worked successfully in these countries. The secret to their success is explored in the sections to follow.

Even though Singapore has a high long-term score, global leaders from short-term orientation countries usually feel very comfortable working there. Singaporeans adapt well to the expectations of these global leaders. The explanation lies in the fact that Singapore is truly a global city. It is at the crossroads of major international trade routes, so for years Singaporeans have learned to live and work with people from all parts of the world. Their predominantly English education, combined with modern internet technology, gives them easy access to cultures from all around the world, enabling them to build skills and knowledge to navigate cultural differences.

Indulge: To Indulge or Not to Indulge, That Is the Question

Indulgence–restraint is a relatively new dimension in research.[22] Indulgence is a value that tolerates and sometimes promotes self-gratification. Activities that are fun and are likely to make people happy are pursued by societies that believe in indulgence. Restraint, on the other hand, is a value that discourages self-gratification, and when that value is high, human desires for fun and happiness-generating activities are likely to be highly regulated.

In indulgent societies, the pursuit of happiness is an important priority. Everything that contributes to happiness becomes important such as greater leisure time, a higher rate of participation in sport and lenient sexual norms. People also believe that they are in control of their lives and therefore their own happiness.

Conversely, in restrained societies the pursuit of happiness is not important. Leisure is a low priority, fewer people are actively involved in sports, and sexual norms are more stringently imposed. In this environment, people do not feel that they are in control of their lives or what happens to them. Hofstede have rated ASEAN and other countries on the indulgence dimension as follows: Indonesia (38), Malaysia (57), Philippines (42), Singapore (46), Thailand (45), Vietnam (35), Australia (71), Germany (40), with the highest the UK (69) and the USA (68).[23]

With the exception of Malaysia, ASEAN countries are restrained societies. Similarly, with the exception of Germany, Australia, the UK and the USA are indulgent societies. The contrast is pronounced. But global leaders who were interviewed had not noticed the difference, and that is not uncommon. Restraint and self-denial in many ASEAN cultures may not be on public display, nor are they practiced by everyone. Restraint may be practiced by middle- to low-income groups, and it may be achieved with finesse and subtlety in places where expatriate global leaders do not go. Indeed, it may be easier for global leaders to notice power distance behavior because this is displayed at work, where it is inescapable as part of the workplace dynamics. But identifying and understanding restraint behavior that is not immediately visible requires sophisticated skills of observation.

Some readers may ask whether it is critical to understand restraint behavior if it is generally out of sight. The simple answer is yes. If a global leader takes the trouble to understand such less-obvious behavior, it will signal to local colleagues and direct reports that they matter. This will help the global leader to build understanding, trust and relationships. So why does this matter? The answer lies in the importance the people from ASEAN countries place on relationships. Relationship is the universal currency for getting things done in this part of the world. Without relationships, nothing happens – or at best, it happens at a very slow pace. It is this deeper level engagement and nuanced understanding that really successful global leaders strive for.

Global Leadership in ASEAN: Skills Development or Mindset Change

So, what are global leaders in ASEAN doing to be successful and effective? What unique capabilities do they bring to unfamiliar cultural environments? What can we learn from their experiences? Even today, where there is so much information about how to prepare global leaders before deployment, very few businesses take this preparation seriously. Most of the interviewees for this chapter did not have any preparation for their assignment. Others have had some rudimentary preparation. The underlying assumption by their employers is that cross-cultural capabilities are not mission-critical. Even organizations that recognize the importance of those capabilities do not know how to develop them.

Nevertheless, global leaders who were interviewed do have a deep appreciation of the importance of cross cultural capabilities for their work, with the Director of global Supply Chain business, headquartered in KL, mentioning that "Working successfully in ASEAN requires a mindset change. It is willingness and an openness a curiosity about the world."

This person went on to say that cross-cultural development programs that are skills-focused are too shallow. Very few programs focus on mindset change. Mostly they are skills-based development programs which may help engender cross-cultural capabilities, but there is no guarantee that these skills will be used, or used effectively. However, a program that aims for mindset change will produce changes in capacity and an openness and commitment to engage with people from other cultures. In every respect, the mindset change is more profound than acquiring greater cross-cultural capabilities. If global leaders are open and willing to engage with bosses, colleagues, direct reports and partners from other cultures, they will continue to learn new skills taught by the people with whom they are trying to work. So cross-cultural development is not something that is done before the start of a deployment and then forgotten. It is an ongoing process that never ends. Global leaders are always discovering new complexities about the world in which they live and their reactions to them. Development programs should set up global leaders for this kind of *generative* mindset change.

Stages in Global Leadership Work

What should one do to be a successful global leader? The stories of global leaders in the ASEAN region give some clues about what to do. The discussion in the previous section identifies the range of *capabilities* for cross-cultural engagement. This section will identify the *stages* in cross-cultural engagement. It is a step-by-step process to get people from different cultural backgrounds to work together to achieve better business results. It applies to situations where global leaders are interacting with bosses, colleagues and direct reports. It is just as relevant when they are engaging with business partners, competitors and external stakeholders.

For a global leader, almost every interaction is a cross-cultural interaction. There are people from all around the world working at all levels of an organization. In addition, the majority of the workforce will be host country nationals. So what roadmap could help them navigate this rich cultural landscape? How should they communicate in town halls? How will they increase engagement in their workforce? How will they deliver bad news to the workforce? How would they build a relationship with a business partner? The Business Engagement Across Cultures (BEAC) (see Fig. 11.1) framework provides some answers. Based on the Cultural Dialogue for Change Across Cultures (CDAC) Framework,[24] the model shows stages of ever deepening engagement between partners in business who come from different parts of the world.

Observe, Analyze and Understand

The foundations for effective cross-cultural business engagement are: observe, analyze and understand. Observation involves gathering information with an open mind. Not prejudging what was said by others with one's cultural values, but seeking more information by asking questions like *What? When? Who? and How?*

Objective data gathering may be difficult at first, as it often challenges deeply entrenched habits. Observation and judgment is a single, seamless act. When we catch ourselves engaging in habitual behavior it signals an opportunity to develop new habits.

Communication and Building Shared Value

The next step is to share information that was collected so that everybody is involved in sense-making. There a couple of ways of doing this. Global leaders can refer to the Hofstede model to help them to understand the information. Then, to be absolutely sure, they will have to check with those

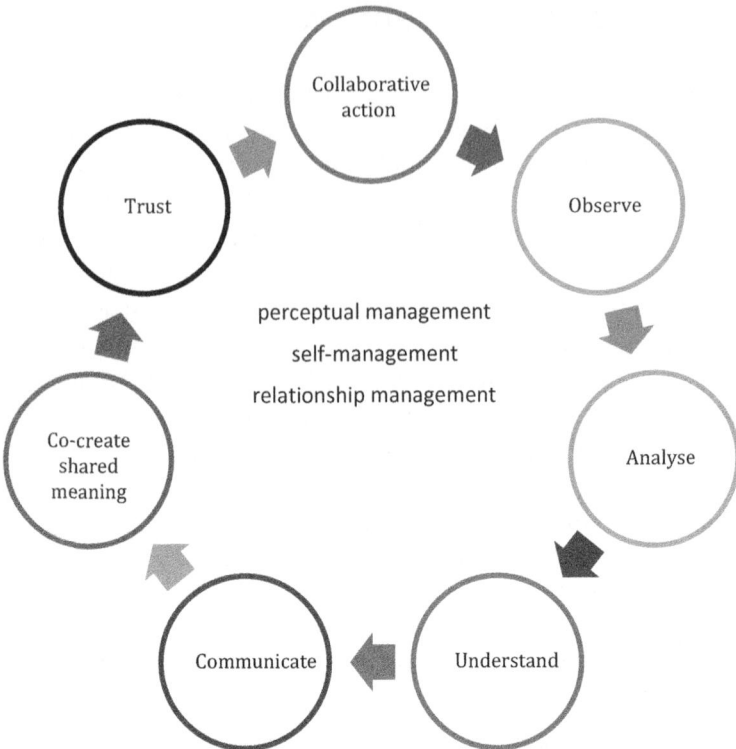

perceptual management

self-management

relationship management

Fig. 11.1 The BEAC framework (*Source:* Adapted from Rhodes, D. and E. Antoine (2015). *Practitioners' Handbook for Capacity Development: A Cross–Cultural Approach* (third edition), Gisborne, Inkshed Press and Leadership Strategies)

they are engaging have understood the message correctly. This is an iterative process to ensure all parties understand each other. It is even better if all parties can explain the values behind their message. Making the values explicit gives everyone a deeper understanding of the meaning of what was said.

The way this works is best illustrated by an incident that one of the interviewees shared with the author. He said that he realized that a certain staff member would ring in sick most Monday mornings. At first he believed him, then realized there was a pattern, and he treated subsequent phone calls with disbelief. What alternative approach might he have taken? He could have suspended his judgment and had a conversation with the staff member about his regular absences. This could have confirmed his suspicion – but on the other hand, it could have given the global leader a better understanding of the meaning behind the staff member's absences. Also, the communication would have given the staff member a better understanding of the global leader's perception of the situation. This interaction could have brought the two closer together and resulted in the staff member attending work on Mondays more frequently.

Develop Shared Meaning

Once information and values are understood by all, the parties are ready to work together to co-create shared meaning. Together everybody will discuss the values to which they wish to commit as the basis of their relationship. They may even agree on shared ways of working together. In the case of the global leader and his staff member, this means they might agree on one or two values to which they will both commit, such as mutual openness, transparency and empathy. Their agreement about working with each other may include getting to work on Mondays more often than not, and getting a medical certificate every time they are sick. If appropriate, the staff member could work at home on some Mondays, if that does not impact on other team members.

Building Trust

Once shared meaning is created, the parties are on the way to building trust. Shared meaning takes away second-guessing about what is meant by people in the conversation. Instead, implicit trust begins to grow as part of the relationship. If it is to grow even stronger, parties will have to demonstrate vulnerability, self-disclosure, openness, support and a willingness to listen. The global leader and his staff member could share stories about themselves, which would place them in a vulnerable position, but they would do so in the firm belief that they were safe in the company of the other. This would inevitably build trust between them.

Collaborative Action

Once trust is well established, the parties are usually very willing to collaborate. In the case of the global leader and his or her staff member, when they get to this stage, absenteeism will be a distant memory and he or she will have a high-performing team member.

The BEAC can be used in relatively uncomplicated relationships between a global leader and his or her direct report. It can also be used in complex contract negotiations, mergers and acquisitions, change-management initiatives and resolving cross-border supply-chain issues. Some global leaders may think the BEAC model is unnecessarily high on interpersonal engagement, and that the same outcomes could be achieved without such a high degree of reliance on trust. But the contrary is true. The degree of trust that is required is proportionate to the complexity of the business transaction. This is especially true in the ASEAN region, where the people place a high premium on interpersonal trust for just about anything.

Conclusions

If global leaders are to work successfully in the ASEAN region what should they do? A fundamental principle that successful global leaders in ASEAN acknowledge is that cultural values influence business behavior. It is not the only influence on people's behavior, but values are critical when working in a borderless world. It is not only the values of bosses, colleagues and direct reports that matter. It is also the cultural values that global leaders bring with them. Once these two sets of values are explicit, then people's behavior will be better understood. A plain-speaking and direct American senior executive will then have a better understanding of his Javanese colleague, who would prefer a more nuanced approach. Similarly, the Javanese colleague will not interpret the direct speaking style of the American as an assault on her integrity. This mutual understanding will create a shared meaning on common issues. Without this understanding, relationships between global leaders and people from other cultures will be tentative, conflicted and even chaotic.

Working in ASEAN countries requires a mindset change for global leaders. Cross-cultural training may be helpful in developing skills for engaging with people across cultures, but underpinning those skills must be a willingness to work with people who are culturally different, and sometimes may even hold diametrically different values from one's own. As one global leader who was interviewed said, a mindset change is a pre-disposition, an attitude which can be characterized as 'humility, awareness, curiosity, a willingness to connect with people and creating the right climate to work together.' This cannot be learned in a cross-cultural workshop focused on building skills. Nor can the mindset change come about from a single pre-departure training for global leaders. It is an ongoing process of continuous learning. Global leaders are always discovering new complexities about the world and their reactions to them. Development programs should set global leaders on the path to this kind of *generative* mindset change.

Global leaders need to focus on building relationships and trust with all business relationships if they are to work successfully in the region. One global leader – a senior executive from a global Supply Chain business in Kuala Lumpur put it like this: "I demonstrate trust, respect and openness to make it easy for my team to become more engaged and work in partnership with me". And another CEO, from ASEAN, reiterated that "[…] here you must lead with compassion, you lead with empathy, you lead with understanding. You make an effort to understand the cultural differences."

These relational qualities offset the distance and remoteness created by the unequal distribution of power between global leaders and their direct reports. It brings global leaders closer to their direct reports, thus building trust and enabling collaborative work. An invitation to their direct reports to share and contribute signals trust and respect. It says, 'I value what you can bring to the table.' This leader said that he always found people from the ASEAN region would respond warmly to such an invitation.

Relationship is just as important when working with business partners. Once trust is established, business will flow more easily. But there is a delicate balance between good business and good governance, and there have been numerous cases of global leaders tipping the balance in favor of profitability and compromising on principles of good governance, as occurred with Leighton in Malaysia.[25] Walking this tightrope is an important leadership challenge for global leaders in ASEAN. For the majority of business transactions, the balance is easily struck and parties are happy, but in many transactions, the intersection of interests is problematic. This usually involves large contracts, sometimes affecting national and security interests. In addition, negotiations may be closely associated with the governments of the respective countries. Almost always there are other global businesses competing for the same business, and with potential to offer more benefits. The temptation is to match an offer made by a competitor in order to win the contract. There is no single solution that fits all situations. But an approach that will be helpful is to have a culturally-mixed negotiation team. Such a team can bring new perspectives and options for breaking the impasse. Members of the team will be mindful of asking culturally-relevant questions that will generate a greater range of options than otherwise the case.

Leading in a borderless world is exhilarating and challenging in equal measure. And it is not possible to have one without the other.[26]

Notes

1. Javidan, M., R. J. House, P. W. Dorfman, P. J. Hanges and M. S. de Luque (2006). 'Conceptualizing and Measuring Cultures and Their Consequences: A Comparative Review of GLOBE's and Hofstede's Approaches.' *Journal of International Business Studies* 37(6): 897–914; Mendenhall, M. E., M. J. Stevens, A. Bird and G. R. Oddou (2008). 'Specification of the content domain of the Global Competencies Inventory (GCI).' *The Kozai Working Paper Series* 1(1): 1–43; and Osland, J.S., M. Li and Y. Wang (2014). Introduction: The State of Global Leadership Research. In *Advances in Global Leadership*, vol 8, J. S. Osland, M. Li and Y. Wang (eds), Emerald, 1–16.

2. van Dierendonck, D. and K. Patterson (Eds) (2010). *Servant Leadership: Developments in Theory and Research*. Basingstoke and New York: Palgrave Macmillan; and Parris, D. L. and J. W. Peachey (2013). 'A systematic literature review of servant leadership theory in organizational contexts.' *Journal of business ethics* 113(3): 377–393.

3. Hofstede, G. (1980). Culture's consequences: International differences in work related values. Beverly Hills, CA Sage. (Second edition 2001).

4. Readers interested in considering the critical scholarship in greater depth might refer to exchanges between McSweeney (2002), Hofstede (2002) and Williams (2002), between Hofstede (2009) and Ailon (2008, 2009), or between Hofstede (2006) and the GLOBE researchers (Javidan et al. 2006) and other commentators (Earley 2006; Smith 2006). However, the studies by Hofstede and his successors have made a significant contribution by giving researches a useful way to think about differences in terms of dimensions of culture, and continuing debate is valuable, enabling research to evolve (see Minkov and Hofstede (2011)). Hofstede (2015) now argues for expansion of his cultural dimensions' approach to the maintenance and development of culture. We refer to a number of interesting studies that have been a source of intellectual inspiration for this contribution:

   - McSweeney, B. (2002). 'Hofstede's model of national cultural differences and their consequences: a triumph of faith; a failure of analysis.' *Human Relations* 55(1): 89–118; McSweeney, B. (2002). The essentials of scholarship: A reply to Hofstede, *Human Relations,* 55. 11: 1363–1372;
   - Ailon, G. A. (2008). 'Mirror, mirror on the wall: Culture's consequences in a value test of its own design.' *Academy of Management Review* 33: 885–904; Ailon, G. A. (2009). Reply to Geert Hofstede, *The Academy of Management Review*, 34(3): 571–573;
   - Earley, P. C. (2006). 'Leading Cultural Research in the Future: A Matter of Paradigms and Taste.' *Journal of International Business Studies* 37(6): 922–931;

- Hofstede, G. (2002). 'Dimensions do not exist: A reply to Brendan McSweeney.' *Human Relations* 55(11): 1355–1361;
- Hofstede, G. (2009). 'Who Is the Fairest of Them All? Galit Ailon's Mirror.' *Academy of Management Review* 34(3): 570–571
- Hofstede, G. (2011). Dimensionalizing Cultures: The Hofstede Model in Context. *Online Readings in Psychology and Culture* 2 (1) 1–26; Hofstede, G. J. (2015). 'Culture's causes: the next challenge.' *Cross Cultural Management* 22(4): 545–569;
- Hofstede, G.J. and G. Hofstede (2005) *Cultures and organisations: Software of the mind.* McGraw Hill;
- Javidan, M. and R.J. House (2001) 'Cultural acumen for the global manager: Lessons from Project Globe,' *Organisational Dynamics,* 29 (4): 289–305
- Kets de Vries, M.F.R., P. Vrignaud, and E. Florent-Treacy (2004). Global Executive Leadership Inventory: Development and psychometric properties of a 360–degree feedback instrument. *International Journal of Human Resource Management,* 15, 3: 475–492
- Kozai Group, Inc. (2002) *The Global Competencies Inventory.* St Louis, MO Kozai
- Lim, R. (2012). 'Singapore wants creativity not cramming.' BBC *Business News,* 23 May 2016 http://www.bbc.com/news/business–17891211 accessed 5 May 2016
- Migliore, L. A. (2011). 'Relation between big five personality traits and Hofstede's cultural dimensions: Samples from the USA and India.' *Cross Cultural Management* 18(1): 10–20
- Minkov, M. and G. Hofstede (2011). 'The evolution of Hofstede's doctrine.' *Cross Cultural Management* 18(1): 10–20;
- Smith, P. B. (2006). 'When Elephants Fight, the Grass Gets Trampled: The GLOBE and Hofstede Projects.' *Journal of International Business Studies* 37(6): 915.

5. Hofstede, G.J. and G. Hofstede (2005) *Cultures and organisations: Software of the mind.* McGraw Hill.
6. Hofstede, G.J. and G. Hofstede (2005) *Cultures and organisations: Software of the mind.* McGraw Hill.
7. Hofstede Centre. (2016). http://geert–hofstede.com/national-culture.html
8. Hofstede, G.J. and G. Hofstede (2005) *Cultures and organisations: Software of the mind.* McGraw Hill.
9. Siddique, S. and L. Suryadinata (1981). 'Bumiputra and Pribumi: economic nationalism (indiginism) in Malaysia and Indonesia.' *Pacific Affairs* 54(4): 662–687.
10. Vieregge, M. and S. Quick (2011). 'Cross–cultural negotiations revisited: Are Asian generations X and Y members negotiating like their elders?' *Cross Cultural Management* 18(3): 313–326.

11. House, R., P.J. Hanges, M. Javidan, P.W. Dorfman and W. Gupta (2004). *Culture, Leadership and Organisations: The GLOBE Study of 62 societies*, Sage Publications.

12. Hofstede Centre. (2016). http://geert–hofstede.com/national-culture.html

13. ibidem.

14. McKenzie, N. and R. Baker,, Building giant Leighton rife with corruption: claims, *Sydney Morning Herald*, 3 October 2013 at www.smh.com.au/business/building–giant–leighton–rife–with–corruption–claims–20131002–2ut2e.html#ixzz47HixBPb5 accessed 30/04/2016.

15. Runco, M.A. and G.J. Jaeger (2012). 'The standard definition of creativity.' *Creativity Research Journal* 24(1): 92–96.

16. Baregheh, A., J. Rowley and S. Sambrook (2009). 'Towards a multidisciplinary definition of innovation.' *Management Decision* 47(8): 1323–1339.

17. Fagerberg, J., M. Srholec and B. Verspagen (2010). 'Innovation and economic development.' *Handbook of the Economics of Innovation* 2: 833–872.

18. Hofstede, G. (2011). Dimensionalizing Cultures: The Hofstede Model in Context. *Online Readings in Psychology and Culture* 2 (1) 1–26.

19. Hofstede Centre. (2016). http://geert–hofstede.com/national-culture.html

20. Gu, F. F., K. Hung and D.K. Tse (2008). 'When does guanxi matter? Issues of capitalization and its dark sides.' *Journal of Marketing* 72(4): 12–28.

21. Hofstede Centre. (2016). http://geert–hofstede.com/national-culture.html

22. Hofstede, G., G.J. Hofstede and M. Minkov (2010), *Cultures and Organizations, Software of the Mind*, 3rd ed., McGraw Hill, New York.

23. Hofstede Centre. (2016). http://geert–hofstede.com/national-culture.html

24. Rhodes, D. and E. Antoine (2015). *Practitioners' Handbook for Capacity Development: A Cross–Cultural Approach*. (third edition), Gisborne, Inkshed Press and Leadership Strategies.

25. McKenzie, N. and R. Baker, Building giant Leighton rife with corruption: claims, *Sydney Morning Herald*, 3 October 2013 at www.smh.com.au/business/building–giant–leighton–rife–with–corruption–claims–20131002–2ut2e.html#ixzz47HixBPb5 accessed 30/04/2016.

26. *Note*: The reflections in this chapter are based on in-depth interviews with eight senior leaders of global organizations headquartered in Kuala Lumpur, Malaysia. One leader is a Global CEO and MD for a business with operations in Asia, Europe and the USA. Global leaders generously contributed their time and were frank about their own experience, being willing to expose gaps in their own knowledge and expectations for the benefit of future global leaders in similar circumstances. I am grateful to them for their contributions.

Afterword

The Challenges of Leadership and Governance in Malaysia

Interview by Ernie Antoine with Alois Hofbauer,
Managing Director of Nestlé Malaysia

Over the last 150 years, Nestlé, a brand synonymous with nutrition, health and wellness has flourished from a small, homegrown brand in Switzerland into the world's leading Food & Beverage (F&B) Company with a presence in over 150 countries around the globe.

In 2016, Nestlé continues to be ranked in *Fortune* magazine's annual survey as one of the World's Most Admired Companies and was named the number one consumer food products company for eight years running.

Alois Hofbauer is Nestlé Malaysia's Managing Director and Region Head of Nestlé Malaysia, Singapore & Brunei. Nestlé Malaysia is the region's No.1 F&B Company with a turnover of over USD1.5 billion. He reveals that it was clear from the very beginning of the company 150 years ago that the only way Nestlé could grow its business was to expand outside Switzerland and to position it as an internationally-known brand.

The company was always guided by a set of basic principles and values which Hofbauer says were built on "the good democratic traditions of Swiss society and its pragmatic no-nonsense approach towards business", it formalized its leadership and management principles during the time of its legendary chairman, Mr. Helmut Maucher, and its then CEO, Mr Peter Brabeck, who is the current chairman of Nestlé S. A.

© The Editor(s) (if applicable) and the Author(s) 2016
P. Verhezen et al. (eds.), *Doing Business in ASEAN Markets*,
DOI 10.1007/978-3-319-41790-5

As the company expanded globally and communication diversified, Nestlé was quick to realize that not only did it need to reproduce its leadership management principles in multiple languages but even more importantly, ingrain its spirit in all Nestlé leaders across the globe. This, Hofbauer attests, has been the basic foundation for what Nestlé does in terms of governance in different countries and different cultures.

Having spent more than 20 years of his 25-year career with Nestlé in Asia – Hong Kong, China, Taiwan, Sri Lanka and Malaysia – Hofbauer has a deep understanding of the consumer and business landscape in the Asian region. According to him, Nestlé's success story in Malaysia started over 100 years ago, but with the introduction of Milo it met a consumer sweet spot for affordable, delicious nutrition, and with that, the company created one of Malaysia's most successful and iconic brands.

Nestlé owes much of its international success to its philosophy of creating shared value (CSV). "This is the foundation of the way we do business", explains Hofbauer. When Nestlé first officially started CSV, a Harvard Business School study confirmed what the company already knew out of its own many years of experience. Businesses that created value for their shareholders as well as for society at large have a much higher chance of succeeding in the long run than the ones that do not.

When we come to a new country, we not only look into how we can add value to consumers but also how can we create value for society in these countries", says Hofbauer. In Malaysia, Nestlé sought ways to add value to the country in terms of water, agriculture and rural development, as well as nutrition, in order to ensure the livelihood of the rural communities and add value to Malaysian society.

"It is our strong belief, that we have not only to add value to our shareholders, and this is where usually corporate governance comes into place, but we must also add value to society, and our other key stakeholders", says Hofbauer. He recalls that during the famous shareholders' movement in the 1990s with its overemphasis on maximizing share value, Nestlé strongly maintained that creating shareholder value would not in itself equate to building a sustainable successful business and insisted on creating value for society as an important concept in its business philosophy and conduct.

Hofbauer says that good governance is a must, not only because Nestlé is a public listed company in Malaysia and responsible to its mother company, Nestlé S.A., but because of Nestlé's abiding principles. He adds, "In the long-term, you cannot maintain a successful business in a society or a country without fully respecting the rules and regulations of the country and add real value".

During the 1980s, when *halal* certification in Malaysia became a necessity, Nestlé not only collaborated with the , Department of Islamic Development Malaysia (JAKIM) to ensure that the company adhered to its *halal* guidelines, but it also became an advocate of *halal* in the Nestlé world.

"We not only followed, but together with the authorities in Malaysia, helped to shape the F&B *halal* industry, this was a key enabler for future growth for us because the company became the global leader in the whole Nestlé world for *halal*", says Hofbauer. He adds that this is one of the reasons why Nestlé experienced an outstanding spurt in its growth. "Today, we export to more than 50 countries around the world and Malaysia's *halal* symbol has become a seal of quality, trusted among Muslims throughout the world".

Not content just to comply with the rules and regulations of a country, Nestlé has gone one step further. Hofbauer says, "We definitely have to fulfill the requirements in Malaysia but we go and apply the strictest available rules". Citing the example of World Health Organization (WHO), he says that Nestlé was the first F&B Company to have signed an agreement with WHO concerningto sugar and salt reduction. However, these commitments are not always easy to implement locally because their local competitors aren't bound by the same rules, but these are the highest standards by which Nestlé chooses to do business and hold itself accountable.

According to Hofbauer, there have been no contradictions or tough calls as to what Nestlé as a company wants, and what is required by the local government because Nestlé does its best fully to adhere to government policies. For example, Malaysia's call to promote racial diversity in the workforce has never been a big issue for Nestlé, "because multiculturalism and diversity is in our DNA".

"As a company, we embraced it at a very early stage because this is what Malaysia has seen as its future and it is fully aligned with our own thinking and Swiss roots, which is all about openness, tolerance and living in a multicultural society", says Hofbauer. He explains that the company worked with the relevant authorities to bring in talent from all races and every religion. "Today, I wouldn't say we are perfect on that part, but over 70 % of our employees are Bumiputras, and 40 % of our managers are females".

Having said that, Hofbauer admits that the only issue of such a policy is the availability of enough local talent. Nestlé Malaysia has not always been able to attract the required number of talents they hoped for. This Hofbauer reveals, is one of the top challenges he has been facing leading Nestlé in Malaysia.

The unavailability of a large pool of well-trained and qualified young talent, says Hofbauer is one economical aspect that is not unusual for Asia, but is rather pronounced in Malaysia which can prove rather challenging. He points out that the way students are schooled in Malaysia could be a contributing factor. Although Malaysia has been at the forefront of possessing English speaking capabilities in the past, Hofbauer says it is the older generation that seems to have a much better command of the language. "The world has become a global village. And the *lingua franca* of business is English. But what I understand is that the quality of local schooling has not been fast enough to catch up, or been in line with requirements of the globalized world".

Today's globalized marketplace has opened up a whole new world of opportunities, but also challenges, and Hofbauer says that means the younger generation needs not only to have a good command of English, but also must be 100% digital-savvy to keep up with the rapid changes. He says that in the past, the education system would have been sufficient and well-equipped to prepare the graduates for their professional careers, but now it is the companies which have to do most of the training required to make graduates job-ready.

"The build-up of a talent pool for the future and the success of any country in the long run depends on the quality and foresight of its education system", stresses Hofbauer, who strongly believes that a quality education is the most important contribution any government can give to its people to ensure its future economic prosperity and growth. He says that in order for a leader to advance his company, he needs to ensure that his team is fully equipped with the necessary capabilities. "As a leader, you can only move as fast as your team can move with you. Human capital becomes the scarcest factor. It's not money, it's not technology. It's human capital. It's one of the things that we in Malaysia have to be aware of and make the development of professional capabilities our number one priority".

When Hofbauer arrived in Asia 20 years ago, he remembers Nestlé Malaysia being a net exporter of highly skilled talent providing resources for emerging markets such as China and other emerging Asian economies. But when he arrived here in Malaysia he saw that the trend was reversed with Nestlé Malaysia at times becoming an importer of talent. He says this was a real wake-up call for him because during his early tenure in China, a big number of Malaysians were being sent there to develop this fast emerging market to provide guidance and to build the business there. To remedy the situation in Nestlé Malaysia has brought in the last couple of years an increased number of young talented university graduates, hiring between 30 and 40 graduates per year to train and develop them in-house. Although grooming such young graduates takes, time, it is essential for the company's long-term success.

"And on top of that today, you're dealing with a very different generation of employees. You deal with the generation X and Y, and Z, and then they encounter generation D. I call our generation D for Dinosaurs", says Hofbauer with a laugh. He admits that leading Nestlé Malaysia & Singapore with a 7000-strong workforce made up of different generations can at times be challenging but it is also very exciting and rewarding.

He dismisses the notion that the younger generation is less diligent, capable or industrious compared to the older generation. But he points out that the latter was maybe more willing to accept directions without questioning them. The younger generation is willing to work hard, but they want to understand the why, in other words, they need a clearer and openly shared meaningful purpose.

According to Hofbauer, the leaders of today need to spend time with the younger generation and explain things clearly. "They want to understand what is happening, why it's happening, why it's good for the company, and why it's going to be good for them and society". He adds, "The older generation in particular needs to listen better and to value the younger generation's views and inputs, but once they are heard and convinced, they are sold, and they will go the extra mile to make it happen.

Hofbauer says that this new generation of employees can pose a challenge, but is also a huge opportunity for traditional hierarchical companies…. Due to the complexity of today's business environment, you need open-minded and fast-acting individuals. At every level you need people who are leaders in their own right on every level, autonomous, and capable of acting quickly and independently in a rapidly-changing business landscape. They must not to be afraid to speak up candidly".

To address these challenges, Nestlé has taken steps to expose its potential future leaders to different cultures in various countries including Switzerland, Germany, China, and around the globe, to help them understand other ways of working and to experience cultural differences. Hofbauer says, "We take them out of their comfort zone to different cultural settings which will help them to mature and become much more open minded and rounded personalities and managers". When these employees return home, they have grown professionally and are much more outspoken after being exposed. "When I talk to them after they come back, all of them will attest to this or they will say, look, today I am a different person because I have seen how other parts of the world, other societies, other cultures are working and I am much more aware of the variety of possibilities to approach problems getting things done".

The other way that Nestlé uses to deal with the hierarchical challenge is to create flat organizations. "We don't want to have more than four to five layers", says Hofbauer, who explains that the company tries to create as few layers as possible to offer more opportunities to contribute directly, establish a less hierarchical structure, and to act as a counter-measure against slow and cumbersome bureaucracy.

According to Hofbauer, the younger generation also has in parts a different set of values and perspectives, and today's employees are much more concerned with the company's value system. "People today want to work in companies which they feel good about. They don't want to work in companies that are perceived to be unethical by themselves or their friends. So these are the things you have to accept and deliver upon as a company if you want to get the best talent".

While Hofbauer says cultural differences are an important issue in the role of leadership, he himself also had to adjust his communication style to fit the Malaysian mindset better. "In this part of the world, financial incentives are important but you also have to win the hearts and minds of the people because this is a more relationship society. This is definitely a challenge if you're coming from a society that tends to be more transactional, and if you don't understand this, you are likely to fail".

According to him, Malaysians expect their leaders to lead with compassion, empathy and understanding. "Cultural differences shouldn't be an excuse for good or bad business. The way of doing good business is the same in every place in the world but the style it is conducted can be different".

According to Hofbauer, Nestlé, being a company with Swiss roots, has its advantages. The Swiss are not only famous for their watch industry and beautiful mountains. The Swiss are very pragmatic business people. And they do not have this idea of superiority because they come from a small place. They immerse and learn from the people and countries they do business in and adjust their approach accordingly without sacrificing their core values.

With a population of only 8 million, *Forbes* reported that Switzerland is a country that is peaceful, prosperous, has one of the lowest unemployment rates in the developed economies, a highly skilled labor force and a per capita GDP that ranks among the highest in the world.

Hofbauer attributes Nestlé's success not only to its pragmatic value driven governance and leadership approach, but also to the adherence to a very basic belief and trust in quality. Quality is non-negotiable for us. We in Nestlé have built our reputation on great quality products and we would never sacrifice on quality whatever it takes. Never, ever," insists Hofbauer.

Notes

1. See Verhezen, P. & G. Martin, (2016), "Corporate Governance matters in Indonesia: an empirical study of listed companies in Indonesia", *Working Paper*, Melbourne Business School. And although research has "proved" that some corporate governance attributes, such as transparency and strict regulations or zero-tolerance to related party transactions, can have a positive effect on financial performance in Indonesia, and concentrated family and state-owned ownership predict lower Net Income or a lower Tobin Q value, only strict regulatory reform and government pressure will induce companies to take action. Without such legal and regulatory reform, implementing good corporate governance remains a distant objective, and this despite the enormous risk advantages of good governance.
2. Zhang, T.; Gino, F. & M.H. Bazerman, (2014), "Morality Rebooted: exploring simple fixes to our Moral Bugs", *Harvard Business School Working Paper*, 14–105, April 2014.
3. See Verhezen, P. (2008), "Guanxi: Networks or Nepotism?", in Zsolnai, Laszlo (Ed.), *Europe-Asia Dialogue on Business Spirituality*, Antwerp; Apeldoorn, Garant, pp. 89–106 for some more insights into the transition from ethical relationships to unethical nepotistic relationships. We also refer to Tabalujan, B. (2008), "Culture and ethics in Asian Business", *The Melbourne Review*, Vol. 4(1): 13–19 for a good understanding of business relationships in Asia.
4. See Meyer, E., (2014), *The Culture Map*, New York, PublicAffairs.
5. Gundling, E.; Caldwell, C. & K. Cvitkovich, (2015), *Leading across new borders. How to succeed as the center shifts*, New Jersey, John Wiley & Sons, pages 35–54. The authors convincingly argue that cultural competency is crucial. Furthermore, they seem to put forward a kind of "supercultural mind" as in a "behavioral adaptation – the ability to adapt conduct and strategy to fit different cultural contexts and to move skillfully and authentically between them" (page 36).

Concluding Remarks

Leadership Challenges and Governance Solutions Across Borders

By Peter Verhezen & Ian Williamson

Since the turn of the century the world has witnessed a systematic and consistent shift in global trade and economic growth from the West to the East. The "East" can be distinguished into three major economic areas: China, India and ASEAN, the last-named comprising ten South-east Asian states. These three Asian regions have been growing steadily since the Asian crisis in 1997. They have also outperformed other countries, such as Russia, Brazil and South Africa, which previously were seen as having high growth potential. Indeed, in recent years these last three have experienced political and economic turmoil along with stagnation and negative growth rates. Today Asian growth is one of the major drivers of global economic growth.

McKinsey estimates that whereas 95 % of the *Fortune 500* companies were headquartered in the developed world in 2000, by 2050 almost half of the world's biggest companies in terms of assets and revenues will be headquartered in other "emerging" markets. Due to the rapid growth in Asian markets, along with mergers and acquisitions, leading global firms once integral to Western-dominated technological prowess now may have Asian or Middle East owners. This change in the global economy is putting pressure on leaders to become more in tune to this new powerful Asian economy. This requires that corporate leaders develop new capabilities and be much more flexible if there organizations are going to thrive during the "Asian Century".

P. Verhezen et al. (eds.), *Doing Business in ASEAN Markets*,
DOI 10.1007/978-3-319-41790-5

Correspondingly, the rise of Asia has prompted an increase in research examining how organizations can realize the enormous opportunities in Asia. However, to date, much of this research has focused on China and more recently on the "opening up" of India. Much less focus has been placed on the ASEAN countries. This is despite the fact that the ASEAN region represents tremendous opportunities for a wide range of industries. Furthermore, the diversity and complexity of the ASEAN market means that now more than ever there is a need for ASEAN-oriented research on the challenges businesses face in the region and the strategies business leaders can take to overcome these barriers.

Obviously, any leader's path to steer his or her enterprise to sustainable revenues is unique. However, the research presented in this book suggests that leaders can prepare themselves for certain common characteristics and risks within the ASEAN market. Leaders doing business in ASEAN markets – with the potential exception of Singapore – can expect to encounter a number of considerable business challenges and specific pitfalls or risks, be they (1) *weak legal institutions and institutional voids* that often result in red tape if not outright coercive corruption that can make legal and judicial certainty a far-fetched dream for many global firms, (2) *ethical leadership challenges* when attempting to finalize deals in these markets, (3) *weak governance structures* and concentrated ownership that make long-term foreign investment less straightforward, (4) *social and cultural misunderstandings* and tensions that can threaten international trade and business, or (5) *political nationalism* that makes long term policy less predictable.

This book has attempted to address some of these leadership challenges, especially at the top executive and board level. We have mainly taken the perspective of foreign investors and managers who are pursuing investments or operations in this attractive region. However, leaders in local ASEAN-based companies are also likely to face the same threatening risks. When doing business in ASEAN, the editors and contributors strongly believe that emphasizing governance solutions may allow both foreign and local parties to avoid unnecessary risks that hinder firms from realizing the enormous opportunities in the region. Having proper foundational governance structures and mechanisms in place makes cultural savvy and responsible leadership better placed to steer and manage their organizations without the negative outcomes many firms have experienced in the past, such as the dissolution of joint-ventures, reputational damage or running large financial losses while learning how to navigate the region. Throughout this book, we believe that most of the solutions offered can be brought back to the following two themes: (1) *institutionalized governance structures and practices and* (2) *accountable, professional and culturally sensitive leadership.* We propose that it is incumbent upon business leaders to implement these two recommended guidelines in a manner that would stand any level of international scrutiny.

"Best" Governance Practices that Are "Contextualized" in ASEAN Markets

In 2004 the OECD published a set of Principles for Corporate Governance defining good corporate governance as a set of relationships between a company's management, its board, its shareholders and other stakeholders. The OECD's Corporate Governance Principles prescribe that a framework should ensure the strategic guidance of the company, the effective monitoring of management by the board, and the board's accountability to the company and the shareholders. Such a foundational organizational framework not only provides the structure through which the objectives of the company are set, but also the means of attaining those goals and the ultimate organizational power to monitor performance of the organization. Indeed, corporate governance can be perceived as the collection of control mechanisms that an organization adopts to prevent or dissuade potentially self-interested managers from engaging in activities detrimental to the welfare of shareholders and stakeholders.

However, as discussed in several chapters of the book, the prevailing corporate governance agency theory in the West may not be fully adopted in an ASEAN context. This is due to institutional limitations in many ASEAN markets, the prominence of concentrated family and state ownership and a legacy of traditional and informal management practices in many ASEAN firms. Thus, while OECD governance guidelines may be taken as valid in the USA, the UK or Australia, the principles were not developed with the ASEAN context in mind and thus they may not always be easily applied when doing business in ASEAN countries.

For example, as discussed in Chap. 8 by Verhezen, Soebagjo and Hardjapamekas, it is well established that the proper functioning of government regulatory institutions enhances the likelihood that firms practice good corporate governance since firms and their boards are more likely to be penalized if they do not comply with minimal governance requirements, and to be shunned by international investors. Conversely, when public governance is weak, as in many ASEAN countries, companies and their owners – be it families or state – may be less motivated to implement best practices. Without such legal and regulatory reform, broad implementation of good corporate governance in ASEAN firms can be more challenging.

Another area of tension is in the conceptualization of the role, function and composition of boards. A key aspect of the OECD governance principles is the inclusion of independent non-executive directors on company boards. The OECD principles propose that independent, "outside" board members will help ensure that boards meet their fiduciary responsibility objectively to monitor and evaluate the actions of top management and provide advice to the executives that ensures they act in the best long-term interest of the company. However, the Anglo-Saxon "outsider" board model with a majority of independent board members would most likely not be the norm in the ASEAN context where there is a tradition of using the "insider" board model. The dominance of an "insider" board model is in part due to the predominance of state ownership or majority family ownership in ASEAN firms. Thus, Western leaders looking to partner ASEAN firms must grapple with how to create a governance structure at the board level which ensures that an "independent state of mind" exists in the board even if the board members are not technically independent from a Western perspective.

There is also a need for organizational leaders to understand the value of exceeding minimal government governance standards and investing in the implementation of best-in-class governance practices to enhance operational and performance outcomes.[1] This point is clearly illustrated by Chambers and Verhezen's examination of joint venture challenges in the ASEAN context (Chap. 7) and Verhezen and Abeng discussion of SOEs (Chap. 9).

Chambers and Verhezen note that joint ventures between foreign and local shareholders in ASEAN markets often fail because: (A) the shareholders did not agree in principle on the governance structure and mechanisms to be put in place, (B) they did merely comply with the (letter of the) legal requirements, hardly spelling out the strategic and operational responsibilities or (C) not all the shareholders fully contribute pro rata to the capital set up which can engender free-riding behavior and moral hazards.

These challenges are made particularly salient by the fact that many ASEAN firms have very powerful and active owners with a high concentration of ownership held by a family or the state either directly or through complex pyramid structures. This is quite different from Anglo-Saxon capital markets, such as Australia, the UK or the USA, which are characterized by dispersed ownership. This can create a situation where powerful majority owners can engage in behavior that is detrimental to minority shareholders and sometimes to the overall value of the company. In the particular case of SOEs, Verhezen and Abeng illustrate how political interference and patronage can undermine the smooth functioning of the board and hinder strategic execution. At the extreme, boards in SOEs can be taken "hostage" by state owners creating political looting or at least political interference in a firm's operations.

However, in the both the context of joint ventures (JV) and in the running of SOEs the voluntary creation of best-in-class governance systems holds the promise of reducing these risks and help firms prevent potentially destructive scenarios. Thus, the minimal governance requirements as practiced in the West may be a good start, but JV and SOE success in the ASEAN is really dependent upon propers check and balances embedded in good corporate governance practices that facilitate trust and subsequent trustworthy behavior between all relevant stakeholders.

We state our strong support for proper governance structures, mechanisms and shareholders' agreement, composition of the board, and role and duties of board members. These governance structures provide the appropriate institutionalized foundations for any long-term investment in ASEAN markets.

Despite the fact that ASEAN countries may apply a unique consensual management style, or may be characterized by specific patriarchic leadership, specific compensation norms and selection processes, or may rely on important interpersonal networks, international businessmen should adopt or "contextualize" those "best" internationally best accepted practices. Implementing such corporate governance principles at the board and in the potential company should remain a guiding benchmark for international investors to measure risk and return. The banking sector underwent an even more strict governance reform after the Asian crisis, as Manggi Habir convincingly argues for the Indonesian banking industry in Chap. 5.

Unfortunately, weak public governance is hampering good conduct at the firm level. Developing rules and regulations supporting good corporate governance will remain an idle and often superficial effort without visionary and responsible leadership in the public domain as Chap. 7 has analyzed for Indonesia.

One can only hope that Indonesian bureaucrats and owners (either conglomerates, family-owned businesses or the state) understand the significance of the benefits of pursuing good corporate governance while acknowledging the high costs when lacking such implementation. If civil society, government, creditors, investors and businesses emphasize their interdependence rather than possible trade-offs and tensions, ASEAN might become a more attractive and less opaque place for business. Having better governance practices in place would not only reduce the overall risks of the organization, it also would attract 'better' investment and allow the organization to retain or get the best managerial talent needed to sustain the organizational value-creation.

Professorial Fellow Howard Dick explores in Chap. 3 the historical context in which companies within ASEAN have tried to leverage the different legal frameworks to their advantage and negotiated a certain arbitrage in the most effective and "business neutral" neighboring country, Singapore. The fact that Singapore has been oasis of legal certainty and proper governance mechanisms and structures has helped to propel the city-state as the primary regional headquarter destination for many multinationals and banks. It has become a hub for international banking with a proper legal and arbitrage system. And although Singapore has become a very expensive place to live, it still grows and attracts the best talent in the region with top universities and business schools providing the needed managerial talent for the city-state itself and also for the ASEAN region as a whole.

Companies in ASEAN markets should focus on reducing corruption and collusion, establishing a more transparent business environment and taking responsibility for corporate activities, including accountability for environmental and ethical challenges relating to the operations of these companies. We have argued that boards, which carry ultimate responsibility and power within any organization, should aim to implement policies and strategies that enhance the overall value of the organization over a prolonged period.

Companies with the appropriate moral values and vision to promote good corporate governance practices have gained trust from the market and investors. Such a reputation attracts slightly superior long-term returns on investments. These shared goals can be translated into inspiring corporate narratives. The entrepreneur Warren Weeks and his co-author Peter Verhezen (Chap. 10) noted that rumors in the media can make or break a brand. Corporate reputation combined with a strong internal ethical compass are prerequisites for success in any global context. The notions of transparency, fairness, accountability and responsibility in a global business are not just management fads, but realities that cannot be ignored anymore. They all contribute to leadership credibility and corporate reputation wherever the firm is operating across borders.

Committed, Responsible and Sensitive Leadership in ASEAN Businesses

Having all the institutional foundations of good corporate governance in place – even hypothetically assuming that business operations would take place within a context of well-functioning institutions with proper law enforcement securing a minimum of legal certainty in those ASEAN emerging markets – would not guarantee the elimination of all possible institutional and organizational risks. Such a formal structure-oriented approach will need to be amended or strengthened by individual leadership capabilities accompanied by a strong internal compass to behave ethically[2] – be it from the CEO and top executives or from the board – to steer the organization through the treacherous murky waters of business competition and risks. In other words, formal governance structures are necessary but not sufficient to secure business success in ASEAN emerging markets. Effective leadership – sensitive to the broader socio-cultural tendencies, and having the competence and skills to develop global mindset capabilities among his or her employees – will be required to make the difference. Indeed, any business executive responsible for investments or operations in emerging markets needs to be culturally tuned in. Global leadership should acknowledge at least the importance family businesses are giving to trusted relationships in business.[3]

Leadership of any multinational or foreign investment or joint venture partnership will acknowledge that ultimately, it all boils down to *trust* between the parties involved. And trust can only be gained when the different parties and partners are transparent and accountable for their respective actions.

Obviously, in order to be locally successful, it can be assumed that foreign leadership tunes in the cultural and socio-political ASEAN context in which they may operate. Such genuine cultural engagement has been tested at Nestle, whose Malaysian Managing Director – interviewed by MBS' senior consultant Ernie Antoine – confirms the importance of leading by example. He also shared his view that being attuned to the local culture and thus being culturally savvy – while at the same time being aware of the enormous remaining differences between Malaysian and Swiss culture – has helped him a lot in developing a cohesive international team.

Whatever the dimensions are in understanding basic differences between cultures, any responsible global leader knows from experience the enormous socio-cultural challenges involved in integrating team members into a coherent functioning entity able to embrace the opportunities and minimize the risks involved. MBS senior consultant Ernie Antoine revealed in Chap. 11 some of those multifaceted though common behaviors in an Asian context. Leaders must accept certain cultural values and norms[4]; and whatever socio-cultural differences might exist, they still need to instill the highest standards and clearly communicate corporate goals in order to remain consistently competitive in an international context. As with "best" governance practices, it seems that effective global leadership will need to be sensitive to cultural diversity.[5]

And yes, the importance that Asian businesspeople place on close relationships is likely to continue as briefly indicated in Chap. 8, but likely expressed in different ways, and the interpretation of such 'bonding' behavior differs from place to place in Asia. Drinking alcohol may be part of developing a relationship in Hanoi, not necessarily in Solo. And although foreigners may still be "respected" in ASEAN, they are not received with open arms anymore as two or three decades ago. Asia has found its self-confidence and Western companies and their leaders will need to be more subtle and "inclusive" in their approach with Asian businesspeople and government officials. Nonetheless, most global leadership is aware that navigating the subtleties of cultural expectations and international standards is an art rather than a science. However, being aware of a number of crucial pitfalls and risks will help to increase the odds for such leaders to maneuver successfully within the ambiguous and complex Asian context.

We are convinced that the economic development of ASEAN countries – within the boundaries of responsible corporate behavior based on good governance practices – should continue to thrive, as long as the huge governance challenges of corruption and inefficient big (often-state owned) firms are addressed. However, good governance, aligned with a more sustainable vision of the economy and underpinned by more responsible and accountable corporate and public leadership, could positively affect the welfare of many citizens in the ASEAN markets.

Seneca, the Roman Senator and Stoic, taught us that "anyone can endure difficulties better if he has previously practiced how to deal with them". Indeed, business luck comes easier and more often to those who are well prepared. This book attempted to contribute to the idea that leadership that is better prepared for addressing specific risks and pitfalls will increase the odds of becoming more successful when doing business in ASEAN.

Index[1]

---

[1] Note: Page numbers with "n" denote notes.

© The Editor(s) (if applicable) and the Author(s) 2016

P. Verhezen et al. (eds.), *Doing Business in ASEAN Markets*,

DOI 10.1007/978-3-319-41790-5

The manufacturer's authorised representative in the EU is Springer
Nature Customer Service Centre GmbH, Europaplatz 3, 69115 Heidelberg,
Germany. If you have any concerns regarding our products, please
contact ProductSafety@springernature.com

Printed and bound by CPI Group (UK) Ltd, Croydon, CR0 4YY
27/04/2026
02097621-0002